ISLAM and
CENTRAL ASIA
An Enduring Legacy or An Evolving Threat?

EDITED BY ROALD SAGDEEV AND SUSAN EISENHOWER

Library of Congress Catalog-in-Publication Data

Islam and Central Asia: An Enduring Legacy or an Evolving Threat?
edited by Roald Sagdeev and Susan Eisenhower
[p. cm.]
[Includes bibliographical references (p.239) and index..]
ISBN 0-9670233-2-7
Library of Congress card number 00-103550

Center for Political and Strategic Studies
1050 17th Street, NW
Suite 600
Washington, D.C. 20036

Table of Contents

Introduction and Acknowledgements

Susan Eisenhower

Seventy years of Soviet indoctrination and religious persecution did not exterminate the deep Islamic roots that existed in Central Asia. After the dissolution of the USSR, the question was not whether Islam would see a revival, but rather what kind of Islam would define the post-Soviet transformation of the Central Asian states that were engaged in the process of nation/state building. Would it be a moderate and tolerant Islam, as had dominated the region historically, or a newly recreated, highly politicized radical Islam with ambitions to establish control far beyond the religious affairs of these states?

These are the central questions we have tried to address in this book. And we owe a great debt of gratitude to a number of people who helped make this book a reality. First, our deep appreciation and thanks go to David Speedie and the Carnegie Corporation of New York for their moral and financial support. We would also like to thank Murad Esenov, editor-in-chief of the Stockholm-based journal *Central Asia and the Caucasus*, who helped on many occasions with authors and contributions for our workshops on Central Asia. We would like to acknowledge, with appreciation, the help of Anara Tabyshalieva and her team who played a key role in organizing our conference on Islam held in Bishkek, Kyrgyzstan in August 1999. My gratitude also goes to Center researchers Peter Zeihan and Bill Sanford, with special thanks to Shawn Howard and Helen Soderberg. Their assistance in producing this book was invaluable. Thanks also to Kim Hasten and Jill Handman of Hasten Design, for their patience and their professionalism. Finally, I would like to recognize the Nixon Center, where I was doing a visiting fellowship, and thank its president Dimitri Simes for providing me with a stimulating yet tranquil environment in which to finish the last stages of this project.

Pulling together this collected volume has been an ambitious undertaking. Similar to other books published by the Center for Political and
Strategic Studies, we made a priority of finding, whenever we could,
native voices so that those professionals living closest to these issues could
speak for themselves. Since we embarked on the project much has tran-
spired within the political and religious landscape our authors sought to
describe. There were incursions into Dagestan from Chechnya, Uzbek
militants invaded Kyrgyzstan from Tajikistan, terrorist violence shook
Tashkent, and a second war in Chechnya was launched. During the con-
ferences and workshops we held on this subject, all our participants
acknowledged that Central Asia and Islam — a subject that had once
been of secondary intellectual interest — is now "front burner." Violent
events, which have taken on a religious coloration, have had their impact
and are now prompting regional governments to shape policies, at the
same time these troubling developments are increasingly occupying the
attention of clerical figures and ordinary people alike.

Given the dynamics of a rapidly changing political environment and
the rather stereotypical view many Americans have of the Islamic faith,
we set out to provide a book whose audience would be somewhat
broader than the scholarly community. Our aim was to make this topic
accessible enough for politicians, business people and opinion leaders to
understand. By bringing together authors representing different professional backgrounds, such as historians, researchers of Islam, political
scientists, clergymen, and journalists, we've tried to produce a book with
authenticity. We hope that this volume will add new insight and depth
to our understanding of the vital spiritual and political processes that
are now underway in this important strategic region and give us the
impetus to craft an effective American policy to address these dynamic
developments.

Part I

Central Asia and Islam
from Within

Chapter One

Central Asia and Islam: An Overview

Roald Sagdeev

HISTORICAL BACKGROUND

The green banner of Islam was brought to the region we now call Central Asia by Arab crusaders about 1400 years ago, but it was not until the ninth century that Islam established itself as the dominant religion of the regional population. Theirs was not an easy conquest. Despite the fact that there had been no unified religious opposition to the penetration of Muslim faith, local tribes and kingdoms were subject to a number of different and often incompatible beliefs, such as Buddhism and Zoroastrianism, or nature worshipping and shamanism. In the end, the final struggle was between different branches of the Muslim faith. Across the region, *Sunni* Islam won more adherents than the *Shi'a* version, in part because it was more capable of accommodating and incorporating the pre-Islamic rituals and habits of the local population. Indeed some of that pre-Islamic culture survives to this day.

Of all the different subdivisions inside of *Sunni* Islam, the Central Asians managed to adopt one of the most tolerant and flexible sects, Hanafi *mazhab* (school of Islamic jurisprudence). In general, this was a fortunate choice because it was capable of giving a strong impetus to the creative development of Islam in Central Asia. The blend of Islam with Iranian culture, then dominant in the region, made Bukhara and Samarkand the cradle of a genuine Islamic Renaissance in the tenth and twelfth centuries. Later these cultural traditions were assimilated by the Turkic people, who now constitute the major component of the Central Asian demographic spectrum. Until quite recently it was commonplace for educated Central Asians in the major cultural centers of the region to be conversant in several languages: a local one (for example Uzbek), as well as Farsi and Arabic (the language of Koran).

Not surprisingly, this epoch in Central Asian history left a noticeable mark on the shape of Islam, even in the places far from this region. Several of the *Sufi* schools (orders or fraternities professing ascetics and mystic rituals in propagating Islamic teachings), which sprang from here, still play a dominant role in Muslim societies as distant from Central Asia as Turkey, Tatarstan and Chechnya. The founders of such teachings originated from Bukhara and other Central Asia centers of culture. Among the best known of them was Bahautdin Naqshband (fourteenth century), whose name to this day is revered by the most prominent Sufi brotherhoods.

From the very beginning, the spread of Islam in Central Asia was not at all uniform. Reflecting the contrasts in ethnic composition and lifestyle of the region's population, Islam first found strongholds among the urban population, in places like Bukhara, Samarkand and Kokand. At the same time the numerous nomadic tribes, migrating with their hoards of livestock across the wide plains of Central Asia, were much more difficult targets for Islam. What they eventually adopted as the Muslim faith was largely superficial, in part because many of these tribes were still undergoing the process of ethnic formation.

The invasion of the Mongol Hordes of Genghis Khan introduced a century-long recession in the development of the region. At the beginning of their conquest the Mongols brought a wave of destruction that spared nothing including Muslim shrines, mosques and centers of culture. However, unlike the case of Bolshevik rule much later, the Mongol conquerors eventually adopted Islam, using it as a political instrument to enhance their power.

It is important to note that the Central Asian form of Islam, with its constantly changing kaleidoscope of khanates and kingdoms, never had theocratic governance no matter how powerful the role of Islam was in the region.

This form of Islam was preserved in Central Asia even when the Russian Empire established its first outposts there. Russian colonial expansion in the eighteenth and nineteenth century was not a crusade to disseminate orthodox Christianity. It was driven instead by practical imperialist goals: the capture of new territories, the acquisition of new markets, and the pursuit of the geographical and military superiority necessary to make Russia an imperial superpower. The Russian Orthodox Church did not have ambitious missionary goals. Largely, the church served the Slavic settlers inside the Russian outposts of Central Asia.

In general, the Russian czars did not try to interfere in the religious affairs of Muslims. The mosques were mostly untouched, except in cases when resistance to Russian expansionism originated directly from the Islamic clergy. Not only did the Russian colonial administrators leave Islamic cultural and educational spheres intact, the local judicial system, based on Islamic law, was still able to function.

Islamic teachings not only survived, they continued to evolve. Bukhara, the major center of Islamic culture at that time, had more than two hundred different Islamic schools. And as Central Asia of the late nineteenth and early twentieth centuries pondered how the Muslim faith should respond to the demands of industrial revolution and Europeanization of culture, the Islamic movement of *jadids*[1] advanced by liberal Tatar mullahs, generated the idea of reform in the Muslim educational system. They demanded that in addition to Islam, religious schools — *madrasas and maktabs* — should also teach European (predominantly Russian) languages, history and geography, as well as the foundation of hard sciences. The ideas of the *jadids* (the promoters of such reforms) went far beyond the area of its origin to other Muslim provinces of the Russian Empire. They also found support in Turkey and in the Middle Eastern countries of that time.

Unlike Russian imperial expansion, the Bolshevik rule had more than geopolitical goals in mind. It carried with it its own ideology, its own communist "religion." The latter could not tolerate any established religious faiths, and the entry of the Bolsheviks into Central Asia signified a frontal attack on Islam. The clergy were subjected to bloody purges, and as a result of that terror many clergymen perished and many mosques were desecrated and destroyed. Those that endured were put under strict communist supervision. The party controlled even the nomination of religious leaders. It is not surprising, under these circumstances, that part of the clergy joined the armed resistance against Soviet power, the so-called Basmachi movement, which managed to keep fighting in the mountains between Tajikistan and Afghanistan until 1930.

The Soviets continued to follow the strategic dictum of their imperial predecessors: divide and conquer. Stalin drew the administrative borders between the different Central Asian republics in a way that would facilitate centralized control. For some parts of the Central Asian population the process of ethnic formation was still unfolding, and in these cases the political dividing lines introduced by the Soviet government were detrimental. Today the legacy of those artificial sub-divisions remains a source of inter-ethnic conflict, and whenever such strife has surfaced, it almost certainly has had religious overtones.

No matter how ruthless the Soviet regime was on Islam, the Muslim faith managed to survive through folk and oral culture, along with the everyday rituals that were part of family traditions. The researchers of Islam called it "parallel" Islam.[2] Knowledgeable Muslim theologians and underground mullahs kept the flame alive through clandestinely written brochures and secretly recorded tapes.

Open cases of disobedience among Central Asian Muslims emerged in the early 1980s, at the end of Brezhnev's period of stagnation. Such defiance could be seen even at the highest levels. During this time, one of the leaders in Central Asia, Secretary of the Uzbek Communist Party, Sharaf Rashidov, was buried according to Islamic rituals, at his widow's insistence. For the authorities such an occurrence was still unimaginable, especially given the political visibility of the case. Nevertheless, Mrs. Rashidova and her family managed to give Rashidov a proper Islamic burial, despite the great displeasure of the government.

Gorbachev's reforms brought the first real relaxation to the religious lives of Soviet Muslims. It allowed the first wave of mosques and church restorations. It also tolerated the first political rise of Islamic self-consciousness. In the 1990s, the Muslim clergy and political activists from different parts of the Soviet Union gathered to attend the first Islamic All-Union Congress. As a result of it, the first Muslim political party — Islamic Revival Party (IRP) — was founded.

THE TRANSFORMATION OF ISLAM IN POST-SOVIET CENTRAL ASIA

The dismantlement of the Soviet Union immediately launched the Central Asian process of nation-state building. Each of the five Union republics of Central Asia proclaimed itself a sovereign state. Simultaneously this impetus gave rise to what many researchers have called the "Islamic Boom." The Islamic faith, as a part of the traditional lifestyle and culture of Central Asians, was used by these newly born states as an important attribute of national self-identification. A construction boom of mosques reached every distant corner of Central Asian towns and villages. Money for this construction came not only from communal or private sources, but also from their respective governments.

The leaders of the new Central Asian states (most of which were run by former communist bosses) immediately sensed that the Muslim faith, as an inherent part of people's self-consciousness, could provide an efficient political instrument. Without much delay, the leadership of these countries packed their suitcases and left for *hajj* (pilgrimage) to Mecca. Not only was this act a signal to their constituencies, it was a message to the rest of the Islamic world that they were looking for support and help. The first aid delivery brought a flood of Islamic literature, articulating not only traditional Islamic teachings, but also the ideas of Islamic radicalism, which by that time had strong roots in some of the Middle East countries and Pakistan.

Since that time, the current generation of political leaders in Central Asia has not been shy about their Muslim identity. Whether it reflects their genuine beliefs or not, many leaders have been politically savvy enough to understand the value of displaying their spiritual side. However, governmental policies have been very different in each of the various republics of Central Asia, and Islam has played a nonuniform role.

From the very beginning, Turkmenistan was ruled by former Communist Secretary Saparmurad Niazov. His political opponents, who have managed to flee the country, accuse him of dictatorship. Islam in Turkmenistan is under complete control and supervision of the government, which controls even hierarchical promotions of the clergy.

In Kazakhstan, like Turkmenistan, the tribes of nomadic origin occupied the largest territory. Their superficial form of Islam had to coexist with the Russian Orthodox Church that the Russian settlers brought when they came. In the ethnic composition of Kazakstan, the Slavic component is nearly the same size as the indigenous Kazak ethnic group, which explains why the issue of inter-ethnic and inter-religious relations is of greater importance in Kazakstan than it is anywhere else in Central Asia. At the same time, the President of Kazakstan, Nursultan Nazarbayev, has been pushing hard to revive the Kazak ethnos, which suffered greatly under Stalin's ruthless policies in the 20s and 30s. Nazarbayev has been ready to accommodate Islam only as a part of his greater ethnic idea. Islam, which is tolerated in Kazakhstan, is mostly for rituals, and has not developed any significant political coloration.

Askar Akayev, the president of the smaller neighboring republic, Kyrgyzstan, has proven himself to be the most tolerant of all the Central Asian leaders to the different forms of religion in his country. It is not accidental that, in parallel to the "Islamic Boom," there has also been an explosion of diverse religious confessions and sects, from Protestants (recruited mostly by American and South Korean missionaries) to Hari Krishnas. Since the Muslim faith is the dominant religion among the Kyrgyz, it is not surprising that Akayev has paid special attention to it. His induction into the office as president was accompanied by a blessing from the chief Islamic leader, the Mufti of Kyrgyzstan. Akayev believes that Islam is a culturally cohesive force that can and will play an important role in the process of post-Soviet nation building. Religious freedom has been proclaimed as a part of the democratic transformation of Kyrgyz society.

Uzbek president Islam Karimov has criticized the liberalism of the Kyrgyz government and the country's religious freedom, which includes some degree of tolerance for radical Islamic teachings. The justification for this criticism, if any, is that historically Uzbekistan has had to deal with much deeper Islamic feelings among its population. Facing the rise of Islamic radicalism, and even attempts to form early Islamic political movements, Karimov has chosen a much tougher stand on the issue of religious freedom. His government tightly controls the activity of religious institutions, and the mosques that fall into the hands of radical mullahs are immediately closed. Confronted by a rising wave of left-wing Islamic activism, Karimov's government often resorts to the use of force, which threatens to lead to a further escalation of civil-religious turmoil.

Post-Soviet Uzbekistan has been shaken by clashes in the Fergana Valley that were provoked by young Islamic radicals. There have also been occasional bloody incidents here and there in Uzbekistan, one of which culminated in major terrorist acts in the center of Tashkent in February of 1999. Some of the young leaders of the Uzbek opposition managed to escape to Tajikistan and then Afghanistan. There they formed military groups, which participated in the Tajik civil war on the side of the opposition. Allegedly some of these young Uzbek militants were even involved in the Chechen war.

This phenomenon of Islamic extremism giving rise to terrorism was recently seen on the southern border of Kyrgyzstan, as well, where the same group of Uzbek Islamic émigrés invaded several remote villages in the mountains and declared the formation of an Islamic republic. They demanded a free passage through Kyrgyz territory to the Fergana Valley of Uzbekistan. The way the Kyrgyz government finally managed to resolve this conflict, by negotiations rather than with direct military force, may well have annoyed the Uzbek government. In the name of regional stability Tashkent has sought to unify the Central Asian leadership in a holy war against Islamic radicals. But Akayev clearly isn't buying that strategy.

THE GREAT SPLIT

"The great split" between traditional forms of Islam in Central Asia and radical Islam, based on ideas brought from the external Islamic world, began during the Soviet period, specifically during the late seventies and early eighties. Central Asian *samizdat* testifies that hot religious disputes between adherents of both wings of Islam were taking place in underground literature. It was during this time that foreign Islamic pamphlets started to penetrate the Soviet borders, as crowds of students from the Muslim world came through official channels as part of cultural and educational exchange programs. The Kremlin considered building ties to the Muslim world to be an important part of their Cold War strategy.

Later, different Muslim organizations in post-Soviet Central Asia established their own dedicated contacts with the external world. Furthermore, the tragic events in Tajikistan in the early nineties sent thousands of Tajiks into exile in Afghanistan and Iran. This series of events was first triggered by a fierce battle between the old communist regime and a broad coalition of democratic forces and politically active Muslims of the newly created Islamic Revival Party (IRP). Then in 1992, there was a brief alliance with the ruling elite when the IRP became a part of the interim government of Tajikistan. Political Islam, as part of the governing structure of the country, was abruptly ended by civil war. At that stage, the IRP and its military arm became the leading opposition force, operating from a number of refugee camps and military bases on Afghan soil.

The Tajik civil war was the bloodiest military campaign conducted anywhere in the post-Soviet space, until the Chechen war of 1994-1996. However, the very origin of Tajik civil war could hardly be related purely to religious roots. A notable clergy was present on the opposite side, too. Even the peace talks between warring Tajik factions often were followed by joint *Namaz* (Muslim prayer), bringing both the governmental delegation and its Islamic rivals to their knees. The true origin of the war can be traced to deeply rooted conflicts between regions, greatly enhanced by the Soviet policy of "divide and conquer."

Eventually the agreed-upon peace settlement, sponsored by the UN and a number of countries around the region, including Russia and Uzbekistan, introduced a power sharing formula. This agreement signified the legitimate presence of a religious party, the IRP, in governing the country. There was concern that repercussions from this development might affect the political future of Tajikistan and possibly the rest of Central Asia. However, so far all the Central Asian states have declared themselves constitutionally secular. Even in Tajikistan, the leaders of IRP occasionally reiterate their support for keeping the nation's secular status. Akbar Turanjonzoda, who until recently was one of the most outspoken leaders among Tajik clerics, has often reaffirmed that the IRP has "no intention of establishing a theocratic fundamentalist state." But on the issue of the legitimacy of Muslim political parties, he advanced the argument that former communists-turned-Muslims "do not understand that religion establishes and defines relationships not only between man and God... but also between man and man, in all aspects of their relationships. Politics is just one aspect of this relationship."[3]

Different countries in Central Asia, however, interpret their secular status differently. Not even a single mullah was elected recently in Uzbekistan to the new Majlis (parliament). None ran for office since it was prohibited by the constitution, unlike even the old Soviet constitution that tolerated the nominal presence of Islamic clerics, as well as Orthodox clergy in the elected soviets. The Tajik civil war demonstrated the power of Islamic slogans to mobilize the people. The peace process provided the Islamic opposition with a legal mandate to engage in political activity in a different environment. After less than a three-year transitional period, the legitimized IRP suffered a crushing defeat in the national parliamentary elections. This new development in Tajikistan has illuminated the generic problems faced by political Islam in contemporary Central Asian politics. Among their challenges are: the lack of support from the democratic reform movement (in Tajikistan the early alliance was only short lived); their incapacity to energize the traditional Islamic majority with radical slogans, and the absence of their own constructive program of nation-state building. The mere existence of such factors, however, does not mean that Tajikistan has recovered from the spell of radical Islamism; it may revive, especially if the current pattern of economic decline and political instability continue.

INTERCONNECTIONS WITH RUSSIA

The moment Russia declared a unilateral divorce from her former subjects in Central Asia, she realized there was no way to separate from them entirely. More than a century of the Russian/Soviet Empire left multidimensional ties in every sphere of life. Economies were designed and built in order to be fully complementary and interdependent. Regional security needs, especially in light of the long southern borders with China, Afghanistan, and Iran, called for collective arrangements. Furthermore, the nearly 10 million people of the Russian diaspora who remained in this Muslim environment hoped that their big brother to the North would not abandon them completely. In addition to this, scattered over vast spaces inside the Russian Federation, 20 million Muslims from diverse ethnic groups have vowed to never let the Russian Motherland, where they reside, ignore the Islamic factor. In the eyes of the newly independent republics of Central Asia, the issue of how Russians treat their own Muslims, in turn, always serves an important litmus test for current relations.

Post-Soviet Russia has tried to maintain its influence over the Commonwealth of Independent States. Central Asian and other former Soviet republics, however, have been determined to build cooperation with Russia on a different basis. At a recent summit of Uzbek and Ukrainian presidents in December of 1999, for example, they unequivocally spelled out that unless Russia stops treating the former republics of the Soviet Union as colonies, no serious cooperation can be possible.

In that context, Islam has always been treated in Russia as a religion of the conquered. The fate of the country's oldest Islamic minority, the Tatars on Volga, illustrates this point. The Tatars (or Bulgars according to their original historic name prior to Mongol invasion) lost their independent statehood in a war against Russian invaders, led by Ivan the Terrible, in the mid-sixteenth century. Kazan, the capital of Tatar Khanate on Volga, subsequently became one of the regional centers of the Russian Empire in its further expansionist drive to the east. Assimilation and conversion to the Orthodox faith started with the Tatar nobility. Today many familiar names of prominent Russians serve as a testimony to that process of *russification*. Sergei Rakhmaninov and the Prince Yusupov are examples. Persecution of the Muslim clergy, along with the capture of church property and land, were widespread acts until the reign of Catherine the Great, who introduced elements of religious tolerance. During the nineteenth century the Tatar Islamic legacy was largely restored.

This new environment, engendered by the industrial revolution, gave rise to progressive reformist thinking (known as the *jadid* movement, mentioned above). Growing cultural and political self-consciousness of these enlightened Islamists, and their popularity among people, eventually earned them a faction in Russia's pre-revolutionary Duma in St. Petersburg.

The Soviet era virtually established a ban on the normal functioning of religious institutions, whether they were part of the Russian Orthodox Church or the temples of the Muslim faith. The small level of religious activity that was allowed had been kept under the tight control of the government. In that atmosphere of religious persecution, however, the Muslim's share of suffering was much greater. Before the end of the Great Patriotic War (WWII) a number of ethnic groups were accused of alleged collaboration with the Nazi occupants and were subjected to massive deportations to Central Asia and Siberia. Almost every Muslim minority group who lived in the war-stricken European part of the Soviet Union fell victim to Stalin's brutal acts. Khrushchev's campaign of rehabilitation failed to bring all of them back, in fact the Crimean Tatars were never returned their land.

The early post-Soviet period brought the end of state-sponsored atheism that in turn stimulated a quick rise of religious political activism. Inside the Russian Federation newly reborn Islamic slogans often merged with demands for self-determination or greater autonomy for minorities. Here again the example of the Volga Tatars is most instructive. Their political movement culminated in a referendum on sovereignty, which even the Kremlin could not prohibit. On the eve of the ballot, Boris Yeltsin appeared on television and issued a thinly veiled warning to sup-porters of Tatarstan's sovereignty. The referendum on sovereignty was overwhelmingly supported by the popular vote. Thus, the issue became how to implement its results in practical terms.

Mintimer Shaimiev, former regional Communist Party Secretary and now President of Tatarstan, managed to calm a potentially explosive situ-ation. He led the Tatars in negotiations with Moscow and signed a new framework agreement that gave the republic certain privileges in domes-tic politics. In exchange, he agreed that Tatarstan would delegate the issues of national security and foreign policy to the Kremlin. Perhaps this agreement was the only way to avoid direct confrontation between the autonomous republic and the Kremlin, along the lines of what developed soon in Chechnya.

Future historians may call the pact between Shaimiev and Yeltsin a final Peace Treaty between Tatarstan and Russia, signed four and a half centuries after the capture of Kazan by Ivan the Terrible. On the domestic front, the policy of Shaimiev appeared to be a clear winner, too: not a single candidate representing the Muslim extremist party, Ittifak, was elected to the local Tatar parliament. A word of caution, however. Tatarstan may not be able to preserve its prior negotiated privileges for much longer. Vladimir Putin, in recent public remarks, indicated an intention to reconsider the issue, in the name of federation-wide consistency and strengthening Russia's stability.

While Tatarstan and its neighbor Bashkortostan represent a moderate wing of the Islamic revival in Russia, Chechnya is clearly on the radical extreme of the spectrum. However, it was not Islamic *jihad* that ignited the Chechens to armed resistance. The driving force behind their insurgency was the deeply rooted idea of national independence. Islamic slogans served to create solidarity and helped solicit the direct support of the Muslim world. The Chechens hardly differ from the other traditional forms of Islam in the former Soviet Union: they belong to the *Sunni* sect and are steeped in Sufi culture. The legendary leader of the nineteenth century resistance against the Russians, Imam Shamil, was the Sufi sheik of the Naqshbandi brotherhood.

In response to the Chechens' appeal for help, the Muslim world sent the needed military assistance: millions of dollars in financial aid and hundreds of *mujahidins* to fight alongside Chechen rebels. Help also came, however, with radical Islamic ideas. The traditional Chechen clergy, and a majority of its parishioners, were alarmed by the aggressiveness of the newly arrived preachers. The introduction of the Islamic component in the Chechen struggle for independence played a negative role. Unlike the nineteenth-century resistance, which was united by the Sufi leaders, today's Chechnya is torn apart by an uncompromising struggle between traditionalists, representing the legacy of Shamil, the Sufi ishan, and extreme radicals, whose Islamic ideals were borrowed from the Wahhabis. A few prominent field commanders, like Shamil Basaev and al-Hattab (a mercenary from Jordan), took the most active role in the latter group. This split quickly became part of Chechen politics after the first war of 1994-96. Thus, the efforts needed to proceed with the next steps in legitimizing the independent status of Chechnya were ruined. The domestic situation inside the region was rapidly destabilized. The government of

President Aslan Maskhadov virtually lost control of the country to a group of powerful warlords — some of whom allegedly established a kidnapping-for-ransom industry, which severely damaged the moral base of Chechnya's drive for independence. At the same time, the leading warlords launched efforts to ignite the sparks of radical Islam in the neighboring Muslim areas of the North Caucasus. Shamil Basaev even declared himself to be the Imam of Dagestan and Chechnya, symbolically following in the steps of his legendary nineteenth-century namesake.

For its part, the Moscow government was given plenty of warning about the serious intentions of the Chechen warlords. Basaev had already established an impressive track record of military adventures, which began in Nagorno-Karabakh (where he fought against the Armenian "infidels") and Abkhazia, (where he led Chechen mercenaries on the side of ethnic separatists). So the August 1999 invasion into Dagestan, orchestrated by Basaev and Hattab, should have been no surprise for the Kremlin. The territorial integrity of the Russian Federation was at least theoretically at risk, should events create a chain reaction that would involve the rest of the Muslim areas of the North Caucasus. However, the Dagestani adventure was a fatal miscalculation of Basaev and Hattab. The local population did not support the Chechen *jihad* and instead collaborated with federal troops. Neither Wahhabi Islam nor the prospects of Chechen domination looked attractive for the Dagestanis, inhabitants of one of the most impoverished autonomous republics in post-Soviet Russia.

Despite being an obvious threat to Russia's unity, the Dagestan war did not provoke an outright Russian invasion of Chechnya. The Russian public at that time was not ready to make the sacrifices necessary to preserve the country's territorial integrity. It was not until the Moscow apartment house explosions that there was popular support for military action against the "terrorists." While it is still unclear who was responsible for the attacks, once Vladimir Putin started the second Chechen war under this pretext, he succeeded in building popular support for the war. Regardless of how brutal the war became, he gradually managed to put the issue of Russia's territorial integrity on top of the national agenda.

Instead of reuniting Chechen society, the second Chechen war exacerbated further its split along religious lines. The Mufti of Chechnya, Akhmed Kadirov, the leader of the traditional Islamic wing, persuaded some of the field commanders to make a separate peace with the Russians and to establish a war-free zone around Gudermes, the second largest Chechen city before the total demolition of Grozny.

EXTERNAL FACTORS IN THE ISLAMIC WORLD

It was only natural for the newly born Central Asian states to identify with their brothers in the rest of the Muslim world. However, the interests and goals of the different Muslim countries are often in conflict with each other, leaving little common ground. Kazakhstan, for example, was the first among Central Asian states to learn this fact. After the collapse of the Soviet Union, hundreds of nuclear intercontinental ballistic missiles were left intact on the Kazak steppe. Many militants among the international Muslim community urged President Nazarbayev to keep these weapons in order to make his country the first Islamic nuclear power. Encouraged by the United States and Russia to become nuclear free, Kazakhstan to its credit agreed to give up the weapons. Even if they had refused, technical experts determined that the country's nuclear status would have remained nominal, since the Russians kept the weapons' electronic codes. However, the very presence of fissile materials surely would have represented a serious risk.

In practical terms Central Asia needed immediate economic assistance, including access to new markets and vital business partnerships that could substitute for the broken ties within the former Soviet economy. That could be done through bilateral cooperation, first of all with the region's neighbors. But no comprehensive economic contacts could be developed without the full spectrum of other types of mutual involvement, including those within the political and cultural spheres. In the case of these Muslim countries, it was thought that the bonds of common faith might provide the needed boost for cooperation. In that respect, two of Central Asia's regional neighbors, Iran and Turkey, offered diametrically opposite models: Iran, the Islamic fundamentalist state, vs. Turkey, a state praised as an exemplary secular model. The Western world hoped that the Central Asian states would adopt Turkey as a role model for their own development, and thus in the process transform the region's political and economic systems. Naturally, the Iranian counterpart to the Turkish model of democratic development was regarded as a worse than worst-case scenario.

Neither of these two models actually materialized in the post-Soviet period in Central Asia. Perhaps in the case of Iran there was one obvious reason. The Central Asians, as predominantly *Sunni* Muslims, were uninterested in accepting influence from a *Shi'a* Muslim society, even though they had some common roots with Iranian culture. The culture of moderate and tolerant Islam, developed in Central Asia throughout its history and blended with the European Russian and Soviet-type educational system, could hardly accept the extremes of Iranian Islamic revolution.

On top of these considerations, the Iranian leadership tried to assure that the Soviet and then Russian government would not boycott the Ayatollah's regime. During the last several years, the development of cooperation with Russia, especially in areas of strategic concern, proved that for Iran this friendship with Russia was one of the most important partnerships it had for breaking the blockade that was established by the Western world. As a result, the Iranian government has backed virtually every Russian move related to Central Asia and the Caspian Sea, including the pacification of Tajikistan, which led to the establishment of a coalition government between the Russian-supported Rakhmonov government and its Islamic opposition.

The practical presence of Iran on the Central Asian scene is rather limited. Perhaps the greatest opportunity for Iran to influence development within a post-Soviet Islamic country has been the case of Azerbaijan. The Azerbaijanis, like the Iranians, are *Shi'a* Muslims. Moreover, they share a common border. However, in a surprising twist in the contemporary "Great Game," the relationship between Iran and Azerbaijan has deteriorated to such a degree that during the Azerbaijani-Armenian conflict around Nagorno-Karabakh the Iranians effectively took the side of Armenians. Indeed Tehran went so far as to help Armenia break the economic blockade established by Azerbaijan, in retaliation for the role Armenia played in Karabakh.

In their religious faith the Azerbaijanis, *Shi'a* brothers of Iranian Islamic revolutionaries, are much more moderate. So far, there have been no serious internal conflicts in Azerbaijan based on religious considerations. Perhaps it is one of the few cases among the post-Soviet Islamic countries where religious factors have not intervened to a noticeable degree in political life.

Turkey is perhaps the only Islamic country that, at least in theory, has all the necessary prerequisites to serve as a secular role model for Central

Asia. It has common cultural, linguistic and historic roots with all of Central Asia except Tajikistan. Historically, Turkey also adopted the same brand of Islam. Turks are not simply *Sunni* Muslims, they also adhere to the Hanafi mazhab (school of Islamic jurisprudence), which is dominant throughout the rest of the former Soviet Union. Even in the Sufi culture the most influential brotherhood in Turkey is Naqshbandi.

Needless to say, the economic success of Turkey, which underwent its own kind of economic miracle, provides an example for post-Soviet countries to follow in their desperate pursuit of development. The geographic location of Turkey, at the gate to the strategic crossroads between the Silk Route region and Europe, makes it even more attractive for the newly emerging states of Central Asia to cooperate with Ankara. Furthermore, the Western democracies support Turkey as the most qualified country to lead the Central Asians in the new, post-Cold War/post-Soviet era.

The legendary founder of modern Turkey, President Kemal Ataturk, who introduced radical secularism, would hardly approve of the pilgrimages of Central Asian post-Communist leaders to Mecca. However, Turgut Özal, who brought moderation to post-Kemalist Turkish policy, would have accepted the role of Islam as an ally in building the national identities of the Central Asian states. Özal's preference in dealing with his Central Asian brothers has been to promote the concept of pan-Turkism. The brief rule of the Islamic Party of Necmetin Erbakan also marked a political shift in Turkey: a turn in the direction of pan-Islamism. Turkey's political roller coaster in the last decade illustrates the ongoing drama of a nation in search of its own true identity.

Despite significant interaction between Turkey and Central Asia, these newly emerging states, once dependent on Moscow, are not looking to become dependent on Ankara; they are not ready to trade in one big brother for another.

In tracing the impact of Afghanistan and Pakistan in the "reislamization" of Central Asia, it is necessary to go back to the Afghan war, which was triggered by the invasion of the Soviet Army. An almost immediate response to this invasion was an all but universal pan-Islamic *jihad* against Soviet intervention. This unified response brought together about 35,000 Islamic mercenaries from many countries of the Muslim world to join the Afghan *mujahidins*. Within this number were hundreds of ethnic Uzbeks, Tajiks, and representatives of other Muslim minorities of the Soviet Union who defected from the Soviet troops in Afghanistan or clandestinely crossed the southern border. Many of the young Soviet Muslims went across to Afghanistan to get a boost to their radical Islamic ideas in Pakistani religious schools. Eventually, the Soviet government came to understand how risky it was to use military servicemen recruited from the Muslim population of the country to fight their brethren in Afghanistan. The withdrawal of the Soviet army predetermined the fall of the Najibulla marionette regime. Nominally it was replaced by the Islamic rule of the Rabbani government. However, in reality the country was still divided between the warlords.

The leaders of the Afghan revolution practiced very strict orthodox Islam which, in part, helps explain the enthusiastic support from radical Islamic circles in Pakistan, Saudi Arabia and elsewhere. At the same time they enjoyed generous help from the Western world, mostly from the United States, which provided shipments of weapons. When the war was over, thousands of young militarily experienced and well-equipped ardent Islamists were left wondering what to do. The genie of militant Islam was out of the bottle. This pool of volunteers now existed that would eventually swell the ranks of the opposition in Tajikistan's civil war and participate on the side of rebels in Russia's Chechen Wars.

The governments of the newly born Central Asian states had to learn how to adapt to a new reality. The arrival of the Taliban on the southern borders of Central Asia completely changed that equation. It immediately alarmed the governments of the Central Asian republics and forced them to seek closer military involvement with Russia. The 1998 "troika" meeting of Yeltsin, Karimov and Rakhmonov produced a political statement calling for mutual cooperation against the offensive of fundamentalist Islam. Despite ups and downs in the Uzbek-Russian relations, and the very transparent attempts of the Uzbek government to establish much closer cooperation with the United States, the dialogue with Russia on military and national security cooperation is continuing to develop. The 1999 meeting in Tashkent resulted in a new treaty signed by Karimov and Putin, reaffirming the need for close cooperation. Almost at the same time, in the fall of 1999, military strategists from the General Staffs of both countries proceeded to develop specific tactical scenarios for retaliatory strikes against the warlords who refused to disarm after the Tajik civil war. One of the obvious potential targets of such joint Russian-Uzbek strikes has been Juma Namangani and his troops, who have recently withdrawn from southern Kyrghyzstan following an unsuccessful attempt to launch an armed resistance across the border into Uzbekistan.

Conflict between Central Asia and the Muslim world, especially the Arab part of it, is not limited to the shipment of young *mujahidins* to join field commanders in Afghanistan, Central Asia and Chechnya. There has also been a substantial financial influx coming mostly from Saudi Arabia and a few other oil-rich states. Until the recent escalation of the second Chechen war, no government would publicly admit to participation in such efforts. Most likely the money was provided by nongovernmental philanthropic organizations and individuals associated with radical Islamic movements.

Another serious threat coming from Afghanistan is represented by the enormous growth in drug trafficking. The Central Asian region has become not only a burgeoning market for these drugs, but also a new trafficking route for their shipment from Afghanistan to Europe and the rest of the world. President Islam Karimov is right when he says that, considering volatile neighbors such as Afghanistan, bringing stability to Central Asia will not be a simple task.

To the east of Afghanistan, Central Asians have a long common border with the People's Republic of China. The immediate neighbors on the Chinese side live in Xinjiang province. They are the Turkic brothers of Central Asians. The Uighurs constitute the major ethnic group among them. The rest of the Muslim population in Xinjiang includes virtually every ethnic type present in Central Asia (Kazaks, Uzbeks, Tajiks and Kyrgyz). This area (Inner Asia) has been part of China since the late eighteenth and early nineteenth centuries, as a Chinese trophy of the Great Game. Unlike the ancient Muslim communities scattered deep inside Central and Southeast China (the so-called Hui Chinese), Muslims in Inner Asia have created a lot of trouble for their Big Brother. Uprisings did not stop with the formation of the People's Republic of China. In order to subdue the restive Muslims, the Beijing government launched a massive resettlement of Han Chinese groups into Inner Asia.

The separatist movements, especially among Uighurs, got a boost from the disintegration of the Soviet Union. Ethnic minorities of Inner Asia hoped to receive independence like their brothers in Central Asia. While facing re-energized separatists in Xinjiang, the Chinese authorities have become particularly wary of the potentially negative impact of the fundamentalist Taliban across the border in Afghanistan. A number of

recent terrorist acts (including the bomb explosions in Beijing) are associated with the clandestine antigovernment groups of the Uighurs.
Allegedly, these groups used secret arms shipments from Afghanistan. The
current governmental policy in Xinjiang represents the uncompromising
suppression of any hint of Uighur separatism. Whenever Islam appears to
be an ally to the separatists, it, too, has become a target for quick governmental rebuttal.

The Central Asian states found themselves in a rather delicate situation vis-à-vis the separatist aspiration of their ethnic brothers on Chinese
soil. For their part, the Central Asian authorities have reaffirmed that they
are not going to provide a home and refuge for separatists from Xinjiang,
thus denying outside support to their Turkic Muslim brothers. However, it
is estimated that between 500,000 and 600,000 Uighurs now live in post-
Soviet Central Asia, some of them having fled the Chinese repression that
began in 1996 when Beijing started its crackdown. Estimated to number
twelve to fifteen million in total, the Uighurs, who call their homeland
East Turkestan, hope someday for a unification of their people. These aspirations, however, keep the Chinese on alert and ready to exercise repressive measures to stem the tide of separatism.[4] This policy is now being discussed among a number of key Central Asian states. On March 30, 2000,
the Defense Ministers from China, Kazakstan, Kyrgyzstan, Russia, and
Tajikistan met in Kazakstan to coordinate their efforts against separatism
and terrorism in the area. The meeting, held annually since 1996, occurred
one day after the point-blank assassination of Nigmatulla Bazakov, the
ethnic Uighur minority leader in Kyrgyzstan.[5]

ISLAM AND REGIONAL PROBLEMS

The moment Central Asia became a patchwork of independent countries
and started to build nation-states, they wanted to identify with their
Islamic brothers everywhere. But the increasingly close interaction with
other Muslim countries brought about a confrontation between traditional Islam and more fundamentalist approaches to the faith.

Today, radical Islam is being blamed directly or indirectly for a spate of
violent outbreaks. Since 1999 alone, three military conflicts have been
launched in Muslim areas of the former Soviet Union, some of more lasting significance than others. There was the Dagestan insurgence from
Chechnya; the Uzbek *mujahidin* invasion into Kyrgyzstan; and the second

Chechen War that is still underway. The spillover of Muslim radicalism with militant actions, like the intrusion into Kyrgyzstan, brings this issue onto the international scene, requiring at least regional cooperation between countries. However, the Kyrgyz case has had the opposite effect. It has led to deterioration in Kyrgyz-Uzbek relations due to the difference between the soft policy of Akaev and hard-line approach of Karimov.

On the political front the most obvious success has been in Tajikistan with the legalization of IRP and its participation in the peace process and elections. The result has been the containment of the political force of the Islamists. However, it is too early to hail the Tajik model: on the periphery of the country there are a number of warlords defying the authority of the central government.

The rapidly growing drug trafficking from Taliban-controlled Afghanistan is further exacerbated by the involvement of these warlords and poses the serious danger of a real spillover into the rest of Central Asia.

The radical, politicized Islam may well be contained to the fringes of the current political landscape of Central Asia. The calls to reject the educational achievements of the recent past and to reverse the process of emancipation for women are not gaining popular support. But should today's secularist regimes fail in their efforts to stabilize and reform their economies, Islamic fundamentalism may emerge as a feasible alternative.

The contemporary history of the rest of the Muslim world, that is, the ongoing drama of competition between the extremes of secularism and Islamism, provides plenty of lessons. Unfortunately, the attempts to find an appropriate blend of both have not come to fruition.

Almost everywhere in the Muslim world the rise of radicalism represents a reaction to the global challenge brought by the Western way of life. Unlike the earlier enlightened *jadid* movement among Muslims of the Russian Empire, which tried to blend the virtues of Muslim faith with the fruits of European and Russian civilization, the contemporary radical Islamic reformers in Central Asia have not yet come up with any original ideas for the nation-building process. Instead they have tried to suggest carbon-copy scenarios developed by the Islamist reformers of the Arab world (such as the teachings of the Muslim Brotherhood in Egypt), which reject the values of Western civilization.

CONCLUSION

The Central Asian states are destined to play an important role in the twenty-first century. Not only will they be important as suppliers of oil and gas, but also as crucial strategic areas between Russia, China, India and a number of major Islamic countries — among which Pakistan recently became the first Muslim outpost to be armed with nuclear weapons. This is why the outcome of the competition for the souls of Central Asian Muslims is so important. Their orientation will emerge as a result of a major interplay between the historic heritage of Central Asian Islam, the legacy of Russian/Soviet domination, and the region's immediate neighbors in the Islamic world. The outcome of this interaction will depend on the roles that will be played by the developed democratic countries and, most crucially, the degree to which they will provide help to these new emerging countries in the underbelly of the former Soviet Empire.

C h a p t e r   T w o

The Kyrgyz and the Spiritual Dimensions of Daily Life

Anara Tabyshalieva

THE ROLE OF ISLAM IN DAILY LIFE

After the collapse of the Soviet Union, a completely new religious situation emerged in Kyrgyzstan as the country moved toward democracy and a market economy. The Islamic "boom" in Kyrgyzstan, like all over Central Asia, spawned the rapid proliferation of *madrasas* (Islamic schools of higher education) and mosques. The number of *hajji* (pilgrims to Mecca) also grew substantially. For example in the South, where there were very few mosques during Soviet times, there are now about two thousand.

Kyrgyzstan contains many sites with great religious significance. These include the city of Osh with Sulemain Mountain, a destination of numerous Muslim pilgrims; and the *mazars* or holy places dotted around the country, which serve a range of cultural and religious functions.

The cult of ancestors and veneration of holy places in Kyrgyzstan are important spiritual matters, and there are numerous tombs of ancestors, Biblical prophets, and legendary heroes in Kyrgyzstan. Around bushes and trees, on rocks and near caves, one may see sticks stuck into the ground with colorful pieces of cloth tied to them; these have been left by pilgrims as reminders of their prayers. Such places are called *mazars*. Many *mazars* — springs, waterfalls and rivers — are venerated. The most popular are hot and medicinal springs. Pilgrims often travel great distances to obtain a blessing, fulfill a vow, cure a sick child or seek a remedy for infertility.

Mazars have a number of important functions in the spiritual life of the Kyrgyz. Very often they are situated close to hot springs, waterfalls, trees, and stones, and they play an aesthetic role. Any pretty architectural monument or natural place can become a *mazar*. As a rule every hot spring is a holy place. Usually the origin and importance of a spring is linked to a Biblical or historical personage. Their veneration not only has a spiritual dimension, it preserves ecologically important areas and marks territorial boundaries of different groups of former nomads, tribes or local communities.

The conventional character of *mazars* has allowed traditional Kyrgyz, Uzbek and Tajik cultures to be maintained. Muslims, regardless of ethnic affiliation, venerate the *mazars*, which have played a healing role. The *mazars* are linked with the resilience of the local traditions. Despite Soviet attempts to demolish and destroy them, the *mazars* have survived this destructive period of history.

The *mazars* are also focal points for local history, places to contemplate ancient legends and epics. The cult of dead ancestors is extremely popular. Many Muslims in Kyrgyzstan believe that the dead pay visits to their surviving friends and relatives particularly on Fridays. Women go to the cemetery on that day to make offerings and libations. In Central Asia women are not allowed into the mosques in the same way as men are, so women tend to be regular visitors to the *mazars*.

OSH AS AN IMPORTANT RELIGIOUS CENTER

Osh is the main city in the south of Kyrgyzstan and one of the most ancient cities of Central Asia. Currently a large amount of material is being collected about ancient settlements there, and attempts are being made to celebrate the 3000th anniversary of the founding of the city. However, the modern city rests on the ruins of the old one and complex research would be needed to confirm its age.

Several legends exist about the founding of the city, the improbability of which only confirm its unusual and ancient roots. According to one of these legends, Alexander the Great founded the city; another legend names King Solomon as the founder; still another legend gives credit to Adam. The most common legend is connected with the biblical character Solomon (Suleiman) who placed a pair of bullocks pulling a plough in front of his army. When the bullocks reached a strange-looking mountain, Solomon said "Khosh" (that's enough). This, according to myth, explains the name of the city (Osh) that was later built there.[1] Muslim tales also connect the mountain with Suleiman, who got tired after flying over the area. He saw the mountain and decided to lie down on it to rest. According to the legend, the mountain still bears the shape of Suleiman's body. He prayed there and built a mosque with his own hands, using camel's milk to prepare the clay because of the lack of water. Another tale suggests that Suleiman was buried there in a mausoleum. With time, the mountain itself — and stones and depressions found on it — acquired the holy status of a second Mecca, becoming a place of pilgrimage for Central Asians. Some of the stones are literally polished by barren women and the sick, hoping to find cures.

The Mountain of Suleiman (Takht-i Suleiman) in Osh is the most popular pilgrimage place of all Central Asia. In 1959 the Mufti in Tashkent published a special *fatwa* (deliberation by chief mullah) against pilgrimages to the mountain. Furthermore, during Khrushchev's movement against "relics of the past," the so-called house of Babur, a *hujra* (chapel) allegedly built by Babur, the founder of the Mogul Empire in India, was blown up at night in 1963. In the archives it was noted that the house was destroyed in accordance with "numerous requests of the working people" and that the streams of pilgrims coming to the mountain disturbed the "well deserved rest of common citizens."

In 1988, a Society for the Restoration of the House of Babur was formed under the auspices of local businessmen. They quickly built a structure, based on a 1920s photograph of Mazar Suleiman, and decorated it in the spirit of modern Uzbek artists of the Fergana Valley. No social scientists were invited to the opening of the new House of Babur. Regarding the *hujra* itself, it is still unknown what it looked like and where on the mountain it was built. Hopefully, scientists and scholars will soon be in a position to further our knowledge of this mysterious topic.

THE KYRGYZ POLICY OF RELIGIOUS PLURALISM

In Kyrgyz villages the pilgrims upon their return from Mecca are treated with a great respect and often are promoted to replace former local apparatchiks with Communist backgrounds. Such occurrences are the testimony of a new climate and a new set of values that are evolving in rural areas. Unfortunately, claims that the *hajj* to Mecca sometimes is used for mercantile purposes and profit are well grounded, too.

There are ten to twelve separate *madrasas* and about forty small *madrasas* attached to mosques in Kyrgyzstan (Osh, Jalal-Abad, Talas, Kara-Balta, Tokmak, Karakol, etc.). There were no religious educational institutions during Soviet time, but quite a few have been opened over the last years: The Islamic Institute in Bishkek and Tokmak, "Emmanuel" Presbyterian educational centers, and the Islam theology department at Osh University (for male and female students). The latter closely cooperates with institutions in Turkey, and students attend the courses of the first two years there.

Two newspapers, *Islam Madaniaity* (in Kyrgyz and Russian languages) and *Shari'at* (only in Kyrgyz), are devoted to issues of Islam in Kyrgyzstan and are printed in Bishkek. Uzbek-language newspapers in the south often include some materials on religious issues. However, the newspapers write on the religious situation mainly in two ways. First, to chronicle religious celebrations and second, to blame the mysterious Wahhabists for creating trouble. For many people it is unclear what Wahhabism means and why this is "dangerous" for society. Ignorance about Islam allows journalists and officials to label different-thinking people as Wahhabists or religious extremists.

Before 1993, Kyrgyzstan's Muslims were subordinate to the Mufti of Central Asia in Tashkent. Now the Kyrgyz Muslim establishment is independent from Tashkent and relatively independent from state authorities, in comparison to neighboring countries. The Russian Orthodox Church in Kyrgyzstan has always been subordinated to the main center in Moscow.

A majority of the Muslim clergy is located in the South, in Osh and Jalal-Abad regions, but overall a shortage of skilled clergymen is a very serious problem in the religious life of Kyrgyzstan. Only a handful of Mullahs have a good command of the Arabic language and an understanding of the Hadiths. Most of the Muslim preachers cannot use Arabic at all. They are not allowed to preach independently, but they are permitted to carry out some rituals, such as weddings, and to interpret Shari'a (Islamic law). The local Mullahs are at a loss in disputes with foreign missionaries, who have stronger theological training. This is why new interpretations of the Koran are becoming more appealing. At present, scores of students from Kyrgyzstan and other Central Asian states are being trained at the religious centers of the Middle East and other Muslim countries. Since they tend to come back with different interpretations of Islam, contradictions between Muslim groups could well be commonplace.

Kyrgyzstan, like all the newly independent Central Asian states, is now witnessing the emergence of a number of new and revived religious movements. The government's policy of religious tolerance has allowed numerous faith groups to flourish in the country. Particularly noticeable among the newcomers are Protestants, Jehovah's Witnesses, Hare Krishnas and the Bahais. There are also new Protestant Christian and Wahhabist Muslim groups in the country, which challenge the historically predominant traditional Muslim and Orthodox Christian structures.

However, there is the widespread view that the Kyrgyz or Uzbek people should be only Muslims. Thanks to the liberalization of religious policy it has become evident that a declared freedom of conscience is not enough. Foreign missionaries' activities have not been analyzed and comprehended. And while missionaries have been arriving from different countries for centuries, the question of Protestant proselytizing has become a sharper and more controversial issue. Thus, a problem has emerged on how to work out a balanced state policy of religious pluralism. In compliance with the Presidential Decree, the government, in 1996, established a state commission. The Inter-Ministerial Council on Religious Affairs is a consultative and coordinating body, established to work out recommendations on the state's religious policy and coordinate the efforts of the state bodies and religious organizations. The Council includes members of parliament, as well as representatives of different institutions and religious organizations.

The building of a civil society, as declared by President Akaev, is the most acceptable way to achieve confessional accord, on the basis of communication, mutual interest and free choice. In Kyrgyzstan, achieving confessional relations without conflict and making progress in democracy building will be connected to the development of a policy of religious pluralism.

Despite the significant work done by governmental and nongovernmental organizations, the scale of their activities, in harmonizing religious relations and creating tolerance in an environment of religious pluralism, are still lagging behind the accelerating process of social disintegration and polarization. Many factors contribute to the destabilization of the ethno-religious situation. For example, the mass media in Kyrgyzstan (mainly Russian-language newspapers), Moscow, and Uzbekistan often exaggerate the Islamic threat in Central Asia. Every so often a dispute arises between Kyrgyz and Russian-language newspapers over interpretations of Islam. Some Russian-language newspapers are very fast to label new Islamic trends as Wahhabist and dangerous, while rival Muslim factions use newspapers to criticize each other, often in an inflammatory way. Despite these problems, Kyrgyzstan — with the advantage of the freest press in Central Asia — has the possibility of developing a new culture of open and constructive discussion on sensitive issues of faith.

Some parliamentary deputies from the South use Islam to appeal to voters with proposals to make Friday a day off, and they are planning to create an Islamic Party of Kyrgyzstan in defiance of the Constitution.[2] Another indication that Islam is being used for political purposes is the establishment of a "Protection of Muslims Rights Committee" in Jalal-Abad. This is the most devout region of the country where the population is 95% Muslim and contains only two major ethnic groups, the Kyrgyz (67%) and the Uzbeks (25%). It is quite possible that in the impending elections, politicians may appeal to the religious identity of voters more widely and openly, playing on their feelings and their dissatisfaction with the real economic situation. At the same time it appears that people in Kyrgyzstan, like in other Central Asian countries, have no feelings of pan-Islamism or pan-Turkism at all. Rather, political appeals to Muslims play on the internal divisions within Islam, concentrating on ethnic fault-lines. The majority of politicians in Kyrgyzstan at the moment come not from religious but from Communist Party backgrounds, with the skills necessary to manipulate the issue of religious identity. A future generation of politicians, growing up with independence, will be better prepared to use Islam constructively to shape the future of Kyrgyzstan.

MUSLIM VERSUS MUSLIM

More than 80% of people in Kyrgyzstan are from traditionally Muslim ethnic groups, such as the Kyrgyz, the Uzbeks, the Tatars, the Tajiks, the Kazakhs, the Uighurs and the Dungans. Because of the exodus of Russians, the influx of refugees and a high birth rate among Muslim groups, the proportion of Muslims is gradually increasing. Religion is one factor contributing to the division of Kyrgyzstan into two parts. This separation is occurring along geographic, economic, cultural and ethnic lines. Relations between the two large ethnic groups (Muslim Kyrgyz and Russians) determine the state of affairs in the North, whereas the primary concern in the South is the state of relations between two mainly Muslim ethnic groups: the Kyrgyz and the Uzbeks. Today the process of Christianization of the northern part of Kyrgyzstan competes with Islamization in the southern part. This religious polarization further complicates the region's ethnic, cultural, geographic and economic divisions between the more prosperous, industrially developed and Russified North and the more populous and poor South, with its overwhelmingly Turkic population.

At the same time, Kyrgyzstan can be divided into three geographic zones, each with its own religious situation. The first zone is Bishkek city and the Chui region, with their large Slavic population. They tend to be more religiously and ethnically heterogeneous than the rest of the country. According to official data, in Bishkek City, the Kyrgyz are a minority — 33%, while a mix of Russians and Ukrainians (usually Orthodox) constitute a majority — 54%. Proportions are similar in the Chui region, where the number of Orthodox is almost equal to the Muslims (the Kyrgyz, Kazaks, and Uzbeks combined). The position of the Orthodox Church and, therefore, Moscow, is stronger in this zone. As a result, some religious pluralism can be seen.

The second zone is the north of the republic; this mountainous region is mainly Muslim, but practicing the traditional Islam of Kyrgyzstan, with considerable pre-Islamic influences and elements of *shamanism* (a primitive tribal religion). Healers will often invoke Allah and traditional spirits in the same prayers. Here there is a strong Kyrgyz majority — 98% in Naryn, 87% in Talas and 77% in Issyk-Kul. In this zone, Protestant missions now successfully proselytize among the Kyrgyz, free of any significant obstacles.

The third zone consists of the Osh and Jalal-Abad regions. They are in the south where Islam is more strictly adhered to and external Islamic missions are the most prominent. In addition to the low number of non-Muslims (3 – 4%), there is a high percentage of devout believers among the Uzbeks and the Kyrgyz. The region also contains the active Muslim centers of Osh, Jalal-Abad, Uzgen, Safid-Bulend, and Iski-Naukat, all-important sites of pilgrimage in Central Asia. There are nine *madrasas* and more than fifty mosques in Osh, the most religious city. In the second major religious center, Jalal-Abad City, thirty-eight mosques operate, only a quarter of which have been registered. There are about three hundred mosques in the Jalal-Abad Oblast. In the last few years their number has increased tenfold.

Compared to the previous years, the number of mosque-goers is constantly increasing. The majority of them are Uzbeks, but the number of Kyrgyz is also increasing. Many of those who go to mosque are young people. A sociological survey carried out by the Institute for Regional Studies (Bishkek) in southern Kyrgyzstan in 1998 indicated that over half of the respondents had copies of the Koran at home. According to the survey, the Uzbeks of the region are twice as likely to attend mosques as are Kyrgyz.

Despite this growth, the Muslim community is split on certain issues. It is divided between two factions: the "true believers," and the adherents of traditional Islam. The "true believers" are those standing up for the purity of Islamic traditions. They are calling for the return of original moral standards and modesty in public life, and they strongly oppose luxury. This group is mainly comprised of adults, as well as young people and their relatives who have completed a pilgrimage to Mecca. This faction is heavily backed financially and practically by benefactors from wealthy Gulf States, which have, in many cases, overcome opposition to their mosques by bribing local authorities to register them.

An alarming trend among some Muslims is the denial of the diversity of Islam and the recognition of only one version as true and absolute. This could aggravate ethnic and religious tensions. The tension between so-called "good" Muslims and "not very good" Muslims (between ethnic groups or within one ethnic group) could lead to new conflicts. The appearance and activities of radical religious activity is worrying.

There is also a trend to divide conditionally the mosques and *madrasas* on the grounds of ethnicity. Thus Kyrgyz, Uzbek, Uighur, and Dungan mosques and *madrasas* can be seen. Though there is an element of conscious desire among the communities to have their own mosques, a significant factor in this situation is the tendency for ethnic communities to live homogeneously. However, as Muslim identity becomes more important, there is a danger that this separation could inflame ethnic tensions.

Like in other parts of the former Soviet Union, traditional religious communities (the Muftiates and Orthodox hierarchies) have maintained alliances that they formed in opposing repression of faith by the Communist authorities. Their main opponents now are the new religious movements in the region.

GENDER ISSUE

Freedom of worship has brought a great opportunity for many women to observe Islam. Mosques have become open to them. Girls and women may study Koran and Islamic common law, *shari'a*, in newly established religious schools. Hundreds of women have made the *hajj* to Mecca.

At the same time, discrimination of women under the pretext of reviving Muslim traditions in favor of a male-dominated society is seen as very significant, and it could lead to serious changes in the post-Soviet society.

An increasing number of women in *hijab* (mainly very young or old) are regarded by society negatively. Most of these women are young and from rural areas, and strongly influenced by missionaries from Middle Eastern countries and Pakistan. The forms of Islam they turn to, under the influence of the foreign missionaries, tend to be extremely patriarchal and at odds with the Soviet understanding of equality between the sexes. This division in society causes many conflicts in everyday life.

In Central Asia, discussions on the benefits of polygamy are becoming, surprisingly, more common. Many men are talking about the observation of all Muslim traditions, including polygamy. They suggest polygamy as a means of alleviating poverty and curbing prostitution. The exaggeration of ethnicity and religious identity in Central Asia (including Kyrgyzstan) makes many politicians and others eager to increase their indigenous population, and they see polygamy as a righteous means towards this.

This desire for a larger population, along with the societal fertility cult, has a huge negative impact on women in the southern region. One result is the chronic lack of access to contraceptives. Abortion is the major form of contraception in the cities of Central Asia. In rural areas abortion, like any contraception, is seen by many as sinful and impious. At the same time, according to both Soviet and Central Asian traditions, a woman has the sole responsibility for the prevention of an unwanted pregnancy: it is not considered to be a man's concern.

Household labor with the three "un-"s — unpaid, unprestigious and unnoticed — has become even more burdensome. Care of children, one's husband, the sick and the elderly is entirely on women's shoulders. Not only the destruction of the system of social protection, but a discriminatory interpretation of Koran in favor of patriarchal traditions has aggravated the difficult situation of women in Central Asia.

A difference in gender relations between the relatively secular North and the more Muslim South is becoming increasingly visible. It is even difficult for the many organizations to invite female teachers to Bishkek City because often their husbands are against their independent travel. Southern women lead more secluded and isolated lives, explaining this isolation as a necessity if they are to observe "their Muslim traditions."

Thus, a significant number of women are in an ambiguous social situation, encouraged in emancipation, while ethnically and religiously subject to "Muslim tradition." This forces them to return to old behavioral norms, where the functions of bearing and caring for children, looking after their men and fulfilling their household duties have been, traditionally, the women's lot.

Furthermore, the quality of a woman's life is often defined by the presence of children and a husband. According to the widespread understanding of the patriarchal model of Islam, woman's professional advancement and aspirations are not usually among the most important elements of the quality of life. The entire system of patriarchal relations, interpreted as righteousness, restricts a woman's opportunity to freely choose a life paradigm.

Many women in Kyrgyzstan (and in neighboring Kazakhstan as well) who are faced with a male-dominated form of Islam, and are searching for religious identity, have converted to Protestant Christianity, Bahaism (a sectarian teaching, which broke off *Shi'a* faith), and numerous other religions that are nontraditional in the region. This is another factor that could cause friction in a new Muslim environment, especially between men and women.

GEOPOLITICAL DIMENSION

Islam tends to be observed less stringently in Kyrgyzstan than in neighboring Uzbekistan and Tajikistan, though some rituals such as circumcision and Muslim burial are almost universal among the country's traditionally Islamic ethnic groups. There is a tendency for certain ethnic groups in Kyrgyzstan, such as the Uzbeks and Tajiks, to be more observant of Muslim rituals than the Kyrgyz, but this is by no means uniform.

Thanks to the government's policies of religious tolerance in Kyrgyzstan, many pilgrims from neighboring Uzbekistan and Xinjiang are coming to smaller Kyrgyzstan to start their *hajj* to Mecca because strict controls and restrictions of power in their countries impede them from observing the pilgrimages. According to local residents, citizens of Uzbekistan falsify documents and go to *hajj* as Kyrgyzstan residents. It is not a secret that they are helped both in militia departments and passport issuing agencies.

Events in Uzbekistan underscore the religious pluralism that exists in Kyrgyzstan, especially in its part of Fergana Valley. The label of *Wahhabist* has become a popular tool for chastising people who have different views and for intervening in the internal affairs of Kyrgyzstan by the Uzbekistani government. On the other hand, the Uzbek Islamic opposition, which has the goal of creating a theocratic state and is now based in Tajikistan, could be a significant destabilizing force in Central Asia. They have threatened to carry out terrorist activities in Kyrgyzstan if the country cooperates with Uzbekistan in the repression of Islamic leaders.

The situation is extremely dangerous because the light arms, the narcotics, the Islamic extremism, the experience of war and the warrior mentality that has accumulated on Tajikistani territory could spill over into Kyrgyzstan. The borders between the three states are not only porous to the drug trade, they are also pathways open to religious extremists. It is important to understand that extremist ideas easily find sympathetic ears among people of the Fergana Valley because of the economic hardships arising out of the fall of the Soviet Union, hardships that have not been seen in the region since the Second World War.

In the context of Central Asia, many ethnic problems could be resolved simply through economic development. However, this will not dispel religious friction. The Fergana Valley has the highest concentration of religious believers and holy places (*mazars*) in the whole of Central Asia. As I previously noted, the most important holy place is Suleiman Mountain in Osh City. However, a significant number of holy places are located close to international borders. The populations of the three parts of the valley have gone on pilgrimage to *mazars* regardless of borders for hundreds of years. Now, however, these holy places, common to all Muslims, are under the control of different states. In conditions of sovereignty, no state can have pretensions of influence in the management of sites in other countries.

Wahhabism and religious extremist tendencies do not play the significant role that people usually ascribe to them. To avoid conflict, it is more important to pay attention to problems associated with the management of holy places. Intervention and usage of historical justifications to lay claim to holy places on the territory of another state could lead to a whole host of conflicts. Confessional relationships should be founded on the current situation with an eye to the future.

CONCLUSION

To other Central Asians, the democratization process in Kyrgyzstan has clearly not been able to solve all problems in the religious sphere. The declaration of religious freedom has to be accompanied by hard work and strong will on the ground to ensure that tolerance is promoted and conflicts are prevented and resolved. The authorities should break from their Soviet mentalities and become more transparent in their dealings with religious issues. Whenever different confessional groups exist within one state or within the international community there might well be friction sooner or later. This would be the inevitable result where traditions, viewpoints and interests of different groups are dissimilar. One advantage of a democratic community is that it allows the agenda to be open and problems to be tackled soon after appearance. Another is the possibility of finding ways to solve problems to mutual benefit.

Maintaining the principles of religious pluralism in Kyrgyzstan is necessary, and it sets a very important precedent in Central Asia. Only purposeful and staunch will, persistent efforts and a clear understanding of the real situation will promote irreversible changes for the better.

Chapter Three

The Islamic Revival in Uzbekistan: A Threat to Stability?

Abdumannob Polat

ISLAM IN TRANSITION

Gorbachev's liberal reforms in the late 1980s relaxed the pressure on religious activity in Soviet life. In no time at all, Islam was openly a part of
life in the Muslim republics of the Soviet Union. In the years right after
the collapse of the USSR most of the governments of the newly independent states — Uzbekistan included — embraced the liberalization
process or at least tolerated a reemergence of religious activity. They
needed Islam as an ally in national self-identification and for the process
of nation-state building now that the Soviet Empire was in ruins. The
Muslim faith, which had been practiced mostly within the privacy of
people's homes, started to blossom. In Uzbekistan alone some 5,000
mosques and dozens of *madrasas* (Islamic schools) were restored or even
built anew during this period. Islamic literature, previously circulated
in the format of samizdat (underground literature) became legally
available. Along with that, the Muslim faithful and teachers of the
Koran resurfaced in public life to deliver the word of Allah. Sufi *sheiks*
(teachers), suppressed during the czarist rule and later forbidden by the
Soviets, reappeared.

However, the champions of Muslim faith of post-Soviet Central Asia
did not come as a unified group. During the Soviet years there was what
researchers called a "Great Split" between traditionalists and reformers.

Most Muslims in Uzbekistan historically practiced *Hanafi*,[1] one of
the major schools of Islamic jurisprudence. This form of Islam, in addi-

tion to promoting loyalty to the existing rulers, tolerated and to some extent incorporated several ceremonies and rites, most noticeably involving funerals and weddings. A few traditional mullahs were officially accepted by the Soviet regime to perform these rituals. In the eyes of many, these mullahs were collaborating with the oppressors and this left a negative imprint on the whole of traditional Islamic teachings.

Opposition to this form of Islam originally started as an attempt to free the faith from layers of local rituals, the old heritage of pre-Islamic culture and religions. Furthermore, Central Asian Muslim thinkers were not immune to reformist ideas coming from the rest of the Islamic world. They were familiar with the radical goals of the Wahhabi movement, which had originated in Saudi Arabia in the nineteenth century. Wahhabis were committed to returning to the practice of pure Islam, like that observed by the early Khalifs. Among the Uzbek clergy — a home-grown group, known under the name Kadimists — also issued a call to purify the faith. From neighboring India, Uzbek *ulema* (learned men of Islam) learned about the Deobandi school of reform that was promoting an educational renaissance in the Muslim world. On local Uzbek soil similar views were advocated by the enlightened Jadidism movement, which emanated from the late ninteenth century.

"The Split" occurred during the time of Mullah Hindustani, one of the most outstanding Uzbek Islamic teachers. Born and later educated at Deobandi Islamic University before the Bolshevik revolution, Hindustani was later imprisoned in the gulag. Eventually released from prison, he was sent to the front lines during the Great Soviet Patriotic War against Nazi Germany. He survived until Gorbachev's perestroika and was the teacher to many among the Uzbek Muslim clergy of modern Uzbekistan. He stood as a true traditionalist in his teachings. However, a number of his best pupils turned into ardent radicals. Rightly or wrongly, they were later labeled Wahhabis.[2]

Despite the label, their views are not necessarily opposed to the *Hanafi* school. But they rejected the Sufi culture and its practices, as a distortion of the true Islam. They categorically opposed complementary rituals (as a rule financially very expensive) that were followed by many Uzbeks and that had evolved in Central Asia over the centuries.

Several mosques in the Fergana Valley and Tashkent became centers of this new movement in Uzbekistan's religious life. By exploiting the intolerance of other views and interpretations of Islam that were widespread among some clergy and activists from both sides, the government succeeded in deepening the split between followers of the traditional (Hanafi) and the newly emerged interpretation of Islam (Wahhabi).

There is an ongoing debate as to whether this radical movement — called Wahhabism or something else — was imported from abroad or whether it originated at home. Nobody can deny the influx of missionaries and radical Islamic literature that came from Saudi Arabia, Pakistan, and even from *Shi'a* Iran — all proclaiming the necessity for renewal.

Internal conflicts inside the *umma* (Islamic community) erupted in the form of open protests in early 1989. A few hundred Islamic activists demanded the resignation of Mufti Shamsiddin Bobokhonov, head of the Board of Muslims of Central Asia and Kazakhstan. They accused Bobokhonov of not fulfilling his duties as the leader of the Muslim community. They declared that he was too passive in his support for the Islamic revival. Bobokhanov was even accused of drinking alcohol. Protesters organized an unsanctioned five-mile-long rally from Tashkent's main mosques in the city's old town to the city center. The head of the Council of Ministers addressed the activists and told them that since state and religion are separate, the government was not in position to intervene and replace the Islamic leader. In a few weeks, however, a new mufti, Muhammad Sodiq Muhammad Yusuf, head of the Tashkent *madrasa* (Islamic higher school), replaced Bobokhonov.[3]

Muhammad Sodiq came from a well-known and respected religious family in the Fergana Valley. Under his leadership, the Board of Muslims began to make significant progress in reviving Islamic life and education. Immediately after becoming the head of the Islamic community, Muhammad Sodiq was elected to the Soviet parliament in Moscow (the Congress of People's Deputies). It was obvious at that time that he had the support of the Uzbek government.

Soon, however, his opponents launched a bitter campaign against him, claiming that Muhammad Sodiq's election to the Council of Ulema (Islamic leaders) was not legitimate and that it had been marred with serious irregularities. Some critics even claimed that there had been no real election at all. Later, Muhammad Sodiq's opponents accused him of selling tens of thousands of copies of the Koran, which had been sent as free gifts to Central Asian Muslims by the Saudi King.

Regarding his policy toward the so-called Wahhabis, Muhammad Sodiq was under fire from opposition on both sides. One of the sides charged the Mufti for allegedly providing support to a newly emerging movement of nontraditional Islamic thought. The other accused Muhammad Sodiq of organizing attacks against reformers.

Many believe that authorities did not want a strong and respected Islamic leader who enjoyed popular support and could have used Islam as a political tool in dividing his followers. The government wanted to keep the Islamic tool in the hands of the authorities, and use it as an instrument of control. Muhammad Sodiq's opponents organized several demonstrations of protest in an attempt to oust him, in fact using tactics similar to the ones that had earlier brought him to power.

In the meantime, the Board of Muslims, led by Muhammad Sodiq, spearheaded the building and restoration of hundreds of mosques and many *madrasas* (religious schools). In such practical matters, the Mufti had a solid reputation. Even his opponents considered him to be one of the most educated Islamic clergymen in Central Asia. In the 1970s and 1980s, Muhammad Sodiq graduated from the *Mir Arab* Islamic high school in Bukhara and from al-Bukhari Institute in Tashkent. A general belief at the time was that student enrollment to these schools — the only two Islamic educational institutions in the whole of Soviet Central Asia — was tightly controlled by government. The role of the regime and its security apparatus was probably even stronger in selecting Soviet students to be sent to the Islamic universities abroad. Thus, the very fact that the Mufti himself had been given a chance to attend the Islamic University in Libya further complicated matters, compromising him in the eyes of his opponents. Opponents did not hesitate to use such accusations in their attacks, labeling all official clergy "red mullahs." However, for the same reasons it would have been difficult to find an alternative Islamic leader among official clergy, at that time, who had a different resume.

To a degree, Muhammad Sodiq was able to find a proper balance between demonstrating loyalty to the government and garnering some independence for the Board of Muslims. Such balance made a significant contribution to stability in Uzbekistan. The typically nonconfrontational and fully nonviolent policies of the Uzbek secular opposition, together with the moderate position of Mufti Muhammad Sodiq and many other Islamic leaders in Uzbekistan in late 1980s and early1990s, also made a decisive contribution to promoting peace. The political climate in Uzbekistan was dramatically different from the situation in neighboring Tajikistan.

SECULAR EDUCATION IN CRISIS

By about 1993, Uzbekistan encountered serious budgetary problems in maintaining the educational system, one of the major achievements of the Soviet period. Most schools and universities did not have funds to pay teachers' salaries. Shrinking state funds were the only source of support, since there was no private financial assistance to educational institutions. On the other hand, numerous sponsors and donors from Muslim countries abroad — in addition to domestic contributors and volunteers — funded most of the mosque and *madrasa* construction. The country, with its educational system in deep crisis, considered Islamic education as the highest priority. Many Uzbeks, including intellectuals, believed that a "true Islam" would resolve the country's problems. The ideological vacuum left after the collapse of the official Soviet system was now filled by Islamic thought. Many of the newly opened mosques had small *mektebs* (Islamic elementary schools), providing the entry level in Islamic education, while many dozens of *madrasas* (Islamic secondary schools) served the next level of advanced religious schooling. The mass media began to provide extensive information on Islam, in addition to numerous books and brochures that were printed by Islamic leaders. Censorship was also largely lifted. In sharp contrast, the government prohibited the advocacy of democratic ideas and banned pro-democratic organizations. Thousands of Muslims from Uzbekistan traveled to Islamic countries, completing a *hajj* (pilgrimage) to the holy cities of the Muslim world. Fewer, but still significant numbers, went to Muslim countries to get an Islamic education. Islamic missionaries from Turkey, Pakistan, Saudi Arabia, and even *Shi'a* Iran, spread their own understanding of the religion, and foreign Islamic books found their way into the country.

The government extensively used the Islamic card to bolster its legitimacy, especially after 1989. At that time secular, democratic, and nationalist movements received some popular support and were able to organize peaceful demonstrations of tens of thousands of people. Uzbek communist authorities, however, vigorously opposed Gorbachev's *glasnost* (openness) policies. Central Asian society appeared to be less ready to fight for democracy. The movements for civil rights and political freedom that emerged in the region were much weaker than those activities in the Western parts of the Soviet Union. This was especially true in Uzbekistan, with its conservative Communist government. For instance, between 1990 and 1991, the republican leadership, in addition to its lack of enthusiasm for democratic reforms, repeatedly stated that it would continue building socialism even if the Gorbachev government introduced capitalism.

While the emerging secular opposition tried to promote democratic change, the Islamic movement focused on education and avoided political activities. As a result, the government considered democrats and nationalists to be a threat to the authorities and treated Islam, if not favorably, at least with sufficient tolerance.

In June 1989, Islam Karimov, the former head of Uzbekistan's State Planning Committee and Finance Minister in mid-1980s — and head of the poorest province in the south of the republic — became the First Secretary of the Uzbek Communist Party. Karimov soon incorporated into his official policies a proposal to grant the Uzbek language state legal status, and to increase the rights of the republic within the USSR structure, in the areas of economics, culture, and politics.

Fighting Gorbachev's *glasnost* reforms vigorously, the conservative leadership in Uzbekistan managed to keep the February 1990 elections under tight control. As a result, the main leaders and activists of the democratic and nationalistic opposition, which emerged between 1988 and 1989, were prevented from running for seats in public offices, although several independent activists did win elections. In March of 1990, Uzbekistan's undemocratically elected parliament selected Karimov to be the President of Uzbekistan — from a candidate list consisting of one name. Despite an increasing tolerance toward Islam, the government tried to prevent any Islamic-based political movements from forming. As a result, neither official clergy nor their opponents received voices in the parliament.

Barred from a legislative role, the growing opposition to official Islam attempted to institutionalize itself. In January 1991, the Uzbek branch of the then All-Union Islamic Rebirth Party was established. Although the authorities managed to disrupt its founding conference within an hour of its opening — and question and fine several organizers — participants did manage to quickly elect a leadership. The official clergy, led by Mufti Muhammad Sodiq, criticized the creation of this Party, arguing that Islam does not recognize political parties or factions. Very soon, Karimov's government issued a ban on any political party created with a religious base. Such a provision was included in Uzbekistan's 1991 law on public organizations. Because the official clergy was loyal to the authorities and considered their opponents in the Islamic community to be radicals, the government supported the Mufti and his followers in this conflict.

Post-Soviet Uzbekistan held its first presidential elections in December of 1991. Some supporters of Muhammad Sodiq wanted to nominate him as a candidate, but the Mufti himself refused to run for the office and backed Karimov instead. However, there were reports that Muslims collected signatures in the Fergana Valley to nominate Muhammad Sodiq.

THE 1991 NAMANGAN PROTESTS

The Islamic militia *Adolat* (justice) was another independent Islamic movement that emerged in the Namangan province in the Fergana Valley in late 1991. Adolat's focus was on combating crime by cooperating with the local authorities. Many members of this youth organization received the status of police volunteer assistants (somewhat similar to Neighborhood Watch in the United States). Adolat quickly received popular support among people in Namangan because they helped reduce the crime rate, a serious threat to local communities at that time. However, there were reports Adolat members were often abusing their power and beating suspects. Furthermore, the government was alarmed on discovering that some of the militia leaders promoted radical Islamic views and enjoyed broad societal support.

In early December 1991, Karimov visited Namangan. He spoke before approximately one hundred local officials, but four representatives of the Islamic community who had been originally invited were prevented from taking part in the meeting. After being shut out, these four people went to mosques and told the Muslim congregation what had happened. As a result, several hundred people came to the main government building and demanded a meeting with President Karimov, who by that time had already departed for Tashkent. Soon, more demonstrators joined the protesters and thousands remained around the government building all night.

Adolat and some affiliated groups (such as *Tavba* and *Islom Lashkari*[4]) organized the protests. They even got some support from official clergymen. Early the next morning Karimov came back to Namangan and met with the people. Though the demonstration was peaceful, some leaders of the protesters (like Tohir Yoldosh, who later became the head of the

Islamic Movement of Uzbekistan in exile) were very aggressive toward the President. Protestors for the first time aired an open call for a political role for Islam, advocating the establishment of an Islamic state in Uzbekistan and introduction of *Shari'a* (Islamic) law. Karimov responded that the idea of an Islamic state would be discussed in parliament and that all decisions would be made within the framework of the Constitution. He promised to be forthcoming on the other items on the list of demands that did not have political connotations. Soon some of the propositions, demanded by the crowd at the demonstration, were indeed implemented.

KARIMOV'S SECOND TERM

After his reelection, Karimov took his oath of office with one hand on the Constitution of Uzbekistan and the other hand on the Koran. Later, Karimov paid an official visit to Saudi Arabia where he had talks with the top Saudi leadership and visited the holy cities of Mecca and Medina with the Saudi King. Government propaganda and the official clergy tried to present this trip as a "small *hajj*" (an undertaking counted as a Muslim pilgrimage).

In March 1992, the government of the then independent Uzbekistan banned Adolat and arrested twenty-seven of its members. Perhaps it was partially in retaliation for how Karimov had been treated by that angry crowd. But the signal was clear: the government was not going to tolerate the political appetite of Islam. Many in Namangan protested against these arrests. The staff of the main government-owned factory in the city went on strike under the leadership of its Chief Manager, Abduvohid Pattaev, a member of parliament. (Soon after, Pattaev was fired from both the parliament and from his factory and was forced to leave the country. He now resides in Bulgaria).

For a while the government did release some Adolat members, but soon after they were arrested again and given long jail sentences.

UZBEKISTAN'S TAJIK ANGLE AND THE UZBEK MUJAHIDIN

Although Uzbek security forces arrested some leaders and activists of Adolat, many escaped. They fled to neighboring Tajikistan where Tohir Yoldosh, head of the radical group Islom Lashkari (warriors of Islam), became the leader of the Uzbek opposition in exile. Soon they joined the Tajik Islamic movement in the Tajikistan civil war that began in May of 1992. In late 1992 and early 1993, many Tajik Islamic fighters and their Uzbek allies moved to the military camps in neighboring Afghanistan.

Afghan *mujahidin*, led by field commander ethnic Tajik Akhmed Shah Masud, provided weapons and military training to Tajik Islamists. This, combined with Russian and Uzbek support to governmental forces in Tajikistan, resulted in the steep escalation of the Tajik war.

After the end of the Tajik civil war, with the signing of the 1997 peace accord, Uzbek *mujahidin* began to move back to Tajikistan. However, there was no room in Tajikistan for them. There were serious allegations that these groups would try to use this closer and more convenient location to launch sorties into Uzbekistan. The concerns of the Karimov regime had some grounds, especially since the Uzbek *mujahidin* groups were getting support from a growing number of radical factions that supported political Islam in Uzbekistan. The rise of Muslim radicalism was caused by disastrous social conditions, wide-scale unemployment among the youth, and the authorities' ever-growing hostility toward Islamic activism.

According to confidential but credible reports, the number of Uzbek Islamic fighters between 1992 and 1995 was between fifty and one hundred, but the suppression of the independent Muslim community in Uzbekistan since 1996 and 1997 increased their number. By early 1998, there were reports of hundreds of Uzbek *mujahidin*. The government in Tashkent claimed there were one thousand fighters in one of the alleged camps.

The next round of the government campaign against Islamic movements began in December 1997, when they used the murder of a few police officials in Namangan as an excuse to crack down. The government arrested hundreds of people, which in turn significantly increased the number of fighters in the camps led by Tohir Yoldosh and his associate, Juma Namangani.

THE 1999 TASHKENT BOMBINGS

The explosion of six bombs on February 16,1999 in Tashkent, in what may have been an attempt to assassinate President Islam Karimov, killed sixteen people and injured more than one hundred. The attack targeted key government buildings and called into question the stability of this strategically located Central Asian nation. The authorities blame militant Islamic groups in Uzbekistan and abroad for the bombings. The Supreme Court of Uzbekistan recently sentenced six bombing suspects to death; sixteen other suspects were sentenced to ten to twenty years of imprisonment.

It is not yet clear who was responsible for the February 1999 bombings, but there were serious allegations that extremist Islamic groups were involved. The government accused the Tohir Yoldosh's Islamic Movement of Uzbekistan (the so-called Wahhabis), Hisb-Al-Tahrir (a group that advocates the return to a pan-Islamic state of all Muslims worldwide, the modern day Khaliphate), and other unofficial Islamic groups. Authorities also blame Muhammad Solih, leader of the Erk (freedom) Democratic Party, a man who has been in exile since 1993 for his alleged political cooperation with Tohir Yoldosh and other militants. Uzbek government accusations that Tajikistan and Turkey supported these Uzbek extremists have severely damaged relations between Uzbekistan and these two countries.

The Islamic Movement of Uzbekistan made several strong statements after the Tashkent bombings. First, it flatly denied the government's accusations. Second, the movement demanded the resignation of President Karimov and the creation of a provisional government. Third, the movement demanded bringing to justice all officials responsible for the harassment and jailing of Islamic activists. Fourth, the Islamic Movement threatened to launch *jihad* to defend Islam, and admitted that it cooperated with all the factions in Afghanistan, including the Taliban. Embedded in these statements were claims that Karimov favors the United States and Isreal because his father was Jewish. Many statements of the Islamic Movement of Uzbekistan were made public by *Mashhad* (Voice of the Islamic Republic of Iran), as well as by the BBC and Radio Free Europe/Radio Liberty's Uzbek Services. The odd nature of these statements was noted by Iranian radio:

> *We were puzzled and wondered whether it would be correct to put it [statement of the Islamic Movement of Uzbekistan] on [the] air because some of the wording in this statement was very emotional... We would like to stress again that these are not our views and observations, that is they do not belong to the radio of the Islamic Republic of Iran.*[5]

Muhammad Solih also denied any involvement with the terrorist acts. However, he admitted cooperating with longtime friend, Zelimkhan

Yandarbiev, a former acting President of Chechen Republic, who'd recently signed the treaty between Chechnya and the Taliban. Solih also admitted he had political contacts with Tohir Yoldosh.

After the February 16, 1999 explosions in Tashkent, Karimov promised to pardon those who would confess to being involved in the extremist Islamic underground. Reportedly, hundreds of young members of unofficial Islamic groups came to law enforcement agencies with confessions. At the same time, there were reports that hundreds of Islamists left Uzbekistan and joined the *mujahidin* based in Tajikistan.

In May 1999, however, strife was reported among Uzbek *mujahidin* in Tajikistan that led to the killing of sixteen soldiers. Many sources, including Uzbek authorities, reported that Tohir Yoldosh and Juma Namangani ordered the murder of these sixteen *mujahidin* because they wished to abandon their weapons, return to Uzbekistan, and surrender themselves to the authorities. However, the Islamic Movement of Uzbekistan, led by Tohir Yoldosh, denied that there were any such killings. The movement claimed that an Uzbek military unit had attacked the *mujahidin* camp. It is not clear yet what truly happened at the military camp of the Uzbek *mujahidin* in Tajikistan, a military camp in the region controlled by the United Tajik Opposition.

Extreme social conditions, a high level of corruption and lack of opportunities for the development of civil society and democracy created many thousands of potential supporters of a radical Islamic movement in Uzbekistan. This, in turn, has created a serious threat to the stability and peace of Uzbekistan, and therefore to the authority of Karimov's government.

Today, there are few Islamic leaders in Uzbekistan, either official or independent, who are willing to express their views publicly if these views are different from those sanctioned by the authorities. Plans by Islamic groups and leaders to create independent structures have been constantly thwarted, while most Islamic community functions, including Islamic education, have become subject again to strict governmental control.

Extremist Islam, especially the 1990s-Taliban and 1980s-Iranian models, has few supporters in Uzbekistan. The secular opposition has a pro-democratic orientation and together with most social and political groups in the country fully supports the independence of the state.

Before the bombings of February 16, 1999, there were no credible reports of terrorist actions by the Islamic groups. Except for some reports of suspicious "bodyguard training" conducted for twenty young Uzbeks in Turkey, and allegations that Solih somehow cooperated with the militant Islamic or pan-Turkish movements, the democratic opposition has been nonviolent. Most representatives of the independent Islamic community — setting aside unproven claims related to the killings in Namangan in December of 1997 — have had mainly educational and peaceful priorities. However, the mass repressions that began in December 1997 have radicalized the Islamic opposition.

INDEPENDENT LEADERS' ATTEMPTS TO ESTABLISH INDEPENDENT GROUPS

There are no established independent Islamic organizations in Uzbekistan. The Islamic Rebirth Party of Uzbekistan, founded in January 1991, has been inactive since the party's *Emir* (Chairman), *Abdulla qoriO'taev*, disappeared in December 1992.[6] According to his wife he was arrested near his home, but Uzbek authorities deny having him in their custody. Adolat and the groups *Tavba* (repentance) and Islom Lashkari, which were created in 1991 in Namangan province, have been banned since March 1992. Many leaders were arrested, but Yoldosh and some of his supporters left Uzbekistan.

Generally, the Uzbek government has succeeded in reestablishing control over the official Islamic clergy. Mufti Muhammad Sodiq Muhammad Yusuf was forced to resign from his position as the official head of Central Asia's Islamic community in 1993, and later had to leave Uzbekistan to avoid charges of helping Tajikistan's Islamic movement. Several leaders of the Islamic community in Namangan and Kokand remain jailed on dubious charges of narcotics or weapons possession.

In August 1995, *Sheikh* (Islamic leader) Abduvali qori Mirzaev, a popular and respected Islamic clergyman in Andijan and considered to be a Wahhabi leader, was reportedly arrested by security police at the Tashkent airport, along with an assistant, Ramazon Matkarimov. Mirzaev advocated Islamic education and community life free from government control. Despite relatively serious scrutiny from the international community, Uzbek authorities have denied that they arrested them, but the two, as well as Abdulla qori Otaev, have still not resurfaced. Eighteen months after the disappearance of the Islamic activists, and after numerous requests and complaints made by Mirzaev's relatives, the authorities published a photo of Matkarimov as a missing person, but they refused to publish Mirzaev's photo. Many monitors consider this to be evidence that Mirzaev is not being held under his own name. Several radical Islamic activists later confessed that the disappearance of Abduvali qori Mirzaev and the jailing of hundreds of peaceful Muslims since December 1997 has forced them to conclude that the only remaining method of advocating Islamic values is through military struggle.

Obidkhon qori Nazarov, another respected and popular Islamic leader in Tashkent with roots in Namangan, is also considered by the government to be a Wahhabi. Because of that he was dismissed from the mosque where he was chief *imam* (supreme leader of the Muslim community) in 1995. In the spring of 1998 he disappeared, and controversial reports on his fate soon followed. Some activists believe that he was arrested by the security service. Many, however, hope that Obidkhon qori Nazarov was only forced to leave Uzbekistan, as many secular opposition leaders were forced to do several years ago.

At the time, Friday and holiday prayers at mosques, led by popular *imams* such as Abduvali qori Mizrayev and Obidkhon qori Nazarov, brought together tens of thousands of Muslims — so many, in fact, that people had to pray standing up. Hundreds of thousands of copies of educational tapes authored by these *imams* have been sold and circulated.

Today Muslims are allowed to listen only to government-approved speeches at mosques and other public places. Fewer people in Uzbekistan attend mosques because of suspected government surveillance, identification checks of Muslims by police, and a general campaign of repression against any independent Islamic activities.

The government's repression is aimed at eliminating independent views and strong, popular leaders. They are well on their way to reestablishing the Soviet-style fear of authorities that was weakened during the limited liberal reform period between 1988 and 1992.

Harassment of independently oriented Islamic activists and many ordinary Muslims, even if they are loyal or indifferent to the government, occurs mostly without reason. Additionally, in May 1998 the authorities enacted a new law on religious freedom and organizations. This new law prohibits the activities of religious groups and communities with fewer than 100 members. The law also creates extremely restrictive regulations for the registration of religious organizations. It bans religious activity and religious education outside of the bodies that are officially recognized by the government, such as the Spiritual Board of Muslims. Foreign missionaries are also prohibited.

GOVERNMENT OPPOSITION TO DEMOCRACY

There might be a number of rationales behind the Karimov regime's delay in democratic reforms: the economic situation; the Taliban factor; developments in Tajikistan, including Uzbek fighters in Tajikistan; and a general government desire to curtail democratization.

There is another likely reason for Karimov's decision to delay political liberalization. There seems to be a calculated policy to limit democratization through the creation of a "constructive" opposition. This takes the form of GONGOs (government-organized non-governmental organizations) and of a "free" media that is in fact subordinated to the almost total control of the authorities. Even the limited liberalization in 1996 was greeted by increasing attempts to limit opposition views and criticism of the government's policies. For instance, at the OSCE's human rights seminar and the HRSU Conference in September 1996, some dissidents — among them two Islamic activists — strongly criticized the human rights policy of the government. Later, one of the top officials of Uzbekistan told an OSCE representative that the September seminar had given their enemies a forum, which they had used to attack the government. This, he said, would not be allowed to happen again.

Clearly, the Uzbek government has sometimes falsified information on events in the country; on government-opposition relations; on the activities of the opposition leaders; and on the goals and interests of the developed countries. In more open societies a relatively free media plays an important role in providing a broader spectrum of reports and views related to the country and abroad. By restricting its own citizens from gaining access to independent ideas and news, the government of Uzbekistan has also deprived itself of important information.

The government considers independent Islamic activists to be the main threat to the regime and the country's stability. Therefore, harassment of advocates and supporters of the independent Muslim clergy and Islamic missionaries from foreign states is much stronger than that of Christian missionaries and other non-Muslim activists. It is believed that there are hundreds, maybe thousands, of Muslim prisoners in the Fergana Valley jailed on what are likely fabricated narcotics and weapons possession charges. There have been numerous reports that police routinely plant narcotics and weapons in the pockets, cars, or homes of suspects. In most cases, advocates that "call for the forcible establishment of an Islamic state and Haliphate" in practice mean the peaceful promotion of a regime based on Muslim tradition. The government's attention is aroused when any contact or affiliation with unofficial Islamic groups takes place or there is involvement in religious educational activities, or travels to Pakistan, Turkey, or even neighboring Tajikistan. It appears that many Westerners and Western institutions that focus on Central Asia are much more aware of the intolerance of Uzbek society and its government toward foreign Christian missionaries than they are of the larger scale harassment of the independent Islamic community.

Monitoring and advocating the religious freedom of minorities, non-violent sects and missionaries are important. Christianity has strong spiritual and political influence in developed democracies. However, nonproportional attention to these issues — accompanied by a lesser interest in the religious freedom of the majority population in Central Asia — discredits this extremely important idea. Many people in the region view the West's preoccupation with the treatment of Christian sects and missionaries negatively because it ignores the suffering of Muslims, which is occurring on a larger scale. The West has been able to become a strong protector of the Muslims in Bosnia and Kosovo who have suffered ethnic cleansing. Although there is not mass violence against Muslims in Uzbekistan such as there was in the former Yugoslavia, a proper balance on this sensitive issue would, most certainly, be in the interests of the United States. Such a balance would decrease the anti-Western sentiments that are growing in the region, and it could help maintain stability.

EXTREME POVERTY AND LACK OF CIVIL SOCIETY MAY PROMOTE ISLAMIC RADICALISM

After some slightly positive signs in the summer of 1996, which created hope for future improvement, the economic situation soon deteriorated again, with the exception of a small number of companies run by high-ranking officials and their close relatives.

The average weekly salary in Uzbekistan is approximately US$15-20 at the market rate of exchange (which is two to three times lower than the black market rate), but this figure is far from adequate in explaining the real living conditions in the country. Prices for many products and services are the same or even higher than in the United States. However, products manufactured or grown locally or in neighboring poor countries are sold at relatively low prices. In general, a significant number of Uzbek families, including many intellectuals, earn very small incomes that cover only bread and tea and local public transportation, the traditional consumption pattern for poor families in the country.

Prices have gone up dramatically, many stores selling imported goods and related joint ventures have closed, and a shortage of goods has begun. In addition to these problems, world prices for cotton and gold (Uzbekistan's main exports) have fallen. Recent cotton and grain harvests did not meet projected targets. Hyperinflation in the country, since the introduction of the national currency in 1994, has been much higher than in Kazakhstan and Russia, by significant factors.

The country's economic and financial situation is close to disastrous. Uzbekistan needs significant foreign investment to restructure its economy. The national currency, the *som*, still is not convertible except for government-approved trade and investment projects. In reality, this often means that convertibility exists only for companies run by close relatives of top-ranking state officials.[7] Laws that are favorable to foreign investment frequently do not function in practice because there is no independent judiciary or other legal mechanisms to enforce them. Corruption and bureaucratic regulations pose monumental challenges to business and economic development in Uzbekistan. Foreign investors have lost interest in the country.

Many people are now angry with the government and believe that independence has worsened their living conditions. However, attempts to replace Marxism-Leninism with a national ideology — with references to the great historical heroes like *Timur* (Tamerlane) — have not produced noticeable results. Islam could easily fill this ideological vacuum. The poverty of the majority, the wealthy lifestyle of a small minority of "New Uzbeks," the absence of a sizeable middle class, when combined with mass harassment, serve only to heighten the appeal of radical Islam.

EXTERNAL PRESSURES: THE TALIBAN FACTOR AND TAJIKISTAN

It is true that the current fundamentalist regime in Kabul is a threat to the stability of Uzbekistan and the entire region. That is why between 1996 and 1997 — concurrent with these economic problems — Karimov's government significantly increased its support for Abdurashid

Dostum, the ruler of the northern provinces of Afghanistan. It was hoped that this would enable Dostum, and his allies, to oppose the Taliban's efforts to gain total control of the country. It is believed that Uzbekistan's support was significant and was not limited to humanitarian aid and free electric power.

During eighteen of the twenty years of war in Afghanistan, its northern provinces remained relatively stable. This was also true of the five years during which General Dostum was the dominant leader in the region. Alas, the Taliban finally defeated General Dostum's forces. The final fall of this and other more moderate, secular leaders in northern Afghanistan meant that Uzbekistan's only non-CIS border is now shared with a radical Islamic state. This has posed many problems, including the threat to the area's stability and the likelihood of thousands of refugees. Additionally, because the Uzbek government supported the anti-Taliban forces for several years, relations between the current regimes in Tashkent and Kabul are strained at best.

Tajikistan has also affected the situation in Uzbekistan. The two republics have close historical ties. The establishment of a coalition government in Tajikistan, where leaders of the armed Islamic movement have strong positions, as well as speculation about the future creation of a religious state there, has contributed to the fears and concerns of the Uzbek government. The Islamic center in Uzbekistan is located in the Fergana Valley, which is currently divided into Uzbek, Tajik, and Kyrgyz zones. Despite extreme measures conducted by the Uzbek authorities to minimize contacts with Tajikistan, influence from this republic will remain strong.

The city of Khojent (the capital of Leninabad, the northern province of Tajikistan) is Uzbekistan's natural ally. The Leninabad province politically dominated Tajikistan for decades during the Soviet period. It is the most developed part of the country and did not directly suffer from the civil war until early November 1998. Khojent, as a part of the Fergana Valley, has much closer economic, geographic and cultural ties to Uzbekistan than it has to the rest of Tajikistan. Therefore, it is natural that the ruling clan and many ordinary citizens in Khojent are sympathetic to Uzbekistan. Approximately twenty-five percent of the population in Tajikistan is Uzbek, and many of them live in the northern regions of the country. However, Khojent is almost totally excluded from the power-sharing arrangements in Tajikistan. The complicated relations between these two neighbors, and the Tajik President's allegations that Uzbekistan was behind some warlords who oppose the current power-sharing arrangements in Tajikistan, are further causes of serious concern for the Uzbek leadership.

Additionally, there were Uzbek units within the United Tajik Opposition, according to many confidential reports, mainly from Namangan and other provinces in the Fergana Valley. These units had been based in Afghanistan and reportedly have hundreds of fighters. It is believed they currently are based in Tajikistan, and have more than one thousand fighters. Since there is no room for these fighters in today's Tajikistan, it is believed that many of them now cooperate with Taliban forces. The best-known leader among these Uzbek fighters is Tohir Yoldosh, former head of Tavba and Islom Lashkari. Karimov considers him to be a serious opponent.

CONCLUSION

Clearly, Uzbekistan is a key country in Central Asia, but its economy is in tatters. Thus, oil or gas-rich neighbors such as Kazakstan, Turkmenistan and Azerbaijan may overshadow Uzbekistan's importance. However, Uzbekistan will play a key role in the future stability and development of this strategically important region. It is the only country in the Caspian region with the potential to become truly independent from Russia. Uzbekistan and Tajikistan have the most educated populations among states in the Muslim world. Uzbekistan, as the key country of the Central Asian region, can play a role similar to Turkey as another bridge between the West and East.

On the other hand, an economic or political disaster in Uzbekistan — or the establishment of a radical Islamic regime in the country — would severely destabilize all of Central Asia and would have a significant and negative impact on the states in the region. Uzbekistan is not Tajikistan, and it would be hard to contain the impact of instability in Uzbekistan for even a short period of time.

Today Uzbekistan's needs are great, economically and spiritually. The collapse of communism left a vacuum in the spiritual life and ideology of the country. The government is trying to cultivate a new secular ideology based on historical traditions and heritage, but it may take years or even decades for this ideology to put down deep enough roots and to be accepted, partially because there are no opportunities to advocate open and pluralistic democracy. Not surprisingly, there are attempts underway to fill this vacuum with Islamic thought; these attempts have succeeded, at least to some extent. Between 1989 and 1994, Uzbekistan's leadership considered the secular democratic opposition the main threat to the authorities and to stability. The government had been much more tolerant of an independent Islamic movement, with the exception of the persecution between 1992 and 1993 of the most radical groups in Namangan and Ququon. As a result, mosques became the only places where people could hear views not under total state control. Islamic thought, including its interpretations independent from the authorities, began to fill the existing ideological vacuum. Now it is independent Islam that is currently being singled out as the greatest threat to stability in Uzbekistan.

The real threat of religious fanaticism spreading from the south has fed the Uzbek government's use of the highly inflated specter of Islamic extremism to justify its denial of multiparty democracy, openness, a free media, and freedom of expression in the country. This same threat forces leaders of the Central Asian nations to seek support — including military support — from Russia. This is inevitable since NATO and the United States are geographically far from Central Asia, and they are not interested in the region except for Caspian oil and gas.

A continued lack of openness and freedom for secular democratic ideas in Uzbekistan could definitely lead to a much larger confrontation between the government and the Islamic movement. Unfair persecution of Muslims who advocate independence from government control could lead to genuine Islamic extremism. The country needs to promote gradual reforms, step-by-step liberalization, tolerance toward other religious views and different interpretations of Islamic practices, and dialogue with moderate Islamic and secular opposition leaders. This seems to be the only way to maintain the current level of stability and prevent a future disaster in Uzbekistan — and all of Central Asia.

C h a p t e r   F o u r

Islam and
the Tajik Conflict
Saodat Olimova

HISTORICAL BACKGROUND

Tajikistan had always been home to a moderate form of Islam, which has been traditional for most of the Central Asian community. However, it became the only country in the region where an escalation of events, involving political Islam, culminated in a tragic civil war.

The dominant form of Islam in Tajikistan has always been *Hanafi mazhab*, known for its moderation and capability of absorbing local pre-Islamic rituals and rites. It was not surprising that Sufi mystics became an organic part of Muslim faith here, the *Naqshbandi* brotherhood being one of the most widespread. The province of Badakhshan was the only stronghold of an alternative Islamic brand — Ismailism — a doctrine that split away from *Shiism* early in the development of Islam. This splinter sect of *Shi'a* Islam is considered to be substantially softer and more tolerant compared to the mainstream of *Shi'a*, but it accounts for 5% of Tajik population.

On the whole, the territory of present-day Tajikistan has always been a rural mountain-outback region, far removed from Central Asia's major Islamic centers such as Bukhara and Samarkand. The geography or mountainous terrain and rural demographics together have established a peculiar life pattern for local population. Interaction even between ethnically close tribes was complicated by the mountains separating them. Settlements in different valleys were isolated from each other. Thus, the role of ethnic identity lost its importance. Religion acquired the dominant position in developing the self-identification of the people in these mountainous patriarchal communities. Religious leadership tended to merge with secular power, and the Sufi religious orders gradually formed a kind of social hierarchy that permeated the everyday life of society. Sufi leaders exerted a powerful influence on the secular activity of every community.

The Soviet regime in Central Asia related to these Muslim societies by adopting a slash-and-burn campaign that was combined with cooperation. As a result, the institutional Islamic clergy was uprooted and an attempt was made to eradicate Islamic law. Perhaps in order to achieve this goal the Bolsheviks endorsed the existence of "popular" Islam, which was then headed by a new brand of clergy that collaborated with the regime and were totally controlled by it. The regime's battle against Ismaili religious leaders was especially ferocious, which ultimately resulted in a notable secularization in Badakhshan.

On the whole, the major drive of the Soviet period was modernization and its central element, urbanization. Tight social control, which was so characteristic of traditional rural Tajik society, was impossible in the cities. The new order had to develop its own mechanisms of regulating social behavior. Urbanization in Tajikistan had certain unique features. To a large extent it was formed with the help of external financial and human resources. As A. V. Vishnevsky points out, "The Soviet model of accelerated conservative modernization suited the historical conditions of the East Slavic peoples at the time."[1] It is precisely for that reason that the speed and scale of modernization in Central Asia was different from that in Russia proper.

Modernization and industrialization in Tajikistan were perceived as alien because the groundwork for such rapid development had not been laid. New imperatives clashed with traditional values; they did not receive popular support and were subject, in fact, to passive resistance. To this very day, the majority of the population does not realize the need for comprehensive radical modernization and wishes to preserve the traditional way of life and value system.

The years of Soviet modernization led to certain negative trends in Central Asian societies, such as steadily mounting demographic pressures, rural overpopulation, and hidden unemployment. From 1972, the proportion of rural population began to grow. In the period between 1992 and 1997 alone, the rural population increased from 67.8% to 72.6%.[2] Today, almost three-quarters of the population reside in rural areas. Per capita income in 1996 was U.S. $5.6 per month.

Thus, the industrialization and modernization effort imposed by the Soviet authorities actually had the effect of freezing the country's historical development, as Tajikistan seemed to be stuck in a rut of ruralism, falling far behind its Central Asian neighbors. Even as the rural economy stagnated, it also failed to push its surplus human resources out into the cities. To a large degree it helped to preserve the traditional social structures, and a way of life and its values. The cities were hamstrung by medieval restrictions, including the absence of the freedom of movement, direct distribution of goods, etc. All of this did not help to build an urban middle class that is often the agent of urban social organization. The peasants as they moved to the cities were socially marginalized. Individualism, a requirement of urban life, did not suit a people who had been raised on collective principles. The Soviet revolution failed to destroy the traditional holistic cultural paradigm. The growing educational level and changing lifestyle coexisted with the traditional sociocultural basis of Islam.

Elimination of the institutional clergy, followed by the imposition of stringent ideological state control and militant atheism, drove Islam underground. Ironically it helped to preserve the most archaic layers of Muslim culture, including Sufism, especially in regions where it had been traditionally dominant. "Popular" Islam gained a disproportionately strong influence as a way of life and method of adaptation to the atheistic regime, on the one hand. On the other hand, it served as a counterweight to modernization.

ISLAM AND THE INTER-TAJIK CONFLICT

Not long before Gorbachev's *perestroika*, in the general atmosphere of Soviet stagnation, Tajik society found itself on the verge of a serious crisis. The population explosion threw the country further into poverty and backwardness. The dearth of investment resources in the past twenty years, which dramatically slowed economic development in Central Asia, hit Tajikistan especially hard. The attempts to continue the course of modernization were intertwined with the build-up of an illegal shadow economy. One of its spinoffs was the emergence of a new elite alongside the official westernized Soviet elite. In its struggle to supplant the old system, the new elite drew on the powerful wellspring of traditionalism.

The fundamentalist idea emerged in Tajikistan just as the other Central Asian countries were being drawn into the modernization process. It started to embrace broad sectors of the population, whose traditional patriarchal mentality had been traumatized by modernization.

The formation of counter-elites supporting Islamist ideology was similar to the situation in Iran, where they mostly originated in the merchant middle class in the 1980s. The new powerful economic groups were not represented in the upper echelons of government. The barriers established by the Soviet nomenclatura in Tajikistan were complemented by a regional selection principle: the governing elite was recruited by the Kremlin from the north of the country. The historic explanation was that people from Karategin (province in Southern Tajikistan) and other regions of Tajikistan were denied government positions since those regions had originally put up the stiffest resistance to Soviet rule.

After gaining independence, the Tajik Communist Party continued to enjoy popular support in the center of the country, the Gissar Valley, which had accumulated a great deal of influence and resources. This included the province of Leninabad, the country's main industrial region, and in the Kulab — the agricultural outback, which traditionally supplied men for the army and police force. All these regions had close ties to the government.

Economically powerful subethnic elite groups from Karategin and Badakhshan, being underrepresented in the central government, supported an alternative, noncommunist ideology — Islamism. Since these regions had always had a tighter bond between secular and religious leadership, it was natural that support for political Islam emerged. The Islamic Revival Party of Tajikistan (IRPT) became a force to be reckoned with, when it was joined by the Karategin Sufi *ishans* (Sufi preachers) and their numerous *murids* (disciples). In spite of their secular lifestyle, the residents of Badakhshan formed their own ethnic society, La'li Badakhshon, which is essentially an ethno-religious political party. On the basis of these groups, a democratic-Islamic alliance was formed in the spring of 1999. What brought the democrats and Islamists together was a shared belief in egalitarianism and communal democracy, which were characteristic of the holistic communities in the region. Even though there were ideological differences between them and within their groups, they managed to keep their solidarity during the civil war of 1992-93. However, later in the post-war period, after the exclusion of the opposition from the political process, a heightened interest in political parties and general political activity among all the sub-ethnic groups began to wane. The old factional differences within all the parties came to the surface again. The ethno-regional solidarity, which had united the democrats and Islamists, became weaker and soon the rank-and-file and mid-level functionaries in different factions of previously united opposition became hostile toward each other.

The governmental camp, on the other hand, also suffered from a fragmentation of political forces. The Soviet policy was to combine modernism with a degree of traditionalism. However, after the collapse of the USSR, a different mix, namely of traditionalism and nationalism, took over. A new brand of traditionalists came to power.

RELIGION IN PRESENT-DAY TAJIKISTAN

Many of the processes taking place in Tajikistan are in one way or another related to Islam — for the simple reason that Islam remains the core element of people's cultural, civilizational, and ethnic self-identification. O. Rua singles out traditional Islam, the Islamic Revival Party, the Wahhabites, and the Tablighies (supporters of the reformist Islamic movement of Jamaat ul-Tablig) as the key religious and political forces present in Tajikistan today. Traditional or official Islam is represented by registered mosques, whose imam-khatibs (chief preacher) have renounced political Islam and are loyal to the Shuroi Ulamo (Council of Ulama, the supreme institutional Islamic authority in Tajikistan). The Movement for Islamic Revival of Tajikistan (MIRT) has as its main component the Islamic Revival Party of Tajikistan (IRPT), as well as a number of smaller Islamic groups, such as noninstitutionalized doctrinal Islam, Ismailism, and the Sufi brotherhoods.

Influence of international Islamic movements became a problem in recent years as young Tajiks began to return home after studying at various Islamic institutions abroad. The growing foreign influence caused a serious concern among traditionalists. An animosity between the two factions developed into a political conflict between fundamentalism and popular Islam.

In Tajikistan — unlike Pakistan, Algeria, and Chechnya — "popular Islam" has turned out to be almost as strong as canonical Islam. Soviet modernization did not destroy the traditional Tajik social infrastructure and later provided refuge to popular Islam, which kept alive the heritage of traditional Muslim roots. Hence, the two forms of Islam are in a political competition: Muslim fundamentalism vs. traditionalist popular Islam.

Popular Islam encapsulates the world view and way of life of the "silent majority," and it represents the traditional system of behavioral models that regulate different ages, sexes, and occupational groups.

According to a number of opinion polls, about 95% of the residents of Tajikistan said they believe in God, and 90% of adults (18 years and older) consider themselves Muslims. Among those Muslims, 13% said they actively practice Islam, 19% were moderately active, and 59% were not active.[3] This can well be seen in the results of recent (1996) polls. Fifteen percent of Muslims in Tajikistan go to the mosque on Fridays; 27% pray five times a day; the rest do not pray at all. The older the respondent, the closer he/she follows the rules and rituals of Islam. While those who do not pray at all constitute 78% of the 15-24 age group, they account for only 32% in the 55-64 age group. Sixty-seven percent of Tajiks in the 65-74 age group pray five times a day. This means the young generation's lax attitude to religious rules is now socially acceptable — which, however, does not make them atheists or secular people. It is assumed that they will change their behavior as they become older. It is the social norm for the older generation to follow the rules and rituals of Islam to the letter.

Most religious associations in Tajikistan have an educational function. This is due to the weakness of the institutional clergy, which has not yet recovered from the hardships of the Soviet epoch. However, even though all Islamic leaders recognize that the primary objective of their associations is enlightenment of the people, the next logical step is to set political goals. A. Malashenko points this out when he says, "politicization of Islam is a natural step in its renaissance."[4] At the time of crisis and civil war in 1992-1993, Islam was able to prove itself as a powerful mobilizing force in the political process.

Political methods prevail in today's struggle between various strands of Islam. This has been demonstrated by the National Reconciliation Commission, on which the government and the United Tajik Opposition have been locked in a year-long debate about removing the word "secular" from Tajikistan's Constitution (Article 100). An important role in politicizing Islam belongs to fundamentalist religious organizations and the *tariqas* (Sufi orders). The authority and influence of the Sufi *ishans* (teachers) is still high in some regions of Tajikistan. It is they who opposed the secular administration in the inter-Tajik conflict. The Islamic Revival Party of Tajikistan has united leaders of powerful Sufi brotherhoods: Karategin *ishans* and a small number of institutional clergy educated in Islamic universities abroad; Turajonzoda, one of the leaders of Islamic opposition in civil war, is a typical example.

The opposing forces (the Rakhmonov government and its camp) have also struck the Islamic chord with the population. They have looked for allies among traditional clergy, which, in conformity with Central Asian tradition, must subordinate its clerical leadership to political authority.

THE ISLAMIC REVIVAL PARTY OF TAJIKISTAN

Among the existing religious associations in Tajikistan, the Islamic Revival Party is undoubtedly the best-organized political force. The party started as an underground youth organization in 1978. (One of its founders, mullah Said Abdulloh Nuri, later headed opposition military forces from their bases in Afghanistan.) The objective of this young group was to study and disseminate the reformist teachings of Hasan Al-Banna (founder of Muslim Brotherhood movement in Egypt) and the ideas of Abul Ala Mawdudi (the ideologist of Pakistani branch of political Islam).

In 1990, the city of Astrakhan, Russia hosted a convention of Muslims from the entire Soviet Union. The conferees founded the All-Union Islamic Revival Party, approved its program, bylaws, and elected a governing body — the Council of Ulama. After returning to Tajikistan, delegates D. Usmon and S. Gadoev petitioned the republic's Supreme Soviet for permission to hold a regional constituent conference of the Islamic Revival Party. The Supreme Soviet responded by banning the Islamic Revival Party's activity in Tajikistan on the grounds that it was incompatible with the republic's constitution and Religious Freedom Act.[5]

Nevertheless, a constituent conference was held on October 6, 1990 at the Chortut Mosque of Dushanbe, in theTajik capital. The punishment was delivered instantly. First, in November 1990, the Central Committee of Tajikistan's Communist Party published a statement, "On Our Attitude to the Attempt to Establish a Tajik Branch of the All-Union Islamic Revival Party against the Decision of the 3rd Session of the Republic's Supreme Soviet Banning It." This was followed by the Tajikistan Supreme Soviet ruling of December 14, 1990, "On Curbing the Activity of Parties and Political Associations Banned under Tajikistan's Legislation." The conference organizers were fined.

In September 1991, Tajikistan gained independence. Protest rallies lasting many days signaled an erupting conflict. On October 22,1991, under the pressure of these protests, the Tajik Supreme Soviet passed a law repealing some of its own acts that prohibited religious parties. The new act also repealed Paragraph 3 of the Supreme Soviet's ruling of

October 5, 1990, which had stated in part: "To consider unacceptable the establishment on the territory of Soviet Tajikistan of a regional branch of the all-Union Islamic Revival Party."[6] Thus, Tajikistan's Supreme Soviet authorized registration of an Islamic Revival Party.

The Party held its first convention on October 26, 1991 with 657 delegates and 310 observers present, including about fifty accredited foreign journalists. A keynote address was delivered by one of the founders of the Party, Muhamadsharif Himmatzoda. He spoke of the need to establish a totally independent Islamic Revival Party in Tajikistan.[7] Other speakers gave unanimous support to this idea. A separate meeting of the board elected Himmatzoda as chairman of the Islamic Revival Party, and Usmon and Gadoev as his deputies. The convention approved the Party's coat of arms and flag. The *Najot* newspaper was to be the Party's official publication.

The Islamic Revival Party of Tajikistan was registered by Tajikistan's Ministry of Justice on December 4, 1991. At the moment of registration the Party had 20,000 members. Its bylaws stated, "As a sociopolitical organization of Muslims in Tajikistan, the Islamic Revival Party of Tajikistan shall follow the principles of Islam. As a parliamentary type of party, the Islamic Revival Party of Tajikistan shall take an active part in election campaigning and shall nominate its members to run for political offices."

The Party's main objectives were stated as follows:

- to promote the spiritual revival of Tajikistan's citizens;
- the achievement of economic and political independence for Tajikistan, etc.

And as immediate goals the Party proclaimed the following:

- spreading of Islam among the peoples of Tajikistan through any mass media available;
- getting Muslims involved in the country's economic, political and spiritual life;
- establishing youth organizations, etc.

After the convention, Party leaders Himmatzoda and Usmon told journalists that at the present stage of development, the Party's political objective is to establish a democratic state committed to the rule of law. It would form a government that the nation could trust — a government that would represent a broad spectrum of political forces.

It should be noted that of all the legalized Islamic parties in Central Asia today, only the Islamic Revival Party of Tajikistan has taken part in national elections. The first time it participated in the fall of 1991 the opposition coalition, in which the Islamic Revival Party of Tajikistan had a leading role, backed an alternative presidential candidate: Davlat Hudonazarov. According to official sources, Hudonazarov got 31% of the vote (he got over 40% according to opposition sources). Such high returns demonstrated the electoral potential of the opposition in the early post-Soviet period. Soon, unfortunately, despite the initial positive dialog between the ruling elite and the Islamists, a conflict could not be avoided.

The Islamic Revival Party of Tajikistan (IRPT) was one of the organizers of unauthorized protest rallies in Shakhidon Square from March 26 through April 23 and from April 25 through May 5, 1992. On April 1 and May 4, 1992 the Ministry of Justice demanded that the Party leaders stop what it termed "the unconstitutional activity." The marathon rallies culminated in the formation of a government of national reconciliation, which included IRPT representatives. Davlat Usmon was made Deputy Prime Minister of Tajikistan.

During the same period the IRPT undertook the role of co-founder of the military organization, the Motherland Salvation Front. Political processes came to a halt. Formation of armed militias eventually led to civil war. After the defeat of the democratic-Islamist coalition in November 1992, the IRPT leadership emigrated. In June 1993, the Supreme Court of Tajikistan outlawed the IRPT, accusing it of violating the Public Associations Act and certain provisions of its own rules. On the basis of the decision of the Supreme Court's Civil Rights Board, the Ministry of the Press and Information revoked Registration Certificate No. 162, which had been granted to the *Najot* newspaper on January 14, 1992.

The IRPT nevertheless continued its political campaigns. In 1993, an Islamic Revival Movement of Tajikistan was formed on Afghan soil. Abdulloh Nuri was elected its chairman, with Akbar Turajonzoda and Muhammadsharif Himmatzoda as his deputies. From military bases in Afghanistan, the Tajik opposition forces were capable of managing successful guerrilla operations against the Rakhmonov regime. In order to protect its client, Rakhmanov, against "the threat of Islamic fundamentalism," Moscow had to keep its 201st division on the Tajik-Afghan border.

Rakhmonov's opposition, on the other hand, was given support by Afghan *mujahidins* under the command of Akhmed Shah Massoud, an ethnic Tajik himself. The Kremlin leadership soon realized that it did not need to risk "a second Afghanistan." The negotiations on settlement started initially in July 1993, during a clandestine trip of Evgeny Primakov (then the chief of Russian Foreign Intelligence) to Kabul. Akhmed Shah Massoud and Primakov agreed to support the negotiating process.[8] Eventually negotiations between warring factions in Tajikistan got multilateral sponsorship, which, in addition to Russia and Afghanistan, included their Central Asian neighbors and Iran under the umbrella of the United Nations. Even then it took several years to reach the peace agreement. Perhaps the impending arrival of Taliban forces to the Afghan-Central Asian borders finally helped to speed up the talks. On June 27, 1997 the two sides met in Moscow to sign a General Agreement on Peace and National Reconciliation in Tajikistan.

On the basis of that agreement, the sides formed a National Reconciliation Commission, which includes IRPT representatives. The Commission has been charged with drafting proposals to amend legislation on political parties, movements, and the mass media. It also calls for developing a mechanism to transform existing military-political movements into political parties.

Today's return of IRPT back to legal political life has not inspired standing ovations. According to a poll conducted by the SHARK Center in January 1999 in Dushanbe, 5% of the respondents support the IRPT, 28% are loyal to the Communist Party, and the two Democratic Parties are backed by a total of 12%. IRPT supporters are mostly males with very low incomes and the unemployed and the self-employed. On a geographic basis the position of the party is the strongest in Karategin province.

On the whole, the IRPT's prestige and the appeal of political Islam in general are rather low. This is partly due to the fact that after more than two years of semi-legal existence (from the moment of signing the General Peace Agreement) the IRPT has not offered any cohesive political doctrine or economic program to get the country out of its economic ruin. Under the 30% quota stipulated by the agreement, the IRPT is now represented at all levels of government. The portfolios of Deputy Prime Minister, Minister of the Economy and Foreign Economic Relations, Chairman of the Customs Committee, Minister of Land Reclamation and Water Resources, Minister of Agriculture, Deputy Foreign Minister, and certain others, have been given to members of the opposition.

ISLAM AND THE STATE

After gaining independence, Tajikistan had to address the problem of what the role of Islam should be in the state structure. As already mentioned, Islam was already engaged in political dialogue with the government (IRPT participation in elections, etc.), but civil war disrupted the reform process in Tajikistan and had a serious impact on the state-building process. As the legacy of the civil war we are now witnessing the emergence of a powerful military elite, which could influence the future political process not only by curbing the spread of Islamism, but also by disrupting democratic transformation. On the whole, the deep-seated suspicion and antagonism between political Islam and supporters of the secular government are hindering the peace process.

The authorities are trying to assume control of the religious organizations. The government has dissolved the Muftiate (the institution, which has supervised religious affairs since Soviet time), and the chairs of *sar-hatibs* (heads of provincial and district mosques). The Muftiate was replaced by the *Shuroi Ulamo* (Council of Ulama, learned men of Islam), which has a consultative function and is actually controlled by the government. The elimination of the *sar-hatibs* has made the *imam-hatibs* (senior priests of the mosques) dependent on the local authorities since an *imam-hatib* cannot be elected without the approval of the local governments.

Major problems emerged after the 9th session of the Majlisi Oli (parliament) passed the Act on Political Parties in May of 1998. It states that political parties in Tajikistan cannot act on a religious basis. The leadership of the United Tajik Opposition strongly protested. In an effort to resolve the political stalemate, President Rakhmonov vetoed the Act and returned it to parliament for revision. A compromise solution was soon found: on November 13, 1998 the 10th session of the Majlisi Oli adopted amendments to Articles 3 and 4 of the Act, which made it possible to legalize the IRPT. However, Article 4 prohibits establishment of political and military organizations in mosques and *madrasa* (religious schools).[9]

There is no unanimity among members of the Islamic movement on its long-term political goals, and each faction within the Islamic Revival Movement has its own political philosophy. The traditionalists, headed by Abdulloh Nuri, Chairman of the National Reconciliation Commission, are among the most influential factions. The leader of the United Tajik Opposition is quoted as saying that Islam should be the private business of every Muslim, not a religious doctrine monopolizing the state.

The traditionalists, themselves, are divided into several camps. The dominant component in the Islamic Revival Movement is a moderate branch of traditionalism. The only thing they have in common with Afghanistan's Taliban movement is the origin of their original theological basis teachings of 19th century reform school of Deoband in India. However, it looks like the Tajik and Taliban interpretations of today have little in common. Another influential group — radical Islamists — shares the traditionalists' views on Islam and its ideological and social function. However, these two groups have opposing ideas on the means of reaching their goals.

Most prominent among the radicals is the outlawed Taqfir Party, which was recently formed in Garm. Led by Mullah Amirhon, the party opposes the Islamic Revival Movement, accusing it of "compromising with the government and selling out Islamic values." However, radical Islam finds no support among the majority of the population. IRPT leader Himmatzoda said at a national conference in February 1999 that his Party's goal is to establish an Islamic state, which would be governed exclusively by Islamic men. This would exclude women, atheists, and ethnic minorities from the political process.

The tangible fruits of Islamization in the territory controlled by the United Tajik Opposition can already be seen. Tajikistan's Ministry of the Economy estimates that before the war there were approximately 2,000 women with a university education and 3,000 women with a community college-level technical education in the Karategin area. Today there are only 178 women with a university education and 759 women with a college-level technical education in that zone.[10]

FALLOUT OF THE CONFLICT

At present, Tajikistan is plagued by political and economic fragmentation, with local elites — composed of government bureaucrats, field commanders and the new rich — coming to power in each separate region. There is a real danger of Tajikistan splitting up into separate subethnic territories, each with its own system of government, economic model, and external center of attraction. Different regions of Tajikistan already have different systems of government, and Islam has a different role in each. A quasi-theocratic form of government has been formed in a number of Pamir Mountain regions, while secular authoritarian governments have been established in certain northern regions of the country, with the clergy occupying a subordinate position. A highly unusual situation has taken shape in the Hatlon and Gorno-Badakhshan regions. In the Hatlon region, almost every conceivable combination of Islamic and secular government authority can be found. In addition, the Sufi sheiks have an exceptionally strong influence there. In the Gorno-Badakhshan region, the secularized population sees Islamism as an ethno-political movement rather than a religion. And yet Islamism is experiencing a revival together with a revival of the Badakhshanians' ethnic awareness.

CONCLUSION

The precondition for stabilization in Tajikistan is settlement of the inter-Tajik conflict and reintegration of the country into coherent social and economic organisms. It could hardly be achieved without integrating the opposition parties and movements into Tajikistan's political life and building a stable multiparty system, based on healthy civil society and its various civic institutions. The mobilizing power of Islam in Tajik life has been proven throughout turbulent history of the post–Soviet period. Despite the major setback of Islamists at parliamentary elections in February of 2000 (IPRT with 8% of votes came only a distant third, behind Rakhmonov's party and the communists), the legalization of political Islam in Tajikistan has taken place. Above all, lasting peace in Tajikistan can only be reached through a consensus of all the religious, ethnic and social groups.

Islam in Turkmenistan: the Niyazov Calculation

Roustem Safronov

INTRODUCTION

Despite common assumptions both in Russia and in the West, Turkmenistan and the other Central Asian republics of the former USSR were not ready for independence. As a result of the Belovezh Accords, which legally dissolved the USSR, both the communist bureaucracy in Turkmenistan and its multiethnic population suddenly faced independence. In 1991, Turkmenistan was forced to leave the nest, as it were, without having first found its own identity as a nation. That search is still going on, and so far one can discern only the first vague contours of a new ideology and role for Islam in shaping the future of the country.

THE ORIGIN OF ISLAM IN TURKMENISTAN

With the Arab conquest of neighboring territories and with the swiftly advancing power of the Arabian Caliphate, in 651 A.D. the Arab armies entered Khorasan, which included today's southern Turkmenistan. From that moment, Islam began its march across the entire region — a march that was by no means unconditionally triumphant or unimpeded. The Turkic and Iranian tribes inhabiting the region, both nomadic and sedentary, were in no hurry to accept Islam, and where they did accept it, the new religion absorbed elements of traditional shamanism, Zoroastrianism, and other various heathen beliefs.

The main events in the process of ethnic formation of the Turkmen occurred in the ninth and tenth centuries A.D. The invasion of Oguz Turkic nomads from the east resulted in their intermixing with the ancient seminomadic Iranian tribes. In the tenth century, the term Turkmen appeared in Arabic chronicles. The Oguz Turkmen worshiped

their male ancestors and venerated their tribal elders. The graves of influential elders and chieftains were treated as shrines. This fact is of great
significance because, despite their conversion to Islam, the Turkmen still
observe this custom today. At the same time, the Oguz Turkmen widely
practiced Islam as early as the eleventh to twelfth century, as noted by
Sergei Demidov who is the foremost authority on the subject.[1]

The extent to which Islam penetrated into the Turkmen people's
belief system and day-to-day life varied from one place to another. The
new faith quickly took root in the oases near the Kopetdag Mountains,
in Serakhs, in Merv, and in the Amur Darya Valley — in other words, in
the agricultural regions. By contrast, territories inhabited by livestock-
herding Turkic nomads were Islamicized only superficially. The effects of
this incursion of Islam can, to a certain extent, be felt to this day.

The Turkmen ethnographers believe that in the early stages of their
ethnic formation, the Turkmen people had "a military tribal democracy
that preceded the formation of a state."[2] The elders of patrilineal clans
regulated life within the commune, while the legitimacy of power was
determined by the personal qualities of the chieftains and their responsibility to the commune. Decisions of local significance were made at a
general meeting of the men by a simple majority voice vote. Women were
traditionally barred from participation in public life, particularly after conversion to Islam. Issues of a tribal level were deliberated at *maslakhats*
(councils of clan elders and warlords). A council of elders elected the
supreme leader of the tribe, the Khan. The Turkmen society remains to
this day based largely on neighbor and commune relations; clan and tribal
solidarity; influence of the *yashuli* (elders); worship of holy sites, and belief
in magic, superstitions, and rituals reminiscent of witchcraft.[3]

FEATURES OF ISLAM IN TURKMENISTAN

Not all tribes inhabiting the territory of modern-day Turkmenistan converted to the *Sunni* version of Islam. Some — primarily the Persian-
speaking population and part of the Turkic-speaking tribes in southern
Turkmenistan (a marginal minority) — took up *Shi'ism*. Bloodshed was
not uncommon between *Sunnis* and *Shi'as* over the true faith. Differences
between the *Shi'a* Iranians and the *Sunni* Turkmen were often sufficient
cause for punitive expeditions against each other. The clergy was often
directly involved on both sides to stir up such campaigns. Not until after

Turkmenistan's inclusion in the Russian Empire in the late nineteenth century did refuge to religious and territorial strife cease.

Another feature of Islam in Turkmenistan is the powerful influence of Sufism, a mystical movement that spread throughout the region in the late Middle Ages. It appealed to the nomadic tribes in that it combined Islamic dogma with traditional Turkmen beliefs. Unlike orthodox Islam, it did not reject nature worship, but to a certain extent enabled its believers to come closer to the Creator through mysticism. This approach aroused bitter hostility on the part of orthodox Islam. Sufi rituals led by *ishans* (local Sufi leaders) incorporated certain older cultural traditions, such as music, chanting, even dance — practices considered heretical by orthodox Muslims. Such practices obviously clashed with the precepts of classical Islam as taught by Arab preachers. Most among early Sufi preachers and dervishes were Iranians.

The following period, from the fifteenth to the early twentieth century, was characterized by relative stability in Turkmen society, and Islam slowly but steadily became the dominant religion. However, both Oriental and European travelers to Turkmenistan described Turkmen as "bad Muslims" in the sense that they were not sufficiently zealous and fanatical in their faith. Islamic law (the *shari'a*) ultimately failed to subordinate native common law (the *Adat*). To this day the Turkmen say, "You can renounce religion, but customs never!" Thus, from the period of Islamization to the present, Adat law has always prevailed over *shari'a* law in people's minds. (This prevalence concerns mostly the rural population, which is not so much exposed to modern influences and has a more established way of life and stable perception of its own identity.)

By comparison, Turkmen's neighbors, such as the Uzbeks, were much more devout. They were a settled people and Islam had deeper roots in their life. In general, Islam was more successful in penetrating the belief system and day-to-day life of sedentary peoples, as manifested by the numerous mosques and *madrasas* (Muslim secondary schools).

The way of life of the Turkmen nomadic livestock herders was not particularly conducive to orthodox Islamic precepts. The Sufis *pirs, sheiks* (top Sufi clerics) almost never publicly officiated at religious ceremonies, but they enjoyed much greater respect than the *mullahs*. This attitude can be attributed to the Turkmen's traditional worship of ancestors; that veneration was also extended to the Sufis as descendants of ancient religious dynasties. On the other hand, the Sufis participated in political life, most notably as go-betweens in relations with neighboring feudal states, particularly with Khiva.

The greatest Sufis were from Khoresm (which was later incorporated in the Khiva Khanate), Bukhara, and other medieval cultural centers. In Turkmen society, the Sufis exerted their influence through the *ishans* (Sufi preachers) who had to receive the blessing of the top Sufi clerics of the two most powerful orders in Central Asia: Kubraviya (in Khoresm) and Nakshbendi (in Bukhara). The order of the Yasaviya enjoyed lesser influence on the territory of Turkmenistan. Members of the major Sufi orders would travel to remote areas of Turkmenistan to seek out *murids* (novices) from among the nomads.

TURKMENISTAN UNDER RUSSIAN CONTROL

The Russian conquest of Central Asia proceeded in several stages. Because of tribal divisions, the Turkmen could not decide what policy to pursue with respect to Russian colonization. The process of ethnic formation of the Turkmen people had not been completed, and they were still divided into tribes. Some of the tribes, such as the Iomud (in western Turkmenistan, bordering on the Caspian Sea), voluntarily accepted Russian rule; others, such as the Ersari (in modern-day Chardjou and Tashauz *velayats* — regional administrative units), offered sporadic resistance but on the whole cooperated with the new Russian administration. The largest tribe, the Teke, did put up the stiffest resistance to the Russian expeditionary corps. The first Russian expedition, headed by General Nikolai Lomakin in 1879, was defeated. Only the second expedition in 1881 against the stubborn Teke brought victory to the expeditionary corps under the command of General Mikhail Skobelev. Still, a number of tribes, after assembling in a *maslakhat*, voluntarily decided to accept Russian Czarist rule in hopes of gaining protection against the constant incursions of neighboring Iranian tribes.

Today the theory of voluntary incorporation in the Russian Empire has been finally rejected as part of President Sapamurad Niyazov's new approach to history that condemns Turkmenistan's colonial past. Under the new ideology, which seeks to justify Niyazov's autocratic rule, it is now politically incorrect to mention any positive impact of Turkmenistan's incorporation in Russia. Nevertheless, Turkmen historians on the whole recognize Russia's positive influence. Most researchers agree that despite the contradictory and often violent character of the annexation, Russian influence was a step forward developmentally for the Central Asian civilization.

Central Asia's development had indeed been held back by the absence of a stable market, by antiquated feudal relations, and by rudimentary communications. Slavery was abolished only after the Russian conquest. The Russians also brought Christianity, but it remained a religion of the colonizers. Whereas in other Russian colonies Orthodox Christian missionaries and priests usually followed the troops and colonizers, this incursion was not the case in Central Asia. A huge wave of Russian migration to Central Asia — in particular the Transcaspian Territory — followed annexation as the Russian government granted land to Russian peasants who gladly moved to a warmer climate. However, the local population preserved total autonomy in lifestyle, customs, and religion, while existing alongside the Russian colonizers who lived their own lives and built Christian churches.

The two cultures and religions coexisted in parallel worlds, as it were, with virtually no points of contact. A Czarist administration governed the Russians in the Transcaspian Territory, while Turkmen mainly followed the laws of *Turkmenchilik* (their ancestors). Unlike other regions incorporated earlier in the Russian Empire, there was practically no assimilation in Central Asia.

Unlike other parts of the Russian Empire, which had been annexed by force and subsequently converted to Orthodox Christianity, religious assimilation did not occur in Central Asia. Instead, the Russian colonization had geopolitical motives. Fearing any further influence of Great Britain in neighboring Afghanistan, and hoping one day to gain access to India and the Indian Ocean (also Peter the Great's dream in the early eighteenth century), the Russian Czarist government regarded the Central Asian states such as Bukhara and Khiva simply as potential vassals, not as new provinces to be totally assimilated. Central Asia was perceived as a buffer zone. Ultimately, Bukhara became a vassal state, while Khiva was absorbed into the Empire after its subjugation in 1872, followed soon after by the whole of Central Asia. Thus, the two buffer zones — the British in Afghanistan and the Russian in Central Asia — were meant to cushion the massive geopolitical pressure of the two competing powers.

Russian peasants learned to live side by side with the local population without much conflict. In doing so they lost their "colonization skill" and coexisted with the local population in different dimensions without any assimilation. Having annexed Central Asia, the Russians did not attempt to change the Turkmen's way of life but left the *qazi* (Muslim judge) courts and the Adat and shari'a law intact. On the whole, this approach was not consistent with the Russian government's practice in its earlier colonies, which had been to establish more-or-less standard forms of administration and legal procedure. In Central Asia, the local population was granted full autonomy in matters of religion and law, although the Soviets did take certain steps to decentralize the power of the *qazis*.

Therefore, the Czarist colonial government left both the tribal structures of Turkmen society and the people's traditional beliefs untouched. A complex tribal structure and intertribal rivalry, in the context of Russian colonial domination, held back the development of a stable national consciousness among the Turkmen. The role of religion was largely limited to ritual. Illiteracy virtually prevented the population from learning the sacred scriptures of orthodox Islam. Before the 1917 Bolshevik Revolution, according to conservative estimates, at least 90% of the population was illiterate.

The Soviet rule throughout Central Asia brought major changes to Turkmen life. Among other things, the Soviets soon wiped out illiteracy and introduced the Turkmen to Russian culture. The Sovietization of the educational system made Russian the state language. Atheism became the official doctrine in Soviet Central Asia. After 1924, the USSR granted the Turkmen people statehood as a constituent republic of the Soviet Union. Before that time, the Transcaspian Territory was part of a single huge territory called Russian Turkestan.

The acquisition of statehood is of special importance, because after the division of Central Asia along ethnic lines and the establishment of the Turkmen Soviet Socialist Republic, Turkmen for the first time became united within one nation-state. The process of ethnic formation of the Turkmen people entered a new phase. The various Turkmen tribes, which in earlier times tended to be absorbed by this or that multiethnic khanate, were now under the roof of one quasi-state entity. Bolshevik agrarian reform (also known as land and water reform) facilitated a transition to sedentary life, and Turkmen began cultivating crops in addition to their traditional livestock herding. While the Soviet government mounted a consistent effort to root out religion, there were not many mosques in the newly formed Turkmen Soviet Socialist Republic. Thus, the traditional way of life changed only slightly and very slowly.

The Muslim clergy played a part in organizing the early anti-Soviet *basmachi*[1] rebellion movement. The Soviets finally suppressed the *basmachi* in Turkmenistan only in the mid-1930s. Still, religion was not the rebels' main driving force; it was the people's struggle for water, land and food. However, the agrarian reform carried out by the Bolsheviks created considerable support for the Soviet regime, and many Turkmen actually fought on the side of the Red Army.

The period of Soviet rule in Turkmenistan not only brought a quasi-European veneer to people's lifestyle — in the form of urban expansion and industrial development — but it also caused major demographic changes. From 1959 to 1979, the republic's population doubled and was increasingly characterized by a constantly growing proportion of youth. The Soviet public health system scored dramatic successes in fighting infant mortality.

In analyzing the present situation in Turkmenistan, one must recognize that the vast majority of the population grew up in a climate dominated by Soviet atheism. The influx of Russians and other Russian-speakers from central Russia, as well as Armenians from Karabakh, gave a multiethnic face to Turkmen cities, particularly the capital, Ashgabat. Such diversity fostered an atmosphere of ethnic tolerance.

Despite the Bolsheviks' success in eradicating illiteracy and their methodical efforts to stamp out religion, Islam remained one of the chief indicators of the Turkmen's social self-identification. The extremely rigid structure of society based on clan relations (regulated not so much by the *shari'a* as by traditional Adat law) fit nicely with Soviet collectivist principles and with the idea of service to the state of workers, peasants and working intelligentsia. Endogamous marriage (i.e., within one's clan or tribe) was and largely still is the norm. For this reason, almost every nationalist-minded Turkmen is, paradoxically, a zealous proponent of tribal purity.

Nevertheless, the Kremlin was more afraid of ethnic nationalism than of an upsurge of Islam. Mirsaid Sultan-Galiev, an ethnic Tatar and commissar in the Communist Party in the 1920s, advocated combining the ideals of Islam with those of the Communist Party. He had considerable support amongst Tatar Communists, but the Bolshevik leadership was quick to condemn his ideas and suppress the Sultan-Galiev movement. Sultan-Galiev himself was ultimately a victim of Stalin's purges, and any organized protest under Islamic banners became virtually impossible. The

Communist authorities concentrated on ethnic nationalism and launched one campaign after another, particularly during the Stalin period. Thus, the Kremlin tried to prevent any resurgence of nationalism that could one day threaten Soviet power. Victims of the purges included not only members of the tribal elite and clergy, but also many Turkmen in the local administration who were loyal to the Soviet government and were actively implementing the Kremlin's policies. The new Soviet Turkmen elite suffered the heaviest losses in 1937-1938 when authorities arrested Kaisygyz Atabaev (First Chairman of Turkmenistan's Council of People's Commissars) and Nebirdai Aitakov (Chairman of the Central Executive Committee of Turkmenistan) on charges of "bourgeois nationalism." The number of victims among the new Soviet Turkmen elite in that period ran into the thousands.

Such campaigns plagued Turkmenistan through to the late 1950s, although toward the end of that period — particularly after Stalin's death in 1953 — the purges took the form of ostracism rather than arrest. The label of nationalism was often used as a weapon in factional strife within Turkmenistan's Communist Party and government, with Moscow as supreme arbitrator. However, the authorities in Moscow would conduct their policies in each constituent republic through the Second Secretary of the local Communist Party, who was always an ethnic Russian and did not wish to become involved in the details of the power struggle among the various tribal clans.

As for the ongoing campaign against "religious and feudal remnants of the past," that effort had become a mere formality in the final thirty years of Soviet rule in Turkmenistan. Virtually every Turkmen Communist Party official followed Adat law in his private life, celebrated the traditional religious holidays in a semisecret fashion, and circumcised his sons. Whenever a party official was persecuted for religious practice, the charges were, as a rule, a pretext to settle personal scores or to topple a rival in the struggle for power. The Muslim customs, traditions, and way of life on the whole remained unaffected by Soviet rule, and the values of *Adat* law remained largely intact. Soviet officials did not make any serious attempt to eradicate the Muslim way of life and tribal-clan relations. Even when authorities launched such campaigns from time to time, such moves usually brought no results.

AFTER THE BREAKUP OF THE SOVIET UNION

In summing up the seventy years of Soviet rule in Central Asia, Russian researcher G. Mirsky wrote, "In the Asian region, it is hard to overstate the importance of the lower, basic level of consciousness and social relations, i.e., the system of subethnic ties — between relatives, between clan members, between patron and client...."[5] Soviet rule actually helped strengthen the clan mentality. The authoritarian and hierarchical Soviet system merged with the traditional system of social relations that were based on collective solidarity and obedience to one's elders. Whereas authorities pursued a dual state/ethnic consciousness to supplant the Muslim macro-level of identity during the Soviet period, at the micro-level the tribal and clan lifestyle and mentality remained unchanged. This consistency led to the development in Central Asia of exceptionally stable and viable hierarchies, which members of the former Communist Party and the government elite have headed in the post-Soviet period.[6]

Nevertheless, the Soviet Communist Party's ethnic policy aimed at increasing the role of native officials among the local Party-and-government elite and nurturing a well-educated Turkmen intelligentsia resulted in the formation of a stable Turkmen elite that grew more and more into a force to be reckoned with. Although post-Soviet independence came as a surprise to this Moscow-dependent power elite, the former Soviet officials were more able to seize the reins of government in Turkmenistan than were the nationalist intelligentsia. The new Turkmenistan inherited from the Soviet period an agroindustrial economy designed to satisfy the USSR's needs for gas and fine-fiber cotton, along with a relatively well-educated population. It also inherited a system of public education, public health and social services.

The turbulent period preceding the collapse of the USSR and the crisis of values in the entire Soviet society stimulated an interest in Islam among Turkmen youth, and triggered a brief boom in the study of Arabic. This situation did not last long. The new Turkmen President Saparmurad Niyazov (formerly First Secretary of the Turkmen Communist Party) quickly established an authoritarian regime and eliminated the sparse liberal democratic opposition in 1992-1993. In addition, the former Communist Party elites that had come to power in the newly independent countries of Central Asia were seriously frightened by the civil war in Tajikistan, where rival territorial clans made extensive use of Islamic slogans. Both the ethnic Russian minority and the Russified urban Turkmen shared those fears.

In this context, the government of Turkmenistan, and above all Niyazov himself, set out to tame Islam and to adapt it to the needs of the state. Government policies took on a tinge of moderate nationalism, which was not limited to the declaration of Turkmen as the official state language. Even though under its new constitution Turkmenistan is declared to be a secular state, the government has recently recommended that the Koran and the fundamentals of Islam be included in the secondary school curriculum. The president's speeches abound in traditional expressions such as "*Khudaya Shukur!*" ("Glory to Allah!") and "*Inshallah!*" ("Allah's will be done!"). Numerous mosques are being built, and the government is cultivating relations with other Muslim countries, including theocracies such as neighboring Iran. How serious is all this change? Is there any fertile soil for radical Islam, such as Wahhabism?[7] Those questions are of immediate concern.

ISLAM AND NIYAZOV'S CULT OF PERSONALITY

The 1991 Religious Freedom and Religious Organizations Act guaranteed religious freedom to all citizens. The government is trying to fill the ideological vacuum by cultivating relationships with Muslim hierarchs, by building new mosques, and by funding the publication of a Turkmen-language version of the Koran. Niyazov has made it clear that any attempt by the Muslim clergy to interfere in affairs of state and other political matters will be nipped in the bud. The Turkmen government keeps a tight grip on religious associations through a network of *gengeshi* (local people's councils which have limited policing authority). The government even reserves the right to confirm nomination of clerics to administrative positions within the Islamic hierarchy. Current legislation prohibits establishing religious political parties and movements.

"The Communists-turned-nationalists are now trying to get close enough to Islam to block its road to power," writes Kadyrov.[8]

How strong is the influence of orthodox Islam, which is government-supported and propagandized, on traditional Sufi beliefs and on Turkmen *ovlads* (people)?[9] The role of Islam should be analyzed in a broader political context. President Niyazov is not just seeking to fill an ideological void and create a semiofficial alternative to a small liberal democratic opposition (which is mostly based abroad), but to develop an official state ideology. Banners proclaiming "*Khalk! Vatan! Turkmenbashi!*" ("Our People! Our Country! Our Leader!") adorn public buildings across Turkmenistan. The new ideology is based on the glorification of Niyazov. Official propaganda portrays him as a leader who brought independence to the Turkmen people and helped them build a national home. He is referred to as "Turkmenbashi" (the nation's leader and head of all the Turkmen). According to official myth, Turkmenbashi is the epitome of wisdom, under whose insightful guidance the Turkmen people are building a secular democratic society based on the rule of law.

Islam is being used as an instrument of policy, subordinated to government. Niyazov controls everything. Not only does he head the Khalk Maslakhaty (Council of People's Representatives, which is the supreme body of government and includes representatives of all branches of government) and handpicks his own cabinet ministers; he is also leader of the Democratic Party. The latter inherited its property and structure from the former Communist Party and currently serves the interests of the Niyazov leadership. Privatization and market reform are proceeding very cautiously, with the old Soviet social safety net being preserved in the form of subsidized food prices, free education and health services. Both the Turkmen and Russian-language population initially hailed this policy, but problems arose in 1993 when Turkmenistan had to introduce its own currency, which proved extremely unstable. The mounting crisis galvanized the opposition-minded nationalist and liberal intelligentsia. Niyazov and his Democratic Party responded by cracking down on the opposition movement and arresting many of its members. Most of them either fled to Russia and the Scandinavian countries or were put in jail until their release in the spring of 1998, coinciding with Niyazov's official visit to the United States.

THE ISLAMIC THREAT?

The phenomenon of Turkmenistan's political Islam can be explained by the government's desire to acquire new allies and economic donors among the rich Islamic countries. Starting in 1995, Turkmenistan has been actively cooperating with Israel despite protests from Iran, a move that illustrates Niyazov's Islamization drive as a matter of political expediency having little to do with spiritual values. The focus of such cooperation is on purchasing Israeli equipment and technology for the gas industry. As for the threat of Islamic fundamentalism or other radical movements spilling over from neighboring countries into Turkmenistan, Niyazov has stated on numerous occasions that such ideology would find no fertile soil in Turkmenistan.

Murad Esenov, editor of the Swedish-based journal *Central Asia & The Caucasus*, believes that in viewing the religious situation, particularly the threat of radical Islam, Central Asia should be seen as two parts. The Fergana Valley in Uzbekistan, where such a threat does exist, and the rest of the region, where the odds of any serious increase in religious extremism are very slim because most of the population consists of formerly nomadic tribes. "The religious renaissance is on the decline. There isn't going to be any sharp increase in the number of religious Muslims; in fact, religion is going out of fashion already," Esenov concludes.[10]

Iranian theologians and politicians have long tried to win over the sympathies of neighboring Central Asian peoples, especially when the Iranian revolution was on the rise and turning radical. The Iranian city of Gurgen beamed Turkmen-language broadcasts — packed with religious propaganda — toward Turkmenistan. Although recent changes in the Iranian regime have resulted in a more moderate foreign policy, the religious broadcasts continue nevertheless. Iran is still looking for an opportunity to use the religious factor to expand its positions in Turkmenistan, both politically and economically.

Shortly before the disintegration of the Soviet Union, a growing spiritual void prompted part of the population to embrace Islam. Turkmen youth turned to nationalism and Islam as an alternative to discredited Soviet values. As a result, Arabic language courses filled to capacity. This excitement was short-lived. Independence came so suddenly that the public was not ready for it. The former Communist Party and government officials, who had no intention of yielding power to the poorly organized radical nationalists, quickly adopted the rhetoric of independence so cherished by the small groups of nationalist-minded intelligentsia within the Agzybirlik ("Unity") movement and the Paisakh ("Reason") club.

Hopes for a religious resurgence soon died simply because there was no force in the country able to make use of them. The clergy was still hobbled from its existence under the tight control of the Soviet authorities. The intellectuals, even those with nationalist and anti-communist sentiments, mostly pushed for national resurgence, while the religious element in their demands was hazy and weak. One reason for this shortcoming was that the existence of an intelligentsia was a product of Soviet society, and after more than seventy years of state-sponsored atheism, the intelligentsia did not possess sufficient knowledge of, or interest in, Islam.

Instead they supported the idea of reviving traditional national values and of giving the Turkmen language a more prominent role in society as the official state language; they had no particular desire to establish a theocracy. Their position reflected the influence of liberal and pro-Western values, combined with the inferiority complex of a colonial elite seeking to become oracles for their people without having to toe Moscow's line.

The religious renaissance did not materialize because there were no leaders who could rally the people, there were no experts on Islam, and there was no particular desire on the part of the people. Underground religious movements did not exist in Turkmenistan during the stable period of Soviet rule, at least not in the 1970s and 1980s. According to surveys conducted in 1993 by Kadyrov, only 11 percent of Turkmenistan's population expressed concerns that Muslim fundamentalists could come to power in the foreseeable future. Characteristically, most of the respondents were ethnic Russians (obviously, this was not a representative survey). In other words, even the most concerned sector of Turkmenistan's population (ethnic Russians who suddenly found themselves residents in and an ethnic minority of a "foreign" country) did not regard the situation as very disturbing.

However, a certain religious renaissance did occur, mainly because the Turkmen government had to formulate some new ideology and, after a period of uncertainty and confusion, Niyazov declared Islam to be part of the national heritage. As early as 1991, architects received contracts to build 200 mosques. Since that time the number of mosques has grown steadily. Whereas in the Soviet period there were only four mosques in the entire republic, by 1994 their number had exceeded 300.[11]

The Turkmen president went on a brief *hajj* (pilgrimage) to Mecca in 1992, becoming the first leader in post-Soviet Central Asia to do so. Kadyrov concludes that curiously enough, from the moment of independence to 1995, only a little over 450 Turkmen citizens have been to Mecca, a tiny fraction of Turkmenistan's population.

Another step in Islamization has been the introduction of religious subjects, such as fundamentals of Islam and the Koran, into secondary school curricula. So far there are no grounds for concern because this curriculum change is being done extremely slowly and inconsistently, and to date the teaching of those subjects is optional. Niyazov's efforts could bring results only sometime in the future.

One can see no evidence of rapid Islamization, to say nothing of fundamentalism. In December 1995, near the town of Bakharden I witnessed the construction of a new mosque, which the entire community was building together. In the opinion of Durdyiev, who was present at the site, the consecration of the mosque and the accompanying rituals were fully consistent with Turkmen (pre-Islamic) traditions, including veneration of the local saints, all of which goes against orthodox Islam. The state-funded construction of mosques is being done on a grand scale, but progress is slow. Much more money and energy is being spent on the construction of presidential palaces, government buildings and international-class hotels. Both the palaces and the mosques have one objective: the consolidation of Niyazov's power and the filling of the ideological void to block the spread of liberal and democratic ideas. Niyazov believes such ideas to be so dangerous that he has gradually cut off all television broadcasts from Russia: in late 1994 it was the Russian Television Station (Channel 2), and in November 1998 Channel 1 of Russian Public Television (ORT Channel 1) was removed.

The construction of some mosques is being funded by private sponsors, and the size and scale of those construction sites is comparable to those funded by the state. H. Ishanov, former General Director of the Turkmenneft oil company, largely funded one such mosque, with room for approximately 2,000 faithful. The multimillion-dollar mosque at Fort Geok Tepe commemorating the Turkmen resistance to General Skobelev's troops, which the French firm Bouigue recently built, is another example of Niyazov's desire to legitimize his power. The mosque is called Saparmurad Hajji (*hajji* is a title of honor given to a Muslim who has made a pilgrimage to Mecca).

According to Durdyiev, the traditional Sufi beliefs of the Turkmen are gradually giving way under the pressure of orthodox Islam. The president's intent to inculcate orthodox Islam is seen not only in the large-scale construction of mosques, but also in sanctioning indirect forms of foreign religious penetration. For example, the government allowed representatives of Saudi Arabia to open a boarding school for orphans. It is quite obvious that the children there will get what the Saudis consider a sound religious education. The Saudis have also built a mosque in the village of Keshi, on the outskirts of Ashgabat.

A religious secondary school for children through age fifteen operates under the auspices of the Turkmen State University. Before being admitted there, the children learn to read and write at religious *madrasas* (Muslim secondary schools). So far the number of students of religion in Turkmenistan totals a mere 200, and the level of instruction is low because of the lack of qualified theologians. There is a Department of Theology at the Makhtumkuli State University, but it has only a few dozen students. The Koran has recently been published in the Turkmen language in a printing of 250,000 copies. One of the reasons rapid Islamization is unlikely is that most Islamic texts are written in Arabic or in one of the Turkic languages using the Latin alphabet. In the pre-Soviet period, only a handful of Turkmen knew the Arabic script (although educated Turkmen used it until 1929). In the early years of Soviet rule the authorities briefly introduced the Latin alphabet. Finally, in 1940 Cyrillic script prevailed in Turkmenistan as a tool of *russification*. These reforms created a huge gap between Islamic literature and the secular lifestyle of Turkmen society. Even if Niyazov were to open fully the doors to foreign Islamic influence, the effect would be felt only in the remote future. Islamization would take time because throughout the entire Soviet period Turkmenistan was politically and culturally cut off from the major centers of Islam.

In today's Turkmenistan, the government's Islamization policy is designed to create a new, artificial ideology for the nation, an ideology directed by one man — President Niyazov. The president will go to any length to build his power, including establishing an Institute of Human Rights (the purpose of which is to justify the president's authoritarian rule in the eyes of the international community), printing a mass edition of the Koran, and setting up contacts with Israel. His pragmatism borders on the Machiavellian. Even the prayers for the health of Turkmenbashi — the Leader — to be offered at all workplaces and educational institutions, as recommended by the country's religious leaders, are meant to serve the president, not Allah. The prayer-like oath that all children from kindergarten through secondary school must intone each day is a pledge of allegiance not only to their country and flag but also to the president.

So far, Niyazov's pragmatism is paying off. On the whole, the situation in Turkmenistan is under control. The liberal-democratic opposition has emigrated, while part of the intelligentsia is actively collaborating with the regime. Political life is at a standstill. The working class — a product of the Soviet period of industrialization — is showing no signs of social activity. The Communist Party has been unable to gain permission from the Ministry of Justice to register as a political party. Ethnic

Russians are trying to emigrate, even though there is no overt pressure on them. Niyazov can boast that he has put an end to street crime, social unrest, and ethnic tensions. However, corruption is rife and the standard of living is much lower than it used to be under Soviet rule. Only a handful of opposition leaders are left in the country, and they are isolated and under police surveillance.

THREAT FROM AFGHANISTAN?

Niyazov has managed to maintain stability on the Afghan border. Not a single armed *mujahidin* group has crossed the border into Turkmenistan since the president took office. Moreover, he is now seeking to establish good relations with the Taliban movement, the dominant political force in Afghanistan. In Niyazov's opinion, the Taliban is the only force that can prevent the disintegration of Afghanistan into warring regions, overcome ethnic strife, and become an integrating force in Afghan society. Niyazov sees the Taliban coalition as a guarantor of stability in the region. Turkmenistan and its president need stability not only for its own sake, but also as an essential condition for solving the country's economic problems. Active negotiations with major transnational corporations and neighboring countries to find ways of transporting Turkmen gas have been going on for years. In 1996, several agreements were signed to transport Turkmen gas across Afghan territory. However, those accords cannot be implemented because of the ongoing war and general instability in Afghanistan, which explains Niyazov's efforts to strike a deal with the Taliban in hopes that the Taliban will put an end to the war.

In 1992 and 1993, after the collapse of the Najibullah regime in Afghanistan, large numbers of ethnic Turkmen living in that country faced persecution because they had supported the Soviet troops during the Afghan War and had later supported Najibullah. After the defeat of the pro-Soviet regime, Afghanistan's ethnic Turkmen appealed to Niyazov for asylum, but Niyazov refused to let them in. Evidently, he understood that Afghan Turkmen, with their totally different social mentality and religious traditions, would have brought drastic changes not only to the demographic scene in Turkmenistan, but also to the sociopolitical scene. The influx of hundreds of thousands of refugees not only would have exacerbated Turkmenistan's economic problems, but also would have led to unpredictable political consequences. Thus, Niyazov sacrificed ethnic solidarity in the interests of national stability.

ISLAM'S FUTURE IN TURKMENISTAN

Prominent expatriate opposition leaders, such as Abdy Kuliyev who resides in Moscow and is head of the Turkmenistan Foundation, are of a more secular and liberal persuasion than Niyazov. They have shown no interest in propagandizing Islamic ideas, nor have Turkmen opposition leaders living in Sweden and Norway. International human rights organizations regard the current situation in Turkmenistan as a moderate resurgence of Islam.

As already mentioned, Turkmenistan's current Religious Freedom and Religious Organizations Act was passed on June 14, 1991 and was published in the Register of the Parliament of Turkmenistan. The government introduced certain important amendments in 1995. Now the law, while proclaiming the freedom of religious faith, ensures government control over the nation's religious life. For example, a minimum of 500 signatures is required to register a religious community. Only the *Sunni* Muslim and the Russian Orthodox Christian communities have been able to meet this requirement.

Having proclaimed religious freedoms, Niyazov tries to keep the religious situation under his personal control. The Council of People's Representatives must approve nominations to all senior clerical positions for Religious Affairs of the Cabinet of Ministers (an agency inherited from Soviet times), while the head Muslim cleric officially holds the rank of minister. Such tight control enables the government to forestall the formation of any fundamentalist religious political groups and to monitor all international contacts maintained by religious leaders.

The symbol of Islam — a crescent against a green background — adorns the Turkmen national flag. In the summer of 1992, Turkmenistan became a full member of the Islamic Conference organization. The motives for joining, however, were purely pragmatic. Within the community of the Commonwealth of Independent States (CIS), Turkmenistan has been staying aloof, and refraining from any attempt to form economic or political ties. Even before Turkmenistan declared its official neutrality in 1995, Niyazov announced that Turkmen troops would not take part in peacekeeping operations in Tajikistan. By comparison, membership in the Islamic Conference organization does not involve any serious obligations because the group's decisions are advisory. In 1996, a desire to diversify its economic contacts and secure new loans for its ailing economy prompted Turkmenistan to join the Islamic Bank.

The main obstacle to the crystallization of an integral national consciousness is the tribal structure of Turkmen society, which has been maintained throughout the centuries through endogamous marriages within each clan. Tribal and clan relations are an important factor in the structure of power. Their importance has become even more evident since the collapse of the USSR, even though the Soviet authorities had made numerous — albeit inconsistent — attempts to eradicate tribalism.

Rivalry among the major Turkmen tribes (the Esari, the Teke, the Iomud, and others) existed under Soviet rule as well, but it was a hidden undercurrent. Now it is becoming increasingly open. The largest and most powerful tribe, the Teke, are eminently pleased that Niyazov comes from their midst. Although Turkmen have many reasons to be dissatisfied with his rule, his belonging to the Teke is undoubtedly a substantial political advantage. Another asset is the fact that Niyazov was raised in an orphanage. His father was killed in World War II, and the rest of his family died in the Ashgabat earthquake of 1948. Thus, he is less bound by allegiance to a particular tribal or territorial clan. In this sense, the various rival groups see him as a compromise figure. In addition, one must consider the demographic changes caused by the advent of a new generation with a lower educational level than young people had during the Soviet period. Mounting economic problems are also a factor. All these considerations are much more important in determining Turkmenistan's future than is religion. The average age of the country's population (now standing at 4,437,000) is twenty-three years with almost half of the population being children or teenagers who are too young to work. Because of its low mobility and high birth rate, the rural population is growing: in 1995 it accounted for 55 percent of Turkmenistan's overall population, compared to 53 percent in 1989. The *yashuli* (elders) wield great influence in rural areas, while political activity in agricultural communities is low. All these factors, at least in the short term, contribute to political stability.

CONCLUSION

Niyazov relies on traditional, unwritten Asian values such as collectivism, communal mentality, respect for one's elders, and reverence for authorities. These values are reinforced by Niyazov's authoritarian rule, with its concentration of property in the hands of a few, debarment of people from government, and lack of checks and balances to control the ruling elite.

It is possible that some day this official cultivation of Islam might backfire, so Niyazov could well be courting disaster. Turkmenistan is becoming increasingly isolated from Russia, with which the educated class has so many links. At the same time, the influence of Turkey, Iran, and other Muslim countries is growing. The West is too remote geographically to play a significant role in the region; its impact is mostly limited to images of conspicuous consumption as seen in glossy advertisements and television commercials. Most Turkmen cannot even dream of reaching a Western standard of living, while the *nouveaux riches* who arrogated the country's wealth in the course of privatization and through unprecedented corruption and embezzlement already enjoy a standard of living surpassing that of the Western middle class.

Even if Turkmenistan does build a pipeline to transport gas to countries that can pay hard currency, any improvement in the people's standard of living will not come soon. In the meantime, tensions in Turkmenistan are gradually increasing. The deteriorating level of education, state-sponsored Islamization, and worsening economic conditions could in the long term lead to unpredictable consequences. In 1996, for example, the government made changes to secondary school curricula. Education requirements for admission to a Turkmen college were lowered to nine years for those studying in Turkmen-language schools, though they remain at ten years for those in Russian-language schools.

The deteriorating quality of education and state-sponsored Islamization could result in social unrest in the future — if political and police control is weakened as a result of some crisis of leadership, such as the president's illness. So far, all power is concentrated in the hands of one man — President Niyazov. Neither the courts, the Cabinet, the Medjlis (Parliament), nor the Khalk Maslakhaty (People's Council) can take a single step without consulting the president. The personality cult of the president has reached grotesque proportions, and the constant adulation of "The Leader" sickens even the humble Turkmen, who are accustomed to authority. In the meantime, economic problems mount, and the country's hard currency reserves continue to dwindle. Food rationing fails to meet people's minimum needs, and most people's monthly wages can feed them for only half a month. In 1995, young Turkmen took to the streets of Ashgabat, protesting economic hardship and demanding democratic reform. The government responded with reprisals.

If the economic situation does not improve, sooner or later the growing dissatisfaction could burst into an open conflagration. In that event, Niyazov's Islamization policy might backfire. In 1997, certain missionaries tried to spread Wahhabi ideology in Turkmenistan. So far nothing has come of the attempt. Nevertheless, some day Turkmenistan's geopolitical isolation could lead to a growth of radical Islam, especially considering the increasing influence of Saudi Arabia, Iran, Pakistan, and other Islamic countries. Islam could finally turn against Niyazov's regime, but only if a radical Islamic trend takes root in Turkmenistan or if the clergy tries to get more power and influence. For now, this scenario does not seem probable.

A lot in Turkmenistan's future hinges on a favorable geopolitical correlation of forces and on whether the situations in neighboring Afghanistan and Tajikistan will be stabilized soon. If all goes well, Turkmenistan could count on Western investments in oil and gas prospecting and pipeline construction, which could bring a diversification of economic ties and gradual political liberalization. In that case, if Turkmenistan takes the road of secular democratic development, the threat of Islamic radicalism would cease to exist altogether. At present, however, it is impossible to forecast such a turn of events.

Islam could well play an integrating role in Turkmenistan without actually becoming a dominant force. Orthodox Islam does not endorse nationalism; it recognizes only the ummah (the community of Muslims based on a common faith, not on ethnic or geographic origin). Turkmenistan's post-Soviet ruling elite wants to see a strong national statehood and will, therefore, seek to prevent any excessive growth of clericalism. The interplay of these two opposing forces has so far resulted in a precarious ideological balance, but radical Islam could assume a larger role if the present crisis in the region continues.

Part II

Russia and Central Asia:
the Interconnections

Chapter One

Christianity and Islam in Central Asia

Archbishop Vladimir
of the Orthodox Diocese of Bishkek
and All Central Asia

TRENDS IN THE ORTHODOX CHURCH IN CENTRAL ASIA IN THE POST-SOVIET PERIOD

What is taking place today in the Central Asian diocese can be described by one word: rebirth. After the collapse of the Soviet system with its forced atheism, scores of Orthodox parishes were reinstated in Central Asia and many churches restored from ruins or built anew. Today the number of parishes in this region has actually exceeded their number before the 1917 Revolution, and churches are now being built even in communities that never had Orthodox parishes before. Four convents and one monastery have been opened. Moreover, we have trained a new generation of clergy, so despite the fast growing number of parishes each of them now has its own priest. Orthodox bishops have been trying since the last century to establish a theological seminary in Central Asia (or Turkestan, as it was called then), but this became possible only in the post-Soviet period. In 1998, an Orthodox seminary opened in Tashkent with the objective of training highly educated priests for the diocese. In Tashkent and Bishkek — the capitals of two major Central Asian states — we are setting up large Orthodox religious centers which will help coordinate our educational and charitable activity across the entire diocese. And we plan to open a Sunday Orthodox University for the laity as part of the Tashkent Theological Center.

Of course, much has been lost. The Bolshevik regime left a trail of destruction in its wake. Unique Orthodox churches and works of art were erased from the face of the earth, such as the majestic cathedrals of the Fergana Valley, a remarkable blend of Slavic Orthodox and Oriental cultures created by Russian and Uzbek craftsmen working side by side. We still have a long way to go to reach the splendor of the Orthodox churches of the late 19th and early 20th century. And yet in a number of communities we have built new churches that would do credit to the Christian Russia of pre-revolutionary times: at Balykchi (Kyrgyzstan), Zarafshan (Uzbekistan), Nebit-Dag (Turkmenistan), Chkalovsk (Tajikistan), and several others.

This revival has been a very difficult process — not only in Central Asia, but also in all the Russian Orthodox Church. Having freed itself from the godless Soviet regime, the Church found itself in an economic stranglehold. Today's government in Russia, while acknowledging the Soviet Union's debts to the West, has no intention of acknowledging its debt to the Russian Church, whose buildings and other property were created by the people over a period of nine centuries and then plundered and destroyed by the Soviet authorities. In a mocking gesture, the authorities have now returned our defaced and ruined churches and said: "Go ahead, restore them!" But how? Without funds, or building materials, or donors, amidst the country's overall economic dislocation? What is worse, in many cases those defaced church buildings were now occupied by various offices, and the Church would have to get entangled in an endless bureaucratic rigmarole to get them back. Many of them have not been returned to this day.

Actually, in Central Asia the process of returning the Church's property has been much smoother than in many regions of the Russian Federation, and we are very grateful to the Central Asian governments for facilitating it. Even so, not everything has been returned to us.

Now instead of doing their main job — that of guiding the flock, which lost its former piety under the Soviet regime — our priests are forced to manage construction crews and wrack their brains over financial problems.

We long for the time when our diocese can stop being a gigantic building site and the clergy can once again focus their energies on the task of enlightening and guiding the faithful. In the not-so-distant future, we hope this will become a reality: the trends we see today are encouraging, and no one so far is putting up any roadblocks.

True, I can only speak for our diocese, which includes four Central Asian countries — Kyrgyzstan, Tajikistan, Turkmenistan, and Uzbekistan.

As far as Kazakstan is concerned, there are actually three Orthodox dioceses there, and I have neither sufficient information nor the authority to make judgments about what is going on there.

THE RUSSIAN ORTHODOX CHURCH AND THE NATIVE POPULATION OF CENTRAL ASIA

The Russian Orthodox Church has few native Central Asian adherents. On the one hand, Orthodoxy is not a proselytizing faith. I cannot imagine an Orthodox priest handing out leaflets in a bus or train, or grabbing people in the street by their sleeves and dragging them to a revival meeting, as many sectarian evangelists do. The place for an Orthodox sermon is, first, in church, and second, in Sunday school. We have had to set up Sunday schools not only for children, but for adults as well, because of the widespread religious ignorance that the Bolshevik system left behind. It is a spiritual quest, a hunger for the higher Truth that brings people to our churches and Sunday schools. We believe it is God that brings them there.

On the other hand, before addressing any audience, one has to understand its world view, its own belief system. In the minds of the Turkic and Persian peoples, Islam is an inextricable part of their national heritage. An Uzbek or Tajik regards the Muslim faith as the basic element of his ethnic identity, so conversion to another faith would be seen as a betrayal of his people. The attempts of certain sectarian evangelizers to shatter this stronghold with the help of leaflets or brochures are at best naive; at worst, courting disaster.

Modern-day Islam does not strive to expand its domain, but it reacts fiercely to any attempt to recruit proselytes in its own midst. History provides many instances of excessive evangelism in Muslim countries ending not only in the death of the missionaries themselves, but in the massacre of local Christian communities as well. The history of medieval Central Asia shows us some of the most dramatic examples of this. After the region's Islamization by the Arabs, a powerful Nestorian Christian Church, which included five metropolitan sees, existed in Central Asia for another six centuries. In the early fourteenth century, the Pope of Rome sent a mission here, which managed to infiltrate the court of the Chinghizid Khans and even to baptize the heir to the throne. This attempt by the Roman Catholics to usurp the Khan's power provoked an outburst of fury among the Muslims. In 1339, the whole of Central Asia became the scene of a huge massacre, which not only brought death to the Pope's missionaries, but to all the Nestorian communities in the region.

Such things never happened, however, whenever Islam came in contact with Orthodox Christianity. There was no religious friction whatsoever when the Tatar Khans came to rule the Mongol Empire (the "Golden Horde"), which included Christian Russia for two and a half centuries (1237-1480). Likewise, there was no religious strife in Central Asia in the nineteenth century when this region was under the sovereignty of the Russian Emperor. And similarly, the Ecumenical Patriarchate of the Greek Orthodox Church at Constantinople survived in the Turkish Sultanate and operates in Turkey to this day. All this is because Orthodox Christians have always observed the primary rule of peaceful coexistence with Islam: noninterference in its internal affairs.

Here are some statistics of conversions throughout the period of over half a century that Central Asia was part of the Russian Empire. Christian converts included eight Qara Kyrgyzes, two Turkmenians, three Sartes (Uzbeks), and one Persian (probably a Tajik). In the same period, ten Russians living in Central Asia converted to Islam, among them even a priest by the name of Gromov. Clearly, those conversions were motivated by personal inner conviction, and this did not in any way affect overall relations between the Muslim and Christian communities.

The grand-sounding statements about the "need for Christian missionary work among the Muslims" express little more than a pipe dream. The Russian Orthodox Church has enough to worry about with its own flock — the Russian people — a large proportion of whom have been alienated from the Church by the Soviet regime.

ISLAM AND CHRISTIANITY AS BELIEF SYSTEMS

Islam has much more Christianity to it than many other denominations that claim to be Christian. A number of Christian sects have invented their own doctrine, which goes against the spirit of the New Testament. They do not worship the saints of the Lord, they do not believe in the immaculate conception of the Christ Child from the Virgin Mother, and they call the miracles performed by Christ, as attested to in the Gospels, a collection of myths. In other words, they deny the basic tenets of Christianity that even Muslims believe in.

Mutual prejudice can be rooted in ignorance and failure to understand each other's beliefs. But the Allah of the Muslims is the same God, the One God, Creator and Lord of the Universe, that is worshiped by the Christians. Just as we do, Muslims believe in the omnipotence, omniscience, and infinite mercy and justice of the Creator. Islam teaches that the dead will rise and there will be a Last Judgment and that rewards await the righteous and punishment the wicked in the afterlife. The Koran tells about the same patriarchs and prophets of ancient times as the Bible: from Abraham (Ibrahim) and Moses (Musa) to St. John the Baptist (Yahiya) and the Apostles of Jesus Christ ("Allah's assistants").

The Koran is not the only sacred scripture of the Muslims; they also recognize the sacred significance of the Pentateuch of Moses (the *Taurah*), the Psalms of David (the *Zarur*), and the Gospels of Jesus Christ (the *Inzhil*). Islam refers to those who profess these teachings as *ahl al Qitab*, or "people of the Book." Muslims are instructed to have a totally different attitude toward "people of the Book" than toward pagans or atheists. Muslims are even allowed to marry "people of the Book," as the Koran prescribes: "You are allowed to take the chaste ones from among the Muslims and the chaste ones from among those who were given the Scripture that came before you" (Sura 5, Ayat 7/5/).

Jesus Christ is described in Islam as one of the greatest prophets. An entire chapter of the Koran (the *sura* entitled "Maryam") is devoted to His immaculate conception by the Holy Ghost and miraculous birth from the Holy Virgin Mary (Our Lady Maryam). Muslims believe that Jesus is the Messiah, in other words, the Christ, referring to Him as "the Word of God" (as the New Testament says: "In the beginning was the Word, and the Word was with God" (John 1:1). For the Muslims, He is the only "Pure and Sinless" among the Prophets: all the others needed first to be forgiven by Allah. The Muslims know that Christ used divine power to heal lepers and blind men and resurrect the dead; the list of His miracles in the Koran is even longer than in the Gospels. Islam also recognizes Jesus Christ's bodily ascension into Heaven: "Allah took Him up to His own Realm, for Allah is great and wise!" (Sura 3, Ayat 156/158/). Muslims believe that Jesus will return to vanquish the spirits of evil and rule over mankind.

The Koran makes its quite clear what our relations should be like: "You will find, of course, that the closest in love to Muslims are those who said, 'We are Christians!' This is because there are priests and monks among them and they are not conceited"[1] (Sura 5, Ayat 85/82/). One of

Muhammad's close friends was a Christian by the name of Waraka ibn Naufal, and the first copyist of the Koran was a Christian named Sergiy. Christians should be "true Nazarenes," faithful to Jesus Christ's behest: "A new commandment I give unto you, That ye love one another [...]. By this shall all men know that ye are my disciples [...]" (John 13:34,35). Only then can we live in love and friendship with true Muslims.

Islam is often called a religion of justice and Christianity a religion of love. But why should Justice quarrel with Love? There is much hatred and untruth in the world. And there is enough room for everyone to do good deeds and try to make this world a better place to live.

At the same time, it should be emphasized that Orthodox Christianity and Islam represent very different world views, and it is impossible to combine the two. Therefore, any theological debate about the subtleties of the Christian and Muslim doctrine are pointless and could even do harm. We should act in a spirit of respect for each other's opinions and cultures, not emphasize our differences. To reach mutual understanding, we need to bear in mind what we have in common and recognize one simple truth: we will come to learn what God and His Kingdom really are when we see them in the next world. But here, on this earth, our job is to live and guide our peoples in prayer and piety and encourage them to listen to their spiritual mentors. We must join hands in fighting godlessness, which is poisoning human societies with immorality and crime.

ISLAM AS A NEIGHBOR

For us Islam is neither a rival, nor is it just a harmless neighbor — it is our friend and ally. We are united in our refusal to accept sin and injustice, and in our desire to instill in our faithful certain high ideals that are common to both our religions — honesty and decency, kindness and respect for one's elders, fairness and generosity. We are united in our desire to see the countries of Central Asia live in peace, prosperity, morality, good will among people, national reconciliation, and constructive labor. We are united in our commitment to charity and mercy, and in our desire to help those in need and those who suffer. We are united in our desire to overcome the grim legacy of the atheist regime and to restore the spiritual values it destroyed. And the fact that mosques and *madrasas*, churches and monasteries are opening throughout Central Asia is our common joy.

The friendship between our nations exists on all levels: virtually every Orthodox Christian has friends among the Muslims and there are friendly relations between members of our clergies. I personally always feel cordiality and complete rapport when I meet with the Muslim leaders of the Central Asian states. It is touching to see the deep respect that Muslims show for Orthodox priests. During my trips throughout the diocese, I often visit not only Orthodox churches, but mosques as well. There I always find myself surrounded by ordinary Muslims who ask me questions, and I often talk to them. Our priests have told me that they, too, get a heartfelt welcome wherever they go, even in communities where no one knows them. As for business contacts, whenever we ask our Muslim friends for help or advice, we always get it. We have never had even the slightest misunderstanding, to say nothing of a conflict.

This partnership of Orthodoxy and Islam in Central Asia — which, I think, presents a unique example for the whole world — is based on a century and a half of our history.

In the middle of the last century, Kazakstan, and partially Kyrgyzstan, voluntarily became part of the Russian Empire. The rest of Central Asia (except for the Bukhara Emirate) was invaded and annexed by the army of Czar Alexander II, who was vying with Great Britain for "spheres of influence" in the region. However, Russian Orthodox Christianity came to the region with humility, not as the missionary religion of a conqueror, and only to minister to the Russian settlers, with no intention of converting the local population.

A contemporary of that time, Hieromonk Khariton, wrote: "The local people are showing sympathy for the poor settlers. Without their help, many would have died of hunger and exposure." But even in those difficult circumstances, the Russian peasants did not forget about their faith. As soon as they settled down, a new rural community would start building a church. That is how the first congregations appeared. Then, about 130 years ago, an Orthodox diocese was established.

I admire the religious policy of the Russian Czarist government, which not only exercised tolerance toward Islam, but also tried to provide protection to the Muslim clergy in every possible way. Russian government officials being assigned posts in Central Asia would take an oath that contained the following stipulation: "To show fairness to the needs and interests of the Muslims." The Muslim clergy's income remained intact and was tax-exempt. In addition, teachers at Muslim schools —

mektebs and *madrasas* — were given a salary by the state. The Russian
Imperial government started publishing Muslim religious literature at its
own expense. A mass edition of the Koran was published in the city of
Kazan (Tatarstan, Russia), and a major portion of the print run was
shipped to Central Asia. On several occasions, the government allocated
substantial funds to meet the religious needs of the Muslims. For example, in 1888, Czar Alexander III donated some of his own money to
restore the Djami Mosque in the city of Tashkent. In a thank-you speech
on that occasion, Qazi Muhammad Muhitdin Hodja, leader of the
Tashkent Muslims, said: "Glory to Allah! Under the white Czar, nothing
is preventing us from following the Adat and Shariah law. Everywhere on
earth and at all times, civilized nations have shown most respect for two
things: religion and knowledge. And every ruler who renders support for
these two things could do no better good."

The Muslims returned the favor in kind, making generous donations
for the construction of "Russian mosques," as they referred to Orthodox
churches. Their donations funded the construction of four Christian
churches in rural areas of Central Asia. One third of the funding for the
construction of St. George's Church in the village of Troitskoye was
donated by the Mullah of Chirchik (one of the few old churches that
survived the Soviet period; today it stands in the only Orthodox
monastery in Central Asia). Muslims contributed not only money, but
their own labor as well, regarding it a great honor to work on the construction of Orthodox Churches. Contemporaries marveled at the splendor of the stucco molding in many Orthodox churches of Central Asia: it
was the work of Uzbek craftsmen. The Kazan Cathedral in Kokand
could be considered a joint creation of Russian and Uzbek art: cast in
the style of seventeenth-century Slavic architecture, it featured much
Oriental ornament because it was built by Uzbek craftsmen under the
supervision of the Russian architect Vassilyev. The Uzbek artist Husto
Hustitdin was awarded a silver medal on a St. Anna ribbon by the
Russian government for his part in the construction. (In the Soviet
period, the cathedral was razed to the ground by the atheist authorities.)
But today, too, I am happy to see Russians taking part in the building of
mosques and Muslims working on the construction of Orthodox
churches. Muslim philanthropists continue giving money for the construction of our churches. Naturally, they have their own religious priorities — first they build a mosque, and only then do they help the
Orthodox community.

In the pre-Soviet period, Muslims and Christians in Central Asia conducted joint charity programs, including the establishment of orphanages. In addition to funds donated by Orthodox communities, Emir Said Salimkhan, who sent 10,000 gold tchervonets "for the good cause," made a large contribution. The orphanages had a mix of children from different ethnic backgrounds, so a mullah taught the Koran to the Muslim children, while an Orthodox priest taught the Gospel to the Russians.

That was how our friendship developed in times of peace and prosperity. But nothing brings people closer together than shared hardship. Under the Soviet regime, friendship between Muslims and Christians grew stronger, and this helped our faith survive the decades of persecution.

During Stalin's purges, thousands of Orthodox priests, monks, and nuns were exiled or fled to Central Asia, including twelve Russian Orthodox bishops. You have only to visit Botkin Cemetery in Tashkent to realize how many members of the Orthodox clergy have found everlasting peace in this kindly soil. There were many cases of Muslims hiding Russian clergymen. And we should not forget that during the Second World War, hundreds of thousands of Slavic refugees from German-occupied regions survived thanks to the hospitality of Central Asian families. To quote the Scriptures, the Muslims are good neighbors for they "showed mercy" on us (Luke 10:37). I always tell my congregation: love and mutual assistance between you should come just as naturally as between members of one family, and if anyone of you should have the opportunity to do a kind deed for a Muslim, regard this as a special favor from God.

I believe our experience of inter-denominational cooperation sets a good example and could be useful far beyond the borders of Central Asia. It seems to me that if Western ideologues would spend less time spreading panic about the "Islamic threat" and "Muslim aggressiveness" and would try to understand their world view, the West would not have such a big problem in its relations with the Muslim world.

ISLAMIC TEACHING AND THE SLAVIC POPULATION

Like Orthodox Christianity, Islam on the whole, and especially in today's context, is not a proselytizing religion. Islam does not have a following among the Slavic population, and the Muslim clergy has not shown any interest in acquiring such a following. This is not only because Islam is seen as something purely Turkic or Tajik. Of course, people of Slavic origin naturally gravitate toward Orthodox Christianity simply because the entire history and culture of the Slavic nations is steeped in the Christian spirit. But in addition, for Muslims, they are "people of the Book," so any attempt to convert them to Islam would go against the Koran. Besides, starting from the time of the Arabian Caliphates, the Islamic mission has always been regarded as the task of the state, not of individuals (and today's secular governments of Uzbekistan, Kyrgyzstan, and Turkmenistan, which support the cause of Muslim education in their countries, follow the same principle).

In the seventh century, in the course of the Arabian conquest of Central Asia, Islam came to this land together with the armies of the Caliphate. As you probably know, the Koran is quite intolerant of any type of paganism. And the conquerors were pretty blunt about it: each family of fire worshipers or Manicheans was forced to provide room and board to an Arabian soldier, who would then make sure that all the household members dutifully performed Islamic rituals. But Christians got favorable treatment: the conquerors showed them respect, calling them "worshipers of the One God," while the Koran referred to them as "people of the Book." The then Patriarch Timothy I of Syria wrote: "The Arabs, to whom God has now given the power to rule the world, as you probably know, not only do not oppose Christianity, but praise our faith and honor our priests and saints, and help our churches and monasteries."

The time of the Arabian Caliphates is called the "golden age of Islam." But even in those days, Muslims showed broad tolerance toward other faiths. "People of the Book" — Christians and Jews — could hold high government positions, they could even be viziers to the caliphs, and their clergy was represented at the court and received government support. Many famous Christian and Jewish men who were scientists, doctors, and philosophers made important contributions to the great Arabian culture. That was the situation in the age of classical, enlightened Islam.

But the wedge of suspicion and hostility was driven between the Christian and Muslim worlds in the Middle Ages by a number of military adventures: the Crusades launched by the Pope of Rome and the so-called Yellow Crusade of the Mongolian Nestorians. The Orthodox Church had nothing to do with those adventures and the Orthodox community managed, albeit with some difficulty, to maintain relations with Islam and to keep intact the Patriarchates of Constantinople, Antioch, and Alexandria in the vast region under Muslim rule.

I believe that the Muslim faith in Uzbekistan, Kyrgyzstan, and Turkmenistan is developing in the direction of establishing an enlightened, classical type of Islam — as it used to be during the Caliphates. Let us hope that Tajikistan will take the same road after it finally emerges from its civil conflict.

PERESTROIKA AND POST-PERESTROIKA: ISLAM AND ORTHODOX CHRISTIANITY

The religious freedom regained after the fall of the Soviet regime is equally precious to us all. However, I must admit that over the eighty years of forced atheism, the Russian Orthodox Church lost more than Islam and now finds itself in a more difficult situation.

There was no particular need to revive Islam in Central Asia: the Uzbeks, Kyrgyz, Turkmenians, and Tajiks were Muslim and remain Muslim. The stability of Islam can be explained by the inner structure of Muslim society. Anyone who is versed in Islamic doctrine can head a religious community: there is no sacrament of ordination, no hierarchical degrees, without which the Orthodox Church cannot exist, and none of the other Christian sacraments that have to be performed in a church by a priest. Islam found refuge from atheist persecution in secret communes and within the family, where the faith was handed down from generation to generation. Atheism was seen here as an official government ideology, and you just had to pay lip service to it at occasional "atheist rituals." But even the First Secretaries of the Communist Parties of the Central Asian republics and local cabinet ministers followed the rules of Islam at home, and after their deaths were given traditional Muslim burials. Therefore, after regaining freedom of religion, Islam simply came out into the open: mosques were restored everywhere within a matter of two or three years, with active support from the government and help from Muslims in other Eastern countries, but mostly as a result of a unanimous nationwide movement. So today the Muslim clergy is busy, not so much reviving the Muslim faith as spreading and deepening religious knowledge among the faithful.

The situation is much more difficult in the Orthodox Church. Since the Communists killed off most of the Orthodox clergy, the Slavic population found itself with no spiritual leaders to guide them. They were like shepherdless sheep. A large proportion of the people had lost the habit of prayer, fasting, going to church, and many of them had become godless after many years of atheist propaganda. When the revival of Orthodox Christianity began, a new generation of clergy had to be cultivated. At the same time the churches had to be restored or rebuilt. This was much more difficult for us than for the Muslims. And finally, the most difficult task was to get the people back into the churches and to nurture a new Slavic flock, a task which requires of our clergy a high moral code and a high level of education. I must say that in our Central Asian diocese, the putrefying legacy of Bolshevism is slowly but surely receding, and we are especially happy to see an influx of Slavic youth into our churches.

But on the whole, both Islam and Orthodox Christianity have equally gained from the return of religious freedom. As far as other creeds are concerned, most of them are now trying to cash in on the spiritual void left by the Soviet regime. Right after religious freedom was proclaimed, Russia and other republics of the former Soviet Union were invaded by swarms of foreign missionaries of every stripe and color. They have at their disposal large financial resources of questionable origin. Those sectarians often acquire converts not by preaching, but by simple bribery, while some "totalitarian sects" also resort to hypnosis, subliminal encoding, mind-altering drugs, and other satanic techniques. The activity of those sectarians leads not to enlightenment, but to a deepening of spiritual discord, which modern-day Russia is already engulfed in. In this regard, Patriarch Alexiy II of Moscow and All Russia said: "We have the impression that these missionaries are not really pursuing religious objectives. Their goal is to split society along religious lines — a society that is already split politically." As for Central Asia, the sectarian intervention here is a direct provocation, an incitement of religious and ethnic strife. And this is also a hallmark of the post-perestroika period.

Virtually every leaflet and brochure circulated by those sectarians contains attacks on Orthodox Christianity. Well, our Orthodox Christians have been hardened by the blasphemy of militant atheists and I'm sure they can calmly withstand this new onslaught. But how long can the Muslims tolerate the scornful and offensive remarks made by visiting evangelizers about Islam and its founder, Muhammad? Will the Muslim community calmly look on while foreign sectarians try to recruit converts among the Muslim youth, to which Islam has always reacted painfully? Do those self-proclaimed "spiritual teachers" really fail to understand what they are doing, or do they understand it all too well? Fortunately, our Muslims can tell the difference between Orthodox Christians, with whom they have been good friends for more than a century, and foreign missionaries.

These sectarians have come here, to the site of some of the most ancient civilizations of the Orient, with an attitude as though we are savages. The peoples of Central Asia have been practicing Islam for thirteen centuries, and the ancestors of our Slavic community adopted Orthodox Christianity more than a thousand years ago. What can these missionaries expect to teach us if their own sects are only a few decades old? What are we supposed to learn from these unwelcome guests who know nothing about our customs, traditions, history, and who do not respect our religious beliefs?

Some of the things those self-proclaimed evangelists do are really outrageous: they invited people to "meet Christ on Lake Issyk-Kul" and "in Moscow's Red Square" and tried to scare the public by announcing the date of the "end of the world" — in 1992, then in 1993, then in 1996, then in 1999. A sect of Jehovah's Witnesses was expelled from Turkmenistan after it allegedly used psychotropic drugs to lure converts, and there was a spate of scandals when so-called missionaries tried to bribe government officials. . . . What does all this have to do with Christianity, or with religion at all?

Unfortunately, not only sectarian "carpetbaggers" but also representatives of more serious creeds are taking part in this missionary intervention. The World Council of Churches has passed a resolution banning proselytism. However, certain member denominations are actively trying to recruit proselytes here in Central Asia. Recently, the Roman Catholic Church made several statements declaring its respect for the Orthodox Church. Why, then, are Catholics trying so hard to infiltrate the Central Asian diocese of the Orthodox Church? For what purpose and for whose sake did the Nuncio of the Pope stationed in Turkey try so hard to establish a Roman Catholic diocese and religious schools in Turkmenistan, where there is not a single Catholic? And why did another Papal Nuncio, stationed in Kazakhstan, have to spend big money to buy the right for a Roman Catholic priest to teach theology at Bishkek's Slavic University? There is only one small Catholic community in the whole of Kyrgyzstan — which itself was only recently "converted" from Protestantism. Was this done by the same financial method?

All these facts cause bewilderment and breed suspicion among Muslims, who know history much too well and remember that they have Roman Catholic missionaries to thank for at least one medieval tragedy in their land.

Don't the Western evangelizers have anything left to do in their own countries? Does Jesus Christ already reign supreme in all the hearts of the people in their own countries? Not at all. We can see that the Western nations need spiritual enlightenment — not less but perhaps even more than the peoples of our land. It is the West that exports films and publications advocating violence, brutality, pornography, and other deadly sins. Do they think our people are so naive as to accept sermons from nations that can tolerate all that themselves? Before preaching the gospel to Muslims, the Western creeds should put their own house in order. The Koran says: "O people of the Book! You have nothing to stand on until you set straight the Torah and the Gospel!" (Sura 5, Ayat 72/68/). The Bible contains a similar thought: "Wherefore lay apart all filthiness and superfluity of naughtiness, and receive with meekness the engrafted word, which is able to save your souls. But be ye doers of the word, and not hearers only, deceiving your own selves" (James 1:21-22).

A delegation of the World Council of Churches took part in the International Christian–Muslim Conference, which was held in 1995 in Tashkent under the motto "Living Together Under One Sky." After studying reports of foreign missionary activity in Central Asia, the delegation had to admit: "Those preachers are acting in error." At that same conference, the Muslim and Orthodox spiritual leaders adopted a joint address to the peoples of Central Asia, which said, in part:

"We have a common interest in the strengthening of Islam among the Muslim peoples and strengthening of Orthodox Christianity among the Slavic population of the Central Asian countries, since these faiths constitute the sacred legacy of our ancestors. Both Muslims and Orthodox Christians see their common objective in building prosperous, spiritually enlightened and highly moral societies in their native countries of Central Asia . . .

"We support religious freedom. However, we are concerned when the growing number of foreign missionary organizations abuses it. We are concerned by their actions which sow discord in our societies, by their disregard for our culture and traditions, by their aggressive religious propaganda, and by the fact that they are taking advantage of people's financial difficulties for purposes of proselytizing . . .

"Islamic and Orthodox Christian leaders, as good neighbors and sincere collaborators in the cause of strengthening our states, are determined to fight any attempt to distort the image of our two great world religions. We will strive to provide our faithful with objective, complete and respectful information about other faiths, which will open up our hearts and minds to respect each other's religious beliefs." In other words, both the perestroika and post-perestroika periods have expanded the horizons of our spiritual life. But these horizons must be clear.

THE GOVERNMENTS AND THEIR ATTITUDES TO RELIGION

During the Soviet period Muslims could hide — or rather, not demonstrate — the ritual aspect of their religion. But the way of life of the Oriental people, from cradle to grave, remains essentially Muslim. Today the governments of the newly independent states have only freed themselves from the old sin of hypocrisy . . . .

The presidents of the Central Asian states and most of the local officials are Muslims. However, despite all that, we have a secular government. That is because the business of the clergy is to provide spiritual guidance to the faithful, not to engage in politics or economics: that is a good way to keep certain people from exploiting religion for political ends. Naturally, when you consider government support for religion on a purely practical, day-to-day level, preference is given to Islam — simply because the majority of the population is Muslim. This is only natural, it is legal, and it is democratic.

However, the government's attitude to the Orthodox Church is very friendly: we also get government assistance at both the national and local levels. President Islam Karimov of Uzbekistan issued an executive order to provide land and financial support for the establishment of an Orthodox Religious Center in Tashkent. President Asker Akaev of Kyrgyzstan issued a similar edict. In addition, Akaev donated large sums of money on several occasions for the construction of Orthodox churches in a number of communities across Kyrgyzstan. President Saparmurad Niyazov of Turkmenistan personally selected and donated to our Church a piece of land in one of the most scenic parts of Ashkhabad so that we could build a church there. And the government of Kyrgyzstan announced that Christmas would be celebrated on a par with the main Muslim holidays, and now Muslims joyfully celebrate Christmas together

with us as the "Birthday of the Sinless Isa" (Jesus). The Committee for Religious Affairs of Turkmenistan has in effect become a kind of "ministry for care of the faithful": its chairman
is the Head Mufti of the Republic, while the Deputy chairman is an Orthodox priest. I can cite dozens of examples of local officials in town and country responding to the needs of Orthodox Christians. The Orthodox population is very grateful for these acts of charity and goodwill.

There is also a purely pragmatic motive in the willingness of the Central Asian governments to help their Orthodox Christian communities. President Islam Karimov of Uzbekistan has praised the "contribution of the Orthodox diocese to the cause of promoting ethnic peace, national reconciliation and friendship among people of different faiths." In the Uzbek towns of Syr Darya and Karsha, which never had Orthodox Christian communities before, the local authorities gave us buildings for us to adapt as Orthodox churches, and they actually encouraged us to form parishes and provide spiritual guidance to the Slavic population. They did all this on their own initiative, without any prompting on our part. The authorities understand that a person brought up in the Christian virtues, such as love for all people, hard work, respect for the law, humility, moral purity — such a person is a model citizen.

The traditional religions — Islam and Orthodox Christianity — are seen in Central Asia as the spiritual pillars of society. With regard to other denominations, the principle of religious freedom is strictly observed: no one can interfere with their right to hold prayer meetings and preach. The only thing that is banned is illegal mind-control techniques. In Kyrgyzstan, for example, there were even totalitarian sects up until recently, but since their activity has had a tragic outcome, the government had to clamp down.

TRENDS OF ISLAM IN CENTRAL ASIA FROM AN ORTHODOX PERSPECTIVE

The new trends in Central Asia relate to Muslim education. This includes the publication of the Koran, *khadises*, and popular Islamic literature in mass editions in the major languages of Central Asia. It also entails the opening of *madrasa* schools in a number of communities, establishment of Muslim religious centers, in-depth study of history, and a growth of Islamic motifs in secular art and culture. All these trends can only be welcomed.

When we consider the mutual influence and interpenetration of Islam and secular government, we should not forget that the sermons of the Arabian theologian Muhammad ibn Abd al-Wahhab, who is considered the founder of Wahhabism, proceed from the premise that government should be separated from religion. More precisely, venal secular government, which has forgotten the laws of religious (albeit dogmatic) morality, should be separated from the "pure" religion of Islam. Still more precisely, religion should be elevated above secular matters, to the point of subordinating the latter to the former.

In addition to demands for "purity of religion," which includes rejecting the veneration of saints and even the Prophet Muhammad (in other words, rejecting any "intermediation" between man and Allah), and banning virtually all types of earthly pastimes which would distract from prayer and spiritual life (including dancing, smoking, and many other things), Wahhabism is also strongly opposed to luxury, albeit in its own narrow understanding of the term.

All this leads to a very serious conclusion. As long as there exists material inequality — and in many countries this is quite conspicuous and stark — and as long as there are people living in poverty who have little opportunity to take part in normal secular life, the impoverished could easily find themselves following the leaders of this extremist trend of Islam.

Clearly, the wealthier a country and its people, in the crass material sense of the word, the less fertile ground there is for Wahhabism. And conversely, Wahhabism can find fertile ground in the poorest countries of the world.

The term "fundamentalism" with respect to Islam is a misnomer. There is nothing fundamentalist in "Islamic fundamentalism" — that is to say, nothing that would affirm the fundamentals of the faith. Essentially, it is little more than ritualism, somewhat similar to Old Belief in Russia, which also had nothing "old" about it and was rooted in religious ignorance. An enlightened Muslim understands that it is not necessary to punish a thief by chopping off his hand — there are other ways of administering justice. Or take the custom of covering a woman's face with a veil and the ban on depicting live creatures — these customs were introduced several centuries after Muhammad, and not in all Muslim countries. Take the *Miraj Nameh*, a fifteenth-century manuscript now kept in France's National Library (inventory number 190): it contains sixty-one miniatures illustrating the Prophet Muhammad's night journey to Jerusalem and His ascension to Heaven (*al-Isra'wa-l-Mi'raj*).

Observing certain details is, after all, a matter of secondary importance — that is not the essence of Islam. But the real fundamentalism, which embodied the dogmatic essence of Islam of that time, was the cornerstone of the enlightened Islam of the Caliphates. But when extremists, fanatics, or politicians use the letter of *shari'a* law to mask their own selfish ends and go against the spirit of Islam, there is nothing fundamentalist about it — in fact, it has nothing to do with Islam.

Here are a few examples. Islam prohibits the consumption of alcohol, and even more so narcotic drugs. The Koran and the *hadises* (narrations of Muhammad by his disciples) equate a drug dealer with one who poisons and a drug addict with one who commits suicide — they are both doomed to eternal suffering in hell after Allah's Last Judgment. Then how can Afghanistan, one of the biggest drug producers in the world, call itself a Muslim nation? By the same token, Chechnya, which is controlled by the drug barons, is a place where kidnappings happen every day, where Muslims kidnap fellow Muslims and even little children. Such a nation can hardly claim to be governed by *shari'a* law. Or how can a terrorist call himself a true Muslim when his acts lead to the death of innocent people? The Koran contains the dire warnings: "He who slays an innocent man is like unto him who has slain all men." The prominent Muslim theologian al-Gazali condemns terrorists as "highway robbers who attack people under the shroud of religion."

However, no religion is guaranteed against fanaticism and extremism. Take for example the Catholic Inquisition and the "children's crusade," the destruction of churches by Baptists in the early stages of that creed, and the sects of self-immolators and self-castrators in the Old Believers movement in Russia. Let us hope that Islam, as a basically peaceful, sober, and tolerant religion, will ultimately overcome such distortions.

POLITICS AND ISLAM

Religion is a heavenly matter, politics an earthly matter. Any attempt to use religion to gain power, honor, or profit, any political speculation on religion is a deadly sin, blasphemy, a crime before Our Lord. This is an axiom both in Islam and Christianity. And yet, politicians can speculate on religion in any country.

Politics under the guise of religion often leads to tragedy. The ongoing civil war in Tajikistan is actually not even over religion. Everyone knows that President Imomoli Rakhmonov and his government pledged their support for Islam and actually did much to support it, so the opposition's attempts to be seen as more Muslim than the government are absurd. The actual motive behind the conflict was a power struggle among clans. As a clergyman, I have no right to take sides. But the fact is that instead of coming up with a civilized power-sharing arrangement, they unleashed a civil war in which brother killed brother. Only now are the two sides trying to reach an agreement. Better late than never. Both Muslims and Orthodox Christians are praying for peace to come to the long-suffering land of Tajikistan.

Has Islam gained anything from the death of thousands of Tajik Muslims, tens of thousands of families who lost everything, and the economy that lies in ruins? No, only the drug barons have profited from this blood bath. It is they who control the transit routes along which drugs are shipped to Russia and Europe.

Wherever there is a politicization of Islam, in other words a desire to mix religion and politics, it proves disastrous for religion. A dramatic example is the activity of the Popes of Rome in the Middle Ages when they laid claim to world secular power and arrogated the right to declare and wage wars. The result was the secularization and extreme moral degradation of the clergy. This caused the emergence of the Protestant movement, which split the Roman Catholic Church.

Nevertheless, Islam is extremely popular, to use a secular expression. So the temptation is to use it as a vehicle for one's personal ambitions. Ambitious people tend to think that they are fighting for a good cause. In reality, however, it can bring tragedy to people and go against the Commandments of our Lord. Moreover, popularity gained from even a good cause could, in this situation, serve evil. That is why religion must at all costs be protected from politics.

One of the dangerous by-products can be terrorism. A terrorist act always results in the death of innocent people, and under Islamic law, this is a horrible crime. But Islam is not at fault. It is the fault of political or nationalist extremists acting under the guise of religious fundamentalism. Muslim leaders have repeatedly condemned terrorists, kidnappers, and other such gangsters, calling them a "disgrace to Islam" and "enemies of Islam." Not surprisingly, certain terrorist groups in the CIS calling themselves "fundamentalists" have made a number of attempts on the lives of prominent Muslim leaders. By attempting to murder religious leaders, these self-styled "Muslim fundamentalists" have demonstrated ignorance of the most basic principles of Islam.

It is revealing what some of these so-called fundamentalists say. For example, Muhammad Solih, one of the men behind the tragedy of February 16, 1999 in Tashkent, is quoted by the media as saying, "It doesn't matter what kind of state will be established — communist, democratic, secular, or religious. The main thing is to come to power."

Fundamentalism is often used as a disguise by political extremists. Wahhabism, on the other hand, is a deviation from mainstream Islam. It is a Muslim heresy that, in addition to certain distortions of Islamic dogma, exhibits an aggressive political tendency. As far as I know, the preachers of Wahhabism, Ahmadiya, Qadyriya, and other Muslim heresies have received a rather cool welcome from the *Sunni* Muslim majority (the orthodox branch of Islam which is predominant in Uzbekistan, Kyrgyzstan, and Turkmenistan) and these heresies have had no success there.

In Uzbekistan, there was a political conspiracy under the guise of fundamentalism, but it got no support from the population. The government's reaction was swift, but mild: the conspirators did not receive any punishment under the law but were simply sent out of the country. By contrast, those involved in the terrorist acts of February 16 in Tashkent got what they deserved and some death sentences were passed. However, their extremism had nothing to do with religion — they simply wanted to seize power.

Similarly in Tajikistan, the government is aware that exploitation of religion will not end until there is peace in the country. The process of national reconciliation has shown this to be true.

CONCLUSION

The fact that part of the Russian population is leaving for Russia has nothing to do with Islam. The exodus was prompted by the atmosphere of upheaval caused by perestroika and the breakup of the Soviet Union, but it tapered down to a trickle after stability returned to Uzbekistan, Turkmenistan, and Kyrgyzstan. And, of course, it is much easier for an Orthodox Christian to find a common language with a Muslim than for an atheist.

There was an incident at the height of the civil war in Tajikistan that was both tragic and comical. A few gunmen from the opposition camp occupied St. Nicholas' Cathedral in the capital Dushanbe and set up a machine gun in the belfry. They tried to reassure the priests by saying, "We're not fighting *you*, we have nothing against you!" Very comforting, to be sure, but it is true that the conflict did not affect the Russian community. Yet it is hard to live in the crossfire of a civil war, and many Russians left. However, characteristically, even during the civil war not a single Orthodox church closed in Tajikistan — on the contrary, two new Orthodox parishes were established.

Central Asia is still home to more than two million Slavs, who have deep roots here. Their ancestors are buried in this soil, Central Asia is their native land, and they have no desire to leave. So given stability and peaceful development in the region, the Central Asian diocese of the Orthodox Church has a good future.

The Islamic Minority in Russia

Marat Murtazin

INTRODUCTION

When people hear the phrase "a Muslim in Russia" they might think "a foreigner in Russia." Indeed, Soviet-era books on Islam (or rather on atheism) give the impression that Islam in Russia is a thing of the past and you can only find Muslims beyond Russia's borders. Yet the events of this past decade have shown that Russia and Islam are not isolated from each other, and that Muslims actually live in Russia alongside Orthodox Christians, Jews, and Buddhists. In fact, Islam has always been the second-largest religious community in Russia, with more than twenty million adherents in the country.

THE ORIGINS OF ISLAM IN RUSSIA

In the mid-seventh century, the first Muslim armies came sweeping across what today is Azerbaijan, and in 642-643 A.D. they reached the city of Derbent, located in today's Dagestan, a republic of the Russian Federation. These were the first Muslims to set foot on what was to become Russian soil, more than 1,350 years ago (1,400 years ago, according to the Muslim calendar based on the Hegira). Those Muslims were not Russian Muslims, of course — they were Arab warriors who came and left, but their brief presence left an indelible mark. Islam spread throughout Central Asia, the northern Caucasus, Azerbaijan, and the Volga region.

In the eighth century Islam became the official religion throughout Central Asia as a result of the Arab conquest, not as a voluntary acceptance of Islam by the local population. Although the Central Asian countries later became independent states, they were part of the Russian

Empire for many decades and later were part of the Soviet Union. Large numbers of descendants of Central Asian Muslim civilizations — such as the Uzbeks, Kazaks, Turkmens, Kyrgyz, and Tajiks today — live within the territory of the Russian Federation.

As far back as the seventh century, the Khazars were familiar with Islam, and many converted to the faith. The Khazars were, in fact, the first Muslims the Russians of Kiev Rus had ever encountered. However, Islam never became the official religion of the Khazar Khanate, and by the eleventh century the Khazars had themselves disappeared.

Following the Caucasus and Central Asia, the Volga Bulgar region accepted Islam as its official religion in 922 A.D., after the arrival of the embassy of the Caliph of Baghdad. The tribes inhabiting the Volga Bulgar region had already been exposed to Islam through merchants sailing up the Volga from Central Asia, Iran, and the Baghdad Caliphate. Many Volga Bulgars professed Islam and performed Muslim rituals. King Almush, the Bulgar ruler, decreed that the *kamat* (second call to prayer) should be uttered with a double invocation of the *shahad* (first postulate of Islam, "There is no god but Allah! Muhammad is Allah's Messenger!"). This decree became the standard practice in Central Asia in the Hanafi *mazkhab* (branch of Islam), even though the Muslim *ulemas* (scholars of sacred law and theology) from Baghdad taught otherwise.

Islam finally became the official religion of the Golden Horde under the rule of Uzbek-Khan early in the fourteenth century, after which it spread among the numerous Turkic tribes over a vast territory from the Crimea to Siberia. Those tribes ultimately formed the greater part of the multimillion Turkic Muslim populations of Russia, Central Asia, and Azerbaijan.

A HISTORY OF MUSLIMS IN RUSSIA: THE EARLY CENTURIES

Early Muslims in Russia, regardless of ethnic origin, lived in their own independent states. These enclaves had their own ideology, religion, customs, and traditions that met the spiritual needs of the peoples, who lived as free members of their communities. However, by the will of Almighty Allah, the rising principality of Muscovy, surrounded by Islamic states, now began to conquer its Muslim neighbors one by one.

The first Muslims appeared in Russian principalities in the thirteenth century, but they were representatives of foreign states, not local residents.

Those Muslims did not feel very welcome, even though the czars allowed them to establish their own Tatar suburb in Moscow, where they lived an isolated life in accordance with their own laws and customs.

In 1445, a large armed force of Tatars (headed by Prince Kassim of the Kazan Khanate) was granted land in the Meschera region and founded the Kassim kingdom on the Oka River. Its Muslim residents lived according to their own customs, built mosques in Russian towns and cities, held administrative positions, and even governed small towns within the Meschera region. Most important, they could openly practice their religion and they had no difficulties because of their Muslim faith. Their descendants, the Mishar Tatars, have kept their faith to this day despite being surrounded by Russians and other non-Muslim peoples, such as the Chuvash and the Mordva.

In the sixteenth century the Russian capture of the city-states of Kazan and Astrakhan, along with the conquest of the Nogai Principality and the Siberian Khanate, added a sizable Muslim population to the Russian state. However, this conquest brought about the decimation of that Muslim population, banishment of many Muslims from the cities, destruction of mosques and other spiritual centers, and attempts to force Muslims to convert to Christianity. Even though the Muslim states of Kazan, Astrakhan, and Siberia kept their names under the auspices of the Russian Czar until the end of the seventeenth century, they were no longer independent — all their central cities and government bodies were in Russian hands.

Muslims became an oppressed minority in Russia. While still living in the land of their forefathers, they suddenly became unwelcome aliens to the government that claimed to protect them. Authorities banished Muslims from the capital and other major cities, destroyed their mosques and schools, and persecuted their scholars and theologians. Here is testimony from a Kazan chronicler of the mid-sixteenth century:

> *"Ish-Muhammad, son of Tugk-Muhammad, was a righteous man. For 36 years he headed a school in the village of Adai, and under him the school flourished and attracted many disciples. Yet in the past 20 years none of his followers have survived...."*[1]

Moreover, besides using force, Russians tried to convert Muslims to Christianity by offering them brides, privileges, and land. Fortunately, the apostates were few and far between, and even they continued to say their prayers. Only after the Orthodox Christian Church was separated from the Russian state was the policy of forced baptism somewhat relaxed, even though the Missionary Anti-Muslim Department functioned in Kazan up to the early twentieth century.

MUSLIMS' LIFE BEFORE SOVIET RULE

What was life like for Muslims living in Kazan, Astrakhan, Nogai, and Siberia? Faith in Allah, patience, willingness to withstand all the trials and tribulations sent by the Lord, and the age-old convictions that "Allah is your Lord! Islam is your faith! The Koran is your Scripture! Muhammad is your Prophet!" characterized their lives, and gave them the strength to endure, live, work, and raise their children. Those Muslims were able to maintain their mosques and *mektebs* (elementary schools) in the villages, but those structures were banned from the cities up to the mid-eighteenth century. Life was hard for Muslims — for the faithful and clergy alike. Religious persecution was one of the grievances behind the uprisings against Moscow that erupted in the Volga region and Siberia throughout the sixteenth and seventeenth centuries.

The Pugachev uprising of 1773 – 1775, which involved the active participation of Muslims from the Volga and Ural regions, forced the authorities to reconsider their attitudes toward Russia's Muslim population. Catherine the Great (Ebi-Patsha, or "Grandmother," as the Muslims dubbed her) came to power within this time frame. She, too, had come to Russia as a "foreigner and heathen" (herself from a German Lutheran background), but, nevertheless, did much for Russia's people. In particular, she fundamentally changed the government's attitude toward Muslims, something none of her predecessors would allow. According to her Act of 1773, Islam was to be tolerated, which meant that Muslims could openly practice their religion and request permission to build new mosques. The Muslim clergy now received royal support through the Mufti of the Orenburg Muslim Ecclesiastical Assembly, which was established in 1788. Starting in 1787, clergy began opening *madrasas* (institutes for higher education is Islamic studies, typically attached to mosques), first in St. Petersburg. In 1802 the Muslim Publishing House in Kazan started printing the Holy Koran and all other religious Muslim literature without restriction. Literacy was widespread among the Tatars, because striving for knowledge constitutes one of the precepts of the Muslim faith, and the *imams* (Islamic leaders) and their wives gathered children into *mektebs* within each mosque. Despite all the criticism leveled at these *mekteb* schools by enlightened Muslim writers in the late nineteenth century, those schools spread mass literacy among the Muslim population, in stark contrast to the overall illiteracy of the Russians and other peoples of the Russian Empire. By the late nineteenth century, entire Muslim communities (mostly consisting of commoners) appeared even in major metropolitan areas such as Nizhni Novgorod, and later in Moscow, Tver, Yaroslavl, and St. Petersburg, where Muslims constructed new mosques and opened *madrasa* schools.

Ismail Gasprinsky, a prominent contemporary author and founder of *jadidism* (to be explained later) described the Muslim community of the late nineteenth century in Russia as follows:

> *Direct your attention and study all the functions of any Muslim community in its smallest unit, the parish commune. Any such commune is in fact a state in miniature, with strong ties between the parts and the whole, and with its own customs, laws, social order, institutions, and traditions, which are constantly supported and invigorated by the Islamic spirit. The commune has its own self-government represented by the elder and the entire parish, whose authority is absolute because it stands on a religious and moral foundation and is rooted in the Koran. The commune has its own totally independent clergy, which does not require any sanction or ordination. Any trained Muslim can be a* khoja *(teacher in a Muslim school),* muezzin, imam, ahun, *and so on, with the commune's consent. The Muslim faith recognizes no social class distinctions and therefore has no caste of priests.*

> *The clerical class established by Russian laws in certain Muslim territories exists only de jure, but de facto does not prevent members of other classes from administering religious rites, provided they have adequate training. Each Muslim commune has its own school and mosque, which is supported by the entire commune or by capital and property (or* wakufs*) specifically bequeathed for that purpose. Muslim* mekteb *schools keep in close contact with the commune and complement family schooling. Through this process each child is exposed to the irresistible influence of his mother and father's upbringing and the spirit of Islam from a very early age. Consequently, a seven- or eight-year-old child has such strong Muslim and tribal values that he will amaze any new observer and will make the zealous Russifier think twice. Several such communes share one Great Mosque [regional mosque]. Several dozen communes have one* madrasa, *a school of higher learning that trains all Muslim theologians, law experts, mullahs, ahuns, teachers, and scholars in*

general. All these institutions and established social orders function tirelessly, from year to year, receiving moral support from the Koran and material support from the commune and its wealthy members, who give generously in the expectation of rewards in the afterlife.

A Muslim commune consisting of 10 to 20 families, no matter where fate takes it, instantly clusters around a mosque or school, both which are often housed in one building, and immediately, in order to nourish itself with spiritual sustenance, joins the nearest madrasa *school, where it sends its children who are meant to receive the highest Muslim learning.*

Such small Muslim communes, scattered around as separate villages, can be seen in many inner provinces of Russia and, despite their age-old coexistence with masses of Russians, have lost none of their Tatar Muslim traits. Even the spread of the Russian language among them is insignificant and is seen only among the men. As for Muslim women, they speak no Russian at all, with very few exceptions. An edifying example and one which proves the extraordinary tribal stability of the Tatars is presented by the Lithuanian Tatars, who are dispersed over a dozen provinces of the Southwestern and Vistula regions of the Russian Empire, totaling some eight to nine thousand persons.[2]

Finally, it would seem all was well. Muslims were free to practice their religion. The great majority of Muslims lived in accordance with Islamic precepts, especially in rural communities where Islam stood on an unshakable foundation established by their ancestors. Tradition was sacred there, and no one dared change anything in the mosques or *mekteb* schools. However, urban Muslims adhered to Islamic principles as well. Most Muslims lived separately from Russians, predominately in *slobodas* (isolated suburbs) or in compact groups, which allowed them to keep their way of life intact. Sticking to tradition was important to preserve the canons of faith, the foundations of religion in society, the respect for one's elders, and to promote good child rearing. The overwhelming majority of Muslim clergy, teachers, and professors supported traditionalism.

MUSLIM INTELLIGENTSIA AND JADIDISM

Yet in any large community, religious or ethnic, there are always those who first gravitate to the margins and then gradually step outside. By the late nineteenth and early twentieth centuries there emerged a large intel-

ligentsia of religious leaders, writers, and scholars who were well versed
in Islam and in the history, languages, folklore, and literature of the
Muslim people. However, this same intelligentsia had also studied
Russian and Western languages, culture, and literature. Progress — if the
manifold influence of Russian and Western culture can be called that —
gradually infiltrated Russia's Muslim community, finding expression in
jadidism. *Jadidism* is a movement for innovation and reform in Muslim
education and culture founded by Ismail Gasprinsky. Without going into
the economic and social roots of *jadidism*, let us look at it through the
eyes of a devout Muslim.

From a religious standpoint, followers of both *qadimism* and *jadidism*
are equally regarded as Muslims because both groups adhere to the basic
dogma of Islam. The difference is mainly in the ritual and in the way
dogma relates to day-to-day living. Because Islam embraces all aspects of
a Muslim's life from the moment of birth to the moment of death, and
because there is no division in Islam between religious and secular life,
the inevitable question becomes how Muslims can relate to the new
socioeconomic conditions of large cities. In the cities Muslims were
compelled to enter a life based on new capitalist relations, to tolerate the
customs and habits of other peoples and other religions, to come in contact with new expressions of cultural life (theaters, concerts, newspapers,
and magazines), and to learn Russian. Conversely, a city-dwelling Muslim
was socially more sophisticated than village folk and appeared to be
divorced from the traditional Muslim way of life. He naturally provoked
a hostile reaction from the mullah and most of the villagers because he
was seen as an agent of immorality and an example of bad manners.
However, even this urbanized Muslim remained within the Islamic faith.
Qadimism and *jadidism* simply reflected two different attitudes to the new
socioeconomic conditions; they did not affect the foundations of the
Islamic way of life for Muslims in Russia.

Most Islamic scholars, both in the Soviet and post-Soviet period,
have expressed wild enthusiasm about the *jadidist* movement in Russia,
evidently because it urged Muslims to embrace modern Western values.
However, some scholars question the necessity or justification for the
movement. Muslims in Russia's interior led a very different life from
Muslims in Central Asia and the Northern Caucasus. Tatars and Bashkirs
(how Muslims of the Volga and Ural regions identified themselves by the
late nineteenth century, as distinct ethnic groups) were surrounded by

and in constant contact with Russians, both in urban and rural communities. A distance of ten or twenty miles that separated a Tatar village
from the nearest Russian town was not an insurmountable barrier, but in
Russia's outlying regions, Muslims lived much farther away from
Russians and even had their own administrative borders defined along
ethnic and religious lines. Perhaps only the Crimean Tatars found themselves in this situation.

THE SOVIET PERIOD

The 1917 Bolshevik Revolution and subsequent events fundamentally
changed the position of Muslims in Russia. Turbulent military and political events and radical economic change marked the first ten years of
Soviet rule and the subsequent formation of the Soviet Union.
Consequently, the Soviet authorities were too busy to deal with the issue
of religion. However, the year 1927 marked the beginning of an all-out
war against religion. *Madrasa* schools were closed everywhere, school curricula were purged of all religious content and reoriented toward atheistic education, mosques were demolished as "breeding-grounds of religious superstition," and the number of *imams* (religious leaders) decreased
sharply. Here are a few statistics from a 1930 report by Rizaetdin
Fakhretdinov, chairman of the Central Religious Administration for
Muslim Affairs in the city of Ufa, Bashkiria, in the Urals region:

> *All Muslim religious organizations are on the brink of complete destruction
> and disappearance from the face of the earth. Eighty-seven percent of all*
> mukhtasibats *(regional Muslim centers) have been closed; more than 10,000
> mosques of a total of 12,000 have been closed; and 90 to 97 percent of mul-
> lahs and muezzins have no possibility of holding religious services.*[3]

Perhaps for the first time in the history of Russia, the government
launched an all-out ideological war against Islam. Local Soviet government agencies kept a tight rein on the mosques and Muslim religious
organizations. Reports on parish meetings, appointments to clerical positions, and texts of the sermons had to be submitted to the administrative
departments and later to special commissioners for religious affairs. The
ranks of the faithful dwindled, because only the elderly continued going
to the mosques. As for children and young people, especially those born
in the 1920s, organizations such as Young Pioneers and Komsomol
worked with the Soviet schools to rear children to be atheists.

In general, persecution and decimation of the clergy and destruction of mosques in the 1930s had a great impact on the social psyche. My own grandfather, Gabdelwali Murtazin, an *imam* in the village of Chechkaby (Buinsk Region), was among those persecuted. The Soviets confiscated his house and land — in fact, everything he owned. He became an outcast in his own village, where he spent his last years in a primitive dugout, and soon died, fortunately of natural causes. While he thus avoided being executed during the Great Purges of 1937, his brother Ibrahim was not so fortunate. The few clerics who managed to avoid arrest continued to hold religious services in the face of mounting persecution. Everyone regarded them as a dying species.

In effect, the Soviet period reversed the position of religion in society. Those Muslims who kept their faith and continued to practice Islam were now outcasts. A young person caught going to the mosque faced public censure, and risked being expelled from school and cut off from any decent job. Congregations were at an all-time low, consisting of the elderly and a few peasants and factory workers. Students and university graduates were rarely seen at the mosques. Those who did remain faithful gathered secretly on Fridays at friends' homes, read the Koran at burial ceremonies and funeral repasts, and fasted during the month of Ramadan. For many, Islam remained an historic tradition and an expression of respect for their ancestors.

Fortunately, the Soviet regime failed to stamp out religious faith. Perhaps realizing the futility of its attempts, and recognizing that religion actually inspired people to overcome hardship, the Soviet authorities relaxed their bans and persecutions during World War II. After the war, the onslaught of militant atheism died down and official attitudes toward the faithful became more tolerant. Still, anyone who openly professed his or her faith could not dream of going to a university, let alone holding an administrative job. The Communist Party's Central Committee continued to hold meetings on ways to step up the campaign against "remnants of religious superstition" and would regularly pass resolutions and establish guidelines.

Staying true to Allah required great courage. A believer and his children would become pariahs if, after reporting to the local Communist Party branch where he would be coaxed into conforming or threatened, they refused to toe the line. Yet at all times there were people in Russia who embarked on the thorny path of service to Allah because they felt they were needed. Muslims kept coming to the mosque to listen to sermons, to address Allah, to pray for their parents and ancestors, to bring offerings, and to cleanse themselves of sins. Even though young mosquegoers were few and far between and the mosques were filled only on holidays, the important thing was that the mullahs (religious teachers) and *imams* were still the bearers of Islamic values, continuing to conduct the services and preserve the traditions. Thus we believers can say, "Glory be to Allah: it was our fathers and grandfathers who survived all the years of persecution, kept the torch of faith burning, and preserved it for us the way it had been for the past eleven centuries." We are grateful to those who survived the Soviet years, because today the Muslim community in Russia still has a single, common spiritual foundation that is not split into separate branches.

PRESENT-DAY MUSLIMS IN RUSSIA

The mid-1980s saw radical changes in the government's attitude toward religion. Gorbachev's *perestroika*, followed by the fall of communism and the disintegration of the USSR, gave the faithful the freedom to practice their religion. Muslims throughout Russia heaved a sigh of relief because the total surveillance of people's spiritual lives had ended. People were no longer afraid to be seen at a mosque; many now openly professed their faith, a practice that no longer triggered public censure and alienation. Parents who used to initiate their children into the mysteries of Islam in secret could now form study groups for children who wished to learn.

The congregations were now swelling with Muslims of every age, social status, and educational level, and even included scientists and business people. What was once branded as remnants of the past now provided answers to gnawing spiritual questions. Communist ideology (which presented an eclectic set of moral values borrowed in part from religion) could offer only a kind of pseudo-religion, a substitute for spiritual sustenance. The collapse of communism gave people an acute spiritual hunger. For many, a return to religion was inevitable. Some people claim that religion today is just a fad and that young people are simply mimicking their superiors and the country's leadership. This conclusion is not correct because the vast majority of people go to the mosque to follow the call of their hearts. It is very important that when they do come to the mosque, they hear a kind word. They should be able to find answers to their burning questions and see a way out of their spiritual crisis. The mission of the *imams* is to return the true faith and values of Islam to the people. Today it is up to the *imams* whether the mosques will become centers of spiritual education or remain mere collection plates.

If we compare the situation in Russia's Muslim community at the beginning of this century and at its close, we see that they are diametrically opposite. Before the 1917 Bolshevik Revolution, the vast majority of Muslims in Russia saw themselves as part of a single spiritual community. They recognized each other as true believers in spite of differing opinions on specific issues such as preservation of cultural traditions and standards of social conduct, development of education, and science. From an early age children and adults alike were exhorted to follow their true faith. They received lessons in Islamic morality and instructed each other on how to live in conformity with Islam.

In contrast, by the end of this century, most members of Muslim ethnic groups in Russia do not have any clear awareness of belonging to Islam as a religious doctrine. The overwhelming majority has been thoroughly steeped in Soviet atheism, and many admit that they do not believe in Allah. Statistical surveys conducted in secondary schools in a number of Russian cities show that 30 to 50 percent of students aged eleven to seventeen are atheists, and even those who consider themselves Muslims do not always recognize the need to strictly follow Islamic precepts.

The Russian public is not ready to accept the idea of making Islam the goal of education in secular schools — either in general schools or vocational training schools. Law separates religion from the schools as well as from the state. In addition, most teachers and parents still view religion with suspicion, and proposals to include religious subjects in school curricula meet with opposition. Muslim children, therefore, can receive religious education only by gaining basic familiarization with Islam from their parents and grandparents, by going to the mosque, attending Sunday *madrasa* school classes, attending Friday and holiday services, learning the basic precepts of Islam, and forming a conscious adherence to them.

Faithful Muslims today constitute less than 1.0 percent of Russia's overall Muslim population, which means approximately 200,000 people who have Muslim roots in Russia today are aware of their faith, recognize the basic principles of Islam, and seek to adhere to the commandments of Almighty Allah. However, the other 99 percent, while feeling a connection to Islam, for various reasons are unable to cross the line between atheism and faith.

THE EFFECTS OF INTERNATIONAL MISSIONARY WORK ON RUSSIA'S MUSLIMS

In recent years many foreign books on Islam have become available in Russia. Most attempt to define what constitutes a "true Muslim." However, clerics who are in Oriental countries and who know nothing about Russia's multiethnic and multireligious society wrote these books. Such authors attempt to transplant the Islamic customs and traditions of the Arab world and of the Middle East to Russian soil. However, they fail to understand that when today's Russian readers open one of their books and learn that Islam (or more accurately certain Islamic movements) encourages people to oppose the authorities, to despise other religions, and to murder infidels, they recoil from Islam. Readers are left with the false impression that Islam as a whole preaches intolerance and extremism. Such books have nothing to do with the true values of Islam; rather, they convey the ideology of certain political movements that are active in many Islamic countries. Such propaganda does even more harm because, by pretending to spread the Islamic faith, it sows the seeds of hostility to other strands of Islam abroad. The antagonism among those movements within Islam attempts to force people to oppose their government. Such condemnation of Russia's traditional Muslim clergy is creating problems and is upsetting Muslims in all parts of Russia.

After Russia opened her borders in 1991, a torrent of Islamic missionaries flooded the country. Most of these missionaries, while calling for a revival of Islam among Russia's Muslims, actually had a different agenda: to draw Russia's Muslims into their sphere of ideological and political influence. These missionaries placed special emphasis on the need to launch an armed campaign against infidels. It comes as no surprise that the recent bloodshed in Tajikistan, Chechnya, and Dagestan has been largely inspired by those who brainwashed politically active Muslim youth and then generously supplied them with arms. As a result, leaders of the local Muslim clergy who spoke out against this militarization of the Islamic movement themselves fell victim to violence. Dramatic examples of this violence include the murder of the Muftis of Tajikistan and Dagestan and the repeated assassination attempts on the Mufti of Chechnya. Therefore, everything possible should be done to protect Russia's Muslims from the influence of those militant movements (and their literature) which have their own political agendas and are not really concerned with spreading the true Islamic faith in Russia.

Not all foreign Islamic organizations are responsible for subversive activity. Russia's Muslim community maintains friendly and useful relations with governmental organizations, as well as many private foundations that are charitable, cultural, or educational. Among the organizations are the Ibrahim bin Abdulaziz Al-Ibrahim Russian Charitable Foundation, the Asian Muslim Committee, and the Agency for Religious Affairs of the Turkish Republic. These organizations have demonstrated a sincere desire to provide assistance to Russia's Muslims, including their support for religious schools and seminaries and their participation in restoring and building mosques. This positive experience provides optimism that constructive relations between Russia's Muslim community and foreign Islamic organizations will continue.

WAHHABISM

Wahhabism has recently received much attention in the mass media and among Russia's political leaders and Islamic clerics. Not surprisingly, Muslims are starting to ask questions. First of all, one must understand that Wahhabism is not a *mazkhab* (branch) of Islam. *Sunni* Muslims recognize four basic branches of Islam, which are named for the *imams* who founded them: the *Hanafi* tradition, practiced by most Muslims in Russia; the *Shafi'i* tradition, practiced by Muslims in the Northern Caucasus; and the *Maliki* and *Hanbali* traditions, which are not practiced in Russia.

In contrast, Wahhabism is a strongly politicized religious movement founded by Muhammad Abd al-Wahhab, who lived in Arabia in the eighteenth century. Al-Wahhab based his movement on the religious beliefs of two scholars of the Hanbali tradition: Ibn Taimiya and Ibn al-Kayim. Al-Wahhab sought to form a movement that would cleanse Islamic dogma and ritual of the numerous changes that had been introduced over the ages by the Arabs themselves and by other peoples practicing Islam. At the same time, he launched a ruthless campaign against promiscuity and immorality, which were rife among Muslims in those days. The movement's political agenda was to free Arabia from the domination of the Ottoman Empire and to establish a theocratic state. This agenda was broadly supported by the sheiks of the numerous Arab tribes. Al-Wahhab's activity provided an impetus to create the state of Saudi Arabia; his doctrine became part of that country's official ideology.

Numerous missionary groups are now exporting Wahhabi ideology to countries with Muslim communities, particularly to regions where the

Muslim population is undergoing a process of spiritual renewal. A case in point is Turkey. When Muslim Turks gained religious freedom in the mid-1950s, many missionaries from the Arab countries went to Turkey to spread Wahhabi ideas. Thanks to the government's firm stand and the local clergy's efforts to preserve the Hanafi tradition, the ideology did not gain wide acceptance in Turkey.

After the Soviet Union disintegrated and Russian Muslims gained religious freedom, Wahhabi propaganda began to spread in Russia, Central Asia, and Azerbaijan. Under the banner of reviving the faith, numerous foreign missionaries, teachers, and members of Islamic organizations began to promote the idea of pure Islam, calling for a campaign against infidels and urging the need to establish an Islamic order. The Wahhabi missionaries typically targeted regions where a volatile situation existed that could lead to armed conflict. It was there that outside forces channeled large financial resources, supplied weapons, and trained armed units in special camps.

In the interior regions of Russia local authorities and Muslim clergy found the strength and wisdom to prevent these radical groups from gaining a permanent foothold in the mosques, *madrasa* schools, and other centers of Islamic culture. However, the Wahhabis established their own centers in less stable regions, such as Tajikistan, Chechnya, and to a certain extent, Dagestan. This establishment of centers would not have presented any threat if their activity had been confined to strict adherence of Islamic precepts and ritual. Unfortunately, problems arise when political extremism begins to dominate religion, as happened with most of those who followed the Wahhabis. Sooner or later such followers demonstrate extreme religious intolerance and adopt terrorist tactics, because one of the postulates of Wahhabism sanctions the murder of anyone who stands in the Wahhabi's way.

In many cases the Wahhabis insist on the need to establish a social order based on the *shari'a* law, which was derived from the Koran, the *Sunnah* (the Prophet's guidance on how to live), and Islamic tradition. Clearly, because of the absence of scholars and experts in *shari'a* law in the former Soviet republics, it would be impossible to set up a workable system of Islamic legislation and government within a short period of time. Moreover, most Islamic states today do not have a pure system of *shari'a* law. Wahhabis urge the faithful to wage war against the power of the *kaffirs* (infidels). In recent years, religious intolerance in the Northern

Caucasus has targeted not so much the adherents of other religions, but the traditionalist Muslims who hold to the kind of Islam practiced by their ancestors. According to the Wahhabis, these Muslims are apostates who deserve to be put to death.

Unfortunately, the word Wahhabi is often used today as a term of abuse whenever someone wishes to denounce an Islamic leader — or any Muslim, for that matter. This labeling tactic has become so popular that any Muslim who prays five times a day, fasts in the month of Ramadan, and abstains from pork and liquor can now be accused of Wahhabi leanings. In fact, even Islamic leaders are now accusing each other of Wahhabism. Recently certain Muslim leaders have sent articles and reports to the central authorities in Moscow in which they accuse a number of Muftis of supporting Wahhabism in return for large bribes. The true motive of such accusations is obviously not to help revive the true faith among Russia's Muslims, but to defame political opponents. One can see that cases of religious extremism among Russia's Muslims reveal a disturbing trend and must be taken very seriously. Yet, one should not be taken in by allegations of Wahhabism made against innocent Muslims.

CONCERN AND ANGUISH OF MUSLIMS IN RUSSIA

Muslims in Russia should be satisfied with the present state of religious freedom because many new mosques are under construction and people's beliefs are no longer under government control. Nevertheless, there are causes for concern. Russia's Muslims are worried about the future of their country. There is the real threat that certain Muslim-majority republics in the Northern Caucasus could secede from the Russian Federation. This is a possibility that worries Muslims throughout Russia because the fate of fellow believers is at stake, no matter how far away those Muslims live or what their ethnic origins are. Every Russian Muslim feels personally involved in the events taking place in any region where his brothers and sisters-in-faith live, especially where there is confrontation with the authorities. At the same time, the image of the Muslim-as-enemy is an idea that, once planted in Russian minds, will be automatically projected onto anyone who professes Islam. Unfortunately, it is typical of Russians to look for scapegoats among non-Russian ethnic groups. No matter how the situation develops in the Northern Caucasus, the majority of Russia's Muslims, more than ten million people, will

remain in Russia — in Tatarstan, Bashkortostan (Bashkiria), the Volga
region, the central Russian Urals region, and Siberia. They will continue
practicing Islam, building new mosques, and raising children in their
native Russian land.

Muslims in Russia are concerned about the future. After all, how the
government is ruled will affect the condition of all Russian citizens,
including believers. Russia's Muslims have a long history of persecution,
yet there is hope that history will not repeat itself and that whoever gains
power will not launch another crusade against Islam.

Russia's Muslims are concerned about the often-rocky relationships
among Islamic leaders within Russia. The clerical hierarchies split from
central government control (which received some local government support in most of Russia's Muslim-majority areas). With numerous internal
financial disputes, this split combined to destroy any central Islamic
authority in Russia. The two former bodies responsible for supervising
Islamic affairs — one for the European part of the USSR, the other for
Siberia and the Northern Caucasus — disintegrated and have now been
superseded by almost forty regional authorities. Admittedly, this could
not be avoided in the Northern Caucasus, where an independent ecclesiastical authority was established in each of the constituent ethnic
republics. However, in the rest of Russia the establishment of independent ecclesiastical authorities in Tatarstan, Bashkortostan (Bashkiria),
Siberia, and the Central European region of Russia resulted from a combination of the inability of Russia's former Great Mufti, Talgat Tadjuddin,
to adjust to the new conditions. At the same time, regional Islamic leaders
were engaging in efforts to gain more independence. Self-styled local
Muftis proliferated: their only interest was to befriend the local and
national administration; to receive financial aid from foreign Muslim
organizations; and to get the support of the business community, the
security service, and the military. From time to time, the rivalry among
religious leaders got into the news in the form of mudslinging matches
and even blatant slander. All this enmity greatly damaged the cause of
Islam in Russia and undermined the prestige of Muslim leaders in the
eyes of the government, of members of other religions, and of Russian
society as a whole. Clearly, Russia's Muftis, representing Islamic ecclesiastical authorities in major regions and constituent republics of Russia,
need to realize their responsibility to Allah and to the Muslims of Russia.
They must find ways to join forces and coordinate their actions to safe-

guard the interests of Russia's entire Muslim community in its relations with the government, other religions, and foreign organizations. The Muslims of Russia implore Allah not to leave them without His mercy and to help them find a way out of this predicament.

LOOKING INTO THE FUTURE

What will tomorrow's Russian Muslims be like? The average Muslim in Russia has an excellent secular education or at least a secondary school diploma, and a large number of today's mosque-goers have university degrees. The modern-day Russian Muslim was raised in a secular, European-type cultural and aesthetic environment; has read Tolstoy, Pushkin and Lermontov; watches television; goes to the theater; and is well versed in art. For that reason, his or her spiritual needs cannot be limited to the traditional Oriental values and standards of conduct. Today, we truly see the well-educated Muslim that Gasprinsky, *jadidism's* founder, once dreamed about. Today, typical Russian Muslims, no matter how strong their faith, will not wear a turban, a full-length robe, or a long beard, because such outward attributes do not constitute the essence of Islam. Moreover, Allah does not require this external appearance of every Muslim because He looks into people's hearts and deeds, not at their clothing or wealth.

For the Russian Muslim, the purpose of the religious quest is to find an answer to the philosophical and world-view challenges that arise in day-to-day life, in work, in contacts with members of other ethnic groups and religions, in reading books, and in watching films. In Islam, Muslims seek protection against the torrent of commercialized filth from the television screen, newspapers, and magazines and against the lies and dishonesty of today's political and community leaders. It is vital that in the mosque Muslims can find a remedy for spiritual torment and an opportunity to embark on the road of true faith.

Russia's Muslims must realize that their religion was granted to all nations, that it is universal in nature, and that this nature ensures its appeal to all people on this earth. This importance explains why today Islam is gaining ground in Europe and America, even among the peoples who have lived in those countries for centuries. In Russia, Islam has deep roots going back to the tenth century; it is almost native to the indigenous peoples of Russia — Tatars, Bashkirs, Chechens, Dagestanis, Balkars,

Karachais, and others — despite the skepticism of some religious experts on this issue. Islam did not come to Russia on the crest of Gorbachev's *perestroika*, as did Protestantism, Krishnaism, and other religions that are not traditional for Russia.

The first priority is to explain to all Russian citizens of Muslim origin, who have not embraced Islam, that this religion is not alien or hostile to their modern way of life. The clergy should welcome well-educated Muslims in the mosques and try not to frighten them off on the first day with rigid rules and taboos. Islam is the straight road that is accessible to anyone who recognizes Allah as the sole object of worship. The one phrase that expresses the essence of Islam — "There is no God but Allah!" — leads to the road of true faith and away from godlessness. Everyone has the potential to recognize this truth, even though it requires some hard spiritual work.

The Western scholar A. Benningsen was right when he said at the start of this century that Russia's Muslims could well have headed the movement for a revival of Islamic science. Today the tremendous intellectual and scientific potential of Russian Muslims could contribute to a revival of religious science that would set off a powerful resonance capable of propelling Russia's Islam to the vanguard of the entire Muslim world.

CONCLUSION

Almighty Allah predestined a thorny road for Islam in Russia — one of trials and tribulations, persecution and oppression. Yet Islam not only has survived in Russia, but also has become firmly established in many people's hearts. Islam has a future in Russia. It has a great number of followers who have received the faith with their mothers' milk, who are turning without fear or misgiving to Allah's Sacred Scriptures. In a few generations Russia will have vast numbers of truly faithful Muslims who will fill today's half-empty mosques. They will follow the basic precepts of Islam, move Islamic science forward, and protect and cherish the religious and cultural traditions of their Muslim peoples, while at the same time respecting the faith and traditions of non-Muslim nations.

We believers, for our part, shall pray that the Almighty sends us His divine blessing, mercy, and success in all our undertakings!

C h a p t e r   T h r e e

Russia, Islam and the North Caucasus
Victor Panin

INTRODUCTION

The Islamic factor is of major importance for Russia, considering her sizable Muslim population and her long southern borders within the vast geopolitical area that is dominated by the Muslim world. Russia's south has already become the target of radical Islamic movements that are contributing to the escalation of political and socioeconomic destabilization in the region.

The total Muslim population in Russia is estimated to be between eighteen and twenty million people. Because of expected demographic shifts, in thirty years the Muslim population will be between thirty and forty million people. Additionally, Muslims are expected to constitute the largest segment of migration to Russia in the twenty-first century. Therefore, by the year 2050 the number of Muslims in Russia is expected to be roughly equal to the number of Orthodox Russians.[1]

The demographic distribution of Muslim population throughout Russia is nonuniform. The history of Russian expansion and its interaction with the indigenous population have left the northern Caucasus the area with a significant Muslim presence. This area has become the center of strategic interest for several Muslim countries, especially Turkey and Saudi Arabia. The Caucasus geopolitical position, its energy resources, the peculiarities of the political formations within some of its territories and the sizable Muslim minorities within its population make this region vulnerable to the influence of outsiders. It is a viable target for Muslim states seeking to expand their influence since the region is rife with internal territorial conflicts, a lingering Soviet inheritance and a severe economic crisis. Such Muslim states regard the Caucasus as the "weak chain" through which its plans of forcing a Russian withdrawal from the region might be realized. Consequently, Islamic extremism is a real and vivid threat to Russian national security.

ISLAM IN THE NORTH CAUCASUS

Only one fifth of the eighteen million inhabitants of the North Caucasus are Muslim. The two largest groups, the Dagestanis and Wainachs, represent most of the demographic base of Islam in the region. Together they constitute about 2.5 million people.[2] Both groups are multiethnic: Dagestanis are subdivided into almost a dozen tribes, each with its own distinct language, culture, and customs; the Chechens and their neighbors to the West, the Ingush, belong to the Wainach group. Binding them together until recently was their common faith. Islamic *jihad* (holy war) mobilized them to fight the early Russian colonial expansion in the nineteenth century. Islam was able to firmly establish itself here, among mountainous tribes of diverse background, rather late — at the end of the eighteenth and beginning of the nineteenth centuries — after being brought by the Sufi preachers of the Naqshbandi order. The latter eventually managed to unite the Dagestanis and Chechens under the rule of Sufi Imams, the legendary Shamil being the most prominent among them. In the first half of nineteenth century Shamil led the thirty-years-long military battle against Russian colonial expansion.

Even later, Chechnya remained one of the most restive ethnic areas in the Russian (then Soviet) Empire. In 1944, Stalin deported the Chechens from their Caucasian homeland to distant Central Asia, as the punishment for anti-Soviet behavior and alleged collaboration with Nazi Germany. In the mid-fifties, the Khrushchev government brought the Chechens and other deported nationalities of the Soviet Union (with exception of Crimean Tatars) back to their historic habitats. Throughout this turbulent period Sufi-dominated Islam persisted among Chechens, as well as among Dagestanis. The early post-Soviet explosion of Chechen nationalism, led by Dzhokar Dudaev, was initially shaped within local Sufi traditions as well. The roots of that uprising originally lay in a separatist movement, just as in a number of other non-Russian ethnic regions of post-Soviet Russia. However, the radical Islamic slogans were quickly embraced in order to reinforce the goals of the nationalist tide.

Soon, the process of the politicization of Islam intensified. One of the most outspoken Muslim philosophers of Russia, Geydar Jemal, said in

1993: "Islam came to be the political force, and its participation in the political activities of society is natural."[3] The first step in this direction was made in June 1990 with the creation of the all-Union Islamic Revival Party (IRP) at the founding conference held in Astrakhan. Ahmedkadi Ahtaev, a Dagestani, became the first chairman of the Party. Though the goals of IRP, as stated at the beginning, were mostly educational, its leaders had greater ambitions. G. Jemal confessed that the IRP, according to its aims and goals, resembles the "Party of Allah," like the one that led to the Islamic revolution in Iran.[4] After the collapse of the Soviet Union, the regional structures of the IRP tried to form parties in the fledgling post-Soviet states. Ahtaev remained the leader of the Dagestani faction of the IRP up to his death in 1998. He was also a member of the Dagestani Parliament, the leader of the moderate wing of the Dagestani Wahhabis, and the leader of the "Islamic Movement of the Caucasus," the umbrella organization formed to coordinate activities of Muslim political groups throughout Northern Caucasus.

FOREIGN INTERVENTION

Foreign aid, mainly from Saudi Arabia, Turkey, Iran, and Pakistan greatly assisted the process of Islamic rebirth. These countries have been using Islam to strengthen their positions in Central Asia, as well as in some national republics of the Russian Federation, particularly in the North Caucasus.

Saudi Arabia

Saudi Arabia is the primary supplier of financial and moral support to the radical Muslim movements of the Caucasus. This does not necessarily mean a direct involvement of the Saudi government. However, the views of King Fahd cannot be ignored: "Islam [today has become] the most important factor of world politics [and] we, the Muslims, must unite to make the Islamic World the major force of contemporary time."[5]

Saudi sources use numerous charitable funds, international Islamic organizations, and cultural centers to channel aid. One of the most influential Saudi-supported structures is a branch of the international Islamic organization, Al Igasa (headquartered in Jidda, Saudi Arabia), which is a member of the World Islamic League that was created in Mecca in 1962. Numerous missionaries of this organization proselytize Wahhabism and call for the creation of an Islamic state in the North Caucasus.

Turkey

According to its 1924 constitution, Turkey is a secular state. As a result,
Turkey does not employ Islamic slogans in its dealings on the international scene. However, the ideology and practice of Turkic nationalism
(pan-Turkism) often guides its foreign policy. Today the government
body that orchestrates Turkish policy toward the Muslim states of the former Soviet Union (FSU) is the Department of Turkish Regions Affairs.
Turkey, in attempting to popularize the ideas of pan-Turkism and to
unify all forces supporting this goal, regularly organizes international
seminars with the participation of Muslims from the FSU. Turkey also
accepts young people to study in its religious universities. Thus, Turkey's
strategic aim is to create a belt of Turkic nation-states that are in the
Northern Caucasus and that are oriented toward Ankara.[6]

It was former Turkish President Turgut Özal who declared: "the
twenty-first century would be the century of Turkey."[7] To this end,
Turkey created a special foreign fund for the study of the Turkish world.
In Ankara the fund supports the North Caucasus Cultural Society and
different nationalistic emigrant groups such as Chechen Terek and the
Dagestan Shamil Funds. The pan-Turkish Party of Nationalistic
Movement, the government-supported Party of Great Union, and the
extremist Boz Kurt (Gray Wolves) have all played an active role in the
Chechen conflict.

Iran

Iran is another country with direct interests in the North Caucasus. It is
the world leader of *Shi'a* Islam. Iran loathes Turkey's success in garnering
influence in the area. As a result, it actively conducts shuttle diplomacy in
the northeastern region of the Caucasus as it tries to win allies there.
Between 1996 and 1998, numerous groups of Iranian diplomats and spe-
cialists visited the region, particularly Dagestan. For the time being Iran is
not interested in undermining Russia, since Iran regards Russia as a
strategic partner in the global confrontation with the United States.
However, Iran still attempts to foster close relations with Central Asia and
the Caucasus by using the Islamic factor, while taking special care to pay
attention to any Russian reaction. While avoiding any extremist actions,
Iran has tried to play a moderating role in Chechnya, acting as a counter-
balance against the policy of Ankara.[8] Nevertheless, in past years one can
observe an increasing economic, cultural, and religious presence of Iran

in the Caucasus, especially in Azerbaijan and Dagestan. Several groups of the Iranian-backed Hezbollah allegedly participated in military actions against Russian troops in the Chechen war.

Pakistan

Another active player on the geopolitical chessboard of the Caucasus is Pakistan. Although its major interests are directed toward Central Asia and Afghanistan, Pakistan does have some influence on events in the Caucasus. It is well known that Pakistani *mujahidins* (Muslims conducting *jihad* against nonbelievers) took an active part in the Chechen conflict. Many Caucasian terrorists were educated and trained in terrorist centers in Afghanistan and Pakistan. In the North Caucasus, Pakistan directly and covertly supports fundamentalist forces and their leaders, such as the influential Chechen field commander E. Gelaev, who wants to establish an Islamic state in Chechnya along the lines of the Pakistani model. Another example is the "charity" organization Tablig, which is engaged in activities to popularize the ideas of political Islam. Tablig began its efforts in Chechnya and then extended its activities into the other North Caucasian republics. Numerous special groups of Pakistani clergymen, including representatives of different religious parties and movements, visit the North Caucasus on a regular basis with the aim of popularizing the ideas of Islamic fundamentalism. Jamaat-e-Islami is one of the most prominent among them.[9]

Since the beginning of 1996, in Dagestan alone more than forty emissaries of foreign Islamic organizations from Turkey, Saudi Arabia, Iran, Somalia, and the Sudan were accused of criminal actions as the result of such subversive activities. Over the past two years approximately 200 foreigners have violated passport and visa rules, and sixteen of them were deported from the country.[9]

To summarize, the "foreign Islamic factor" actively seeks to Islamicize the Muslim-majority regions of Russia using a number of tactics that include efforts to:

• support varied and numerous Islamic missionaries;

• promote exchanges with the leaders of traditional Islamic structures, Islamic parties, and social movements and organizations. (Such work involves inviting those leaders to participate in different religious forums and Islamic holidays abroad.);

- offer invitations to study abroad at higher theological institutions for extended periods;
- provide assistance for constructing mosques, theological universities, and madrasas (Islamic colleges);
- supply experienced Muslim teachers and Islamic literature; and
- conduct numerous propaganda missions to popularize political Islam.

THE DOMESTIC "ISLAMIC FACTOR"

As for the "internal Islamic factor" in the North Caucasus, it would be wrong to label that factor as a unified social force. Different groups represent each aspect of the Islamic movement, each with its own goals and interests. But above all there is formidable clash between the traditional Islam that has been the keeper of the Islamic flame throughout the repressive Soviet era and today's new breed of radical Islamists. The official leaders of traditional religious organizations — the Spiritual Departments of Muslims (SDM) — represent the first group. The old network of the SDMs that existed in the USSR (including the two in the North Caucasus and Transcaucasia) was subdivided into a multitude of smaller institutions. This reorganization has seriously damaged the official Islamic structure. As a result of this process, the North Caucasus suddenly found itself with seven geo-ethnic-based SDMs, located in Dagestan, Chechnya, Ingushetia, North Ossetia, Kabardino-Balkaria, one unifying Karachaevo-Cherkessia and the Stavropol territory, and the last one unifying Adygeya and the Krasnodar territory. This restructuring led to the weakening of the cohesiveness of Islamic traditionalists. This process also fostered conditions for the further polarization and politicization of Islam. This, in turn, led to the appearance of new fundamentalist movements in the region, such as Wahhabism.[10] As a result of this process of polarization and fracturing, a serious split occurred among the Dagestani Islamic leaders on every level.

Russia's Soviet past, waves of private and state-sponsored foreign missionaries, and structural disintegration of traditional Islamic bureaucracy have broken the coherence of Russia's Muslim elite. Consequently, along with the traditional elite, there are new influential groups: public organizations with Islamic coloration, the local quasi-Islamic ethnic organizations, and the fundamentalists.

RUSSIA'S TRADITIONAL ISLAMIC ELITE

Russian federal and regional political elites initially misunderstood the threats connected with politicized Islam. At first the changes were seen only as developments that had weakened the position of Muslim traditionalists. However, the Mufti of Dagestan, M. Abubakarov, bitterly complained that the authorities were ignoring the threat from militant radical groups.[11] After some time, and with the assistance of federal and local leadership, the Spiritual Departments of Muslims managed to strengthen their position among Muslims. Alas, it was too late for Mufti Abubakarov. In August 1998, he was killed in a car bomb explosion. The organizers of the terrorist act were never found, but the local press blamed it on Wahhabites with Chechen connections.

To shore up support, the Muftiates (offices of the chief mullahs) of the North Caucasian republics are working with local political elites through clan-client associations. Such alignments are based on ethnic origin and tribal ties and with Islamic leaders holding high official posts. Nowadays the ruling political elites of all the North Caucasus republics often are formed on the basis of tribal relationships. Muslim clergy play an active role in the local and regional elections, supporting representatives of their own tribes. In the end they gain financial and political benefits from the former candidates in republic offices. It means they also have direct influence on top leadership. The regional SDMs tend to be more independent from the federal central organizations, yet they cannot be the conductors of policy for all Russian Muslim organizations. Without central support, SDMs are sure to spark severe rivalry with different organizations of radical extremist Islamists — especially those groups that are militarized.

To strengthen the position of traditional Islam, to influence political leadership at all levels, and to broaden those leaders' contacts with foreign Muslim centers and groups, Russia's traditional Muslim leaders are increasingly focusing their activities in the following directions:

- Construction of new mosques. Mosques function not only as spiritual centers but also as political centers, thus strengthening the position of traditional Islam in spiritual and political life.

- Creation of new secondary and higher Islamic institutions. This educational outreach will broaden the scope of Islam's influence and will prepare a new generation of active Islamic clergy.[12]

- Formation of Islamic centers. As "secular" organizations, these centers are used for propaganda purposes as they promote traditional Islam through the mass media. Because they are often created with strong financial assistance from local and foreign public organizations, the centers typically are a convenient channel for cooperation with foreign Islamic organizations.

PRO-ISLAMIC PUBLIC ORGANIZATIONS

The second group consists of public organizations, such as the Islamic Revival Party (IRP) or the Union of Russian Muslims (headquartered in Mahachkala, the capital of Dagestan). These organizations have ambitions beyond the regional scene and are trying to have a voice on the federal level. In this way they are positioning themselves as representing Moscow in the regions. Their aim is to subordinate all the regional and local Islamic organizations to a central authority. Lately these organizations have begun to lose their influence. For example, the IRP now functions only formally. Between 1993 and 1994 its active members organized regional parties with an emphasis on ethnic identity. Such branching out often was accompanied with radicalization. For example, the ex-chairman of the All Russian Islamic Revival Party, A. Ahtaev, founded the Dagestani Islamic Party of Rebirth and became the leader of the Wahhabi Islamic Movement of the Caucasus. Mr. Bagautdin became the main ideological leader of the fundamentalist movement in Dagestan and Chairman of extremist organization Islamic Jaamat of Dagestan; Mr. Bidji-Ulu proclaimed himself as the Imam of Karachai.

Nadirshah Hachilaev, who was elected to the previous Russian Duma (in 1996), became the head of the Union of Russian Muslims, which was created the year before. For a while the Union was an influential clerical actor in the political life of Russia. Between 1995 and 1996 it allegedly provided financial, military, medical, and personnel support to Chechen terrorists. Then Hachilaev was accused of supporting the integration of Islamic republics of the North Caucasus into one Islamic state. He and his brother Mohammad Hachilaev, the leader of the Kumic national movement, Kuzi Kumuh, allegedly instigated a riot in Mahachkala on May 20-21, 1998. Soon local authorities arrested M. Hachilaev, while N. Hachilaev escaped to Chechnya. Following the defeat of the Chechen abortive military invasion into the neighboring mountainous area of Dagestan in the summer of 1999, Nadirshah Hachilaev was arrested by federal authorities.

In general, the influence of these organizations is failing for two main reasons. First, they have not successfully dealt with problems of ethnic identity and ethnocultural construction (though in practice Turkic ethnic groups, especially Tatars in the Union of Russian Muslims, dominate these organizations). Second, they are perceived to be part of a federal structure and have failed to find their places in the regional structures. As a result they suffer from severe rivalry with the local ethnoconfessional organizations; this rivalry considerably limits their local social base of support.

LOCAL QUASI-ISLAMIC ORGANIZATIONS

The third and the most influential force in the Islamic movement of the North Caucasus is the quasi-Islamists. These national and nationalistic movements and organizations include the Association of Caucasian People (ACP), the Nogai national movement Birlic, the Kumic national movement Tenglic, the National Council of Balkar People (NCBP), the Congress of Kabardian People (CKP), and Democratic Jamagait. These organizations are playing a larger and larger role in regional and local political structures, thereby effectively manipulating their way through the ongoing social, economic, and political crises. Their use of Muslim rhetoric permits them to buttress their separatist claims with ideological explanations. Despite the fact that some, such as the NCBP and CKP, are presently banned, their leaders continue to play an active political role. The failure of post-Soviet social and economic reforms to produce tangible results has discredited the idea of Western modernization. On the background of an overall nationwide crisis, the social and economic situation in the Northern Caucasus is even more dramatic. Thus, the idea of a special Islamic path of development has become more and more attractive among the local intelligentsia.

THE FUNDAMENTALISTS

The fourth force consists of Islamic groups with fundamentalist orientations that are based on the ideals of Wahhabism. One must note that these fundamentalists cannot be regarded as a monolithic unified force (which is typical for the entire Islamic world). The fundamentalist movements of Islam in the North Caucasus are not united and are unevenly spread across the entire region with the most powerful and organized force of radical Islam in the northeastern Caucasus (Dagestan and Chechnya). According to I. Dabaev, an expert on the Caucasus, the number of Wahhabis in Dagestan alone varies from 2,000 to 5,000, who call themselves not Wahhabis, but Islamists.[13]

If any among the radical Islamic groups could be called a moderate wing, it is the one represented by Ahmadkadi Ahtaev, a respected Russian Islamic figure. He headed his faction during most of post-Soviet time until his death in 1998. This faction has been tolerant of the Sufi brotherhoods and other religious movements within Islam that are popular in the region. Ahtaev and his followers showed no penchant to forcibly seize political power. On the contrary, they showed an eagerness to participate in the activities of legitimate political structures. After Ahtaev's death, the Islamic Movement of the Caucasus, which he had founded, was taken over a prominent Chechen, Zelimkhan Jandarbiev, who served as acting president of Chechnya after the death of Dudaev. He is well known for his anti-Russian, separatist position. Until the onset of the second Chechen War, Jandarbiev stood in a sharp contrast to Maskhadov, who became president. One of the issues of conflict allegedly was Maskhadov's opposition to Wahhabism. The war again reunited them.

Another prominent faction of radical Islam is represented by Muhammad Bagautdin, the former leader of the Kizil Yurt Center of Wahhabis. Bagautdin is credited with popularizing Wahhabism in the region. His main tenets are the necessity of a *jihad* against nonbelievers, as well as the inevitable emergence of an Islamic state in Dagestan following the Saudi Arabian model. His publishing house, Santlada, which is in Dagestan, produces a large share of the Wahhabi literature that is disseminated in Russia. The leadership of this faction has very close relations with some Middle Eastern countries and is responsible for much of the religious argumentation for the Chechen military's *jihad*. Bagautdin, together with Ibrahim Fattah, a spiritual leader and field commander of Wahhabi armed groups in Chechnya, repeatedly suggested the creation of an Islamic propaganda network for the entire North Caucasian region and coordinating humanitarian aid from Muslim countries. After Bagautdin allegedly organized the Wahhabi attack on the military regiment located in Buinaks (Dagestan) in December 1996, and following the adoption by the Dagestani Parliament of measures to ban some Wahhabi extremism, such as the amendments to the republic's "Law on Religion," Bagautdin and his followers migrated to Chechnya. Once there, he created the radical émigré organization, the Islamic Jamaat of Dagestan in Urus-Martan, and began training growing numbers of Dagestani Islamist recruits. This so-called Insurrectional Army of Imam closely coordinated its activity with the famous field commander Amir al-Hattab, who subsequently led the Chechen insurgency of 1999 into Dagestan.

In Chechnya, Wahhabism started spreading when the first Wahhabi Center opened in Grozny during the Dudaev regime. It spread Wahhabi literature, organized mass prayers, and popularized its ideals through the media.[10] Several reasons explain the choice of the Wahhabi breed of radical Islam:

- The expectation of support from the rich Arabian states where Wahhabism is the official state religion.

- The active participation of well-trained and militarized Wahhabi believers.

- The hope that the spreading of a "strict" and "classical" version of Islam would end religious disagreements not only within Chechnya, but also between all Muslim nations in the North Caucasus. (For this purpose on August 22, 1997, a congress of thirty-five Chechen and Dagestani Islamic parties and movements proclaimed the creation of a socio-political Islamic Nation organization. Its goals are to form conditions for the defense of the Islamic nation against aggression and genocide, the prevention of the anti-Islamic expansion of Russia in the Caucasus, and the creation of conditions for the unification of all nations of the Caucasus on the basis of an Islamic ideal. M. Udugov was elected as its leader, the Amir.[14])

OTHER ISLAMIC ORGANIZATIONS AND THEIR ACTIVITIES

The number of different quasi-Islamic political movements in the Northern Caucasus continued to proliferate almost up to the outbreak of the second Chechen War. Seemingly every distinguished Chechen field commander had to chair an organization of his own. Salman Raduev created the organization of Caucasian solidarity called Caucasian House (and made himself general secretary). The Congress of Peoples of Chechnya and Dagestan became a brainchild of Shamil Basaev. Since the 1994-96 Chechen War, Amir al-Hattab (a Wahhabi emissary from Jordan) gained vast influence. In Chechnya he created and controlled a Sergen Yurt-based network of subversive terrorist training centers named "Caucasus." In addition to military training he places a considerable emphasis on radical Wahhabi brainwashing. This center has prepared approximately one thousand young Dagestanis, Chechens, and Ingush. On the eve of the second Chechen war, the six hundred Wahhabis had taken training courses in Urus-Martan center.[15] Cadets of this center, along with graduates of Muslim high schools from Arab countries, were assigned with the task of further spreading Wahhabism in the Caucasus. According to official Russian mass media sources, the emissary activities of Hattab in the North Caucasus was coordinated and financed by one of the Arab countries of the Middle East. Hattab, himself, never hid the fact that he shares the strategic goals of the Islamist fundamentalists. These goals include the ejection of Russia from the North Caucasus, the creation of a unified Muslim state from the North Caucasian republics, and the enlargement of this new entity's territory by absorbing adjacent Russian regions. In an interview in the newspaper "Al Kaff" Hattab said: "The work of mujahidins is the war against nonbelievers. I work in the Ministry of War . . . with the help of Allah we shall turn Russia in such a state where Chechnya is currently now."[16]

With time, the tactics of Dagestani and Chechen Islamists have undergone considerable change, from organizational-propagandist activities to the use of subversive terrorist methods of struggle against representatives of federal and regional levels of power. In 1998, half of all terrorist actions in Russia were committed in the Northern Caucasus. In Chechnya before the outbreak of the second Chechen War, the neo-Wahhabi ideology became a force that temporarily united all of the opposition to Aslan Maskhadov: Shamil Basaev, Salman Raduev, Amir al-Hattab, Zelimhan Jandarbiev, Movladi Udugov, and others. Maskhadov's attempts to declare Chechnya an Islamic state with *shari'a* law, as an effort to stop the spread of political Islam, did not succeed. This was at least partially due to the fact that he and the opposition did not agree as to what a Chechen "Islamic state" should be. At that time Maskhadov leaned toward "official Islam" (the Chechen SDM) and its leader, *Mufti* Akhmed-Hadji Kadirov, instead of the Wahhabis, who were protégés of his political opponents and their foreign sponsors. The growing conflict between the traditionalists and Wahhabis in the winter of 1998 erupted into a bloody military confrontation on the streets of Gudermes, the second largest city of Chechnya after Grozny. The traditionalist side was represented by the troops of local field commander General Yamadaev. After dozens of people were killed on both sides, the intervention of Maskhadov's Presidential guardians stopped the battle. However, the incident did not cool the Wahhabis. Their aggressiveness only increased. Attacks against militiamen and Russian soldiers became public. Wahhabi camps were blamed for the major rise in crime, including: the kidnapping of common people, the stealing of cattle, as well as robbery and rape. Even President Maskhadov once stated, "All kidnapping cases are made by them (Wahhabis)."[17] Consequently, no one doubts who kidnapped General Gennadi Shpigun, the former commandant of Grozny, because he had been included on the Wahhabis' list of enemies of the Chechen people.

The ideology and practice of the so-called "liberated" movement was described by Muhammad Tagaev in his book *Our Struggle: The Insurrectional Army of Imam:*

> We shall destroy everything — from Dagestan to Moscow, including the Kremlin. We shall write down several bloody pages in the new history, though everyone will have to die on the Earth…. Russians are given 24 hours to leave Rostov, Tsaritsin, Astrahan, Taganrog…. In winter and summer, in fall and spring, at night and day, in the morning and in the evening, we shall burn, blow, cut and kill. Your blood will freeze from the horrors of our retribution.[18]

Another extremist leader, Sultan Gelishanov, declared that the only way to stop the war in Chechnya was to begin military actions in Dagestan. In the three-year interval between the two Chechen Wars, Chechen field commander Shamil Basaev and some of his comrades in arms gave Moscow plenty of warning about how serious they were about bringing Dagestan into an Islamic alliance. Shamil Basaev did not even hide his ambition to make himself the Imam of Dagestan and Chechnya (the title of supreme Islamic leader of these countries), like his legendary namesake in the nineteenth century.

Simultaneously, in Dagestan Islamists tried to create special "autonomous Islamic zones," organized according to *shari'a* laws. The villages of Karamahi and Chabanmahi declared their independence from the authorities. Russian federal troops, supported by Dagestani volunteer formations, defeated the Chechen invasion into Dagestan, and "liberated" these villages. Apparently the Wahhabis had accumulated a lot of arms and managed to convert Karamahi and Chabanmahi into genuine fortresses.

THE INFLUENCE OF WAHHABISM IN THE NORTH CAUCASUS

In general, the influence of the Wahhabis in the Northern Caucasus, among practicing Muslims, is limited. To a degree it was true also in the case of Chechnya. However, the outbreak of the second war dwarfed the confessional disagreements and brought together many of the field commanders and their troops who had been standing on opposite sides of the religious split. Only a small part of the military, led by General Yamadaev, stood to support the Mufti of Chechnya, Akhmed Kadirov, and conclude the separate peace settlement with Russian federal troops in Gudermes.

The majority of the Muslim population in North Caucasus continues to practice traditional Islam and opposes the radical variant. Nevertheless, local analysts have observed the rising activities of radical and extremist Islamic movements such as Wahhabism, even in such a relatively stable area as Karachaevo-Cherkessia.[19] The Wahhabis certainly have not given up the idea of increasing their presence. For example, after the end of the first Chechen war, they considerably increased their mass propaganda activities. The Wahhabis regularly recruited members from among the youth who were intrigued by the romanticism of a half-banned organization. These new members sometimes were paid up to U.S. $3,000 to participate.[20] Their task was to popularize the organization's ideas among relatives and friends. Joining the Wahhabis meant escaping from the problems connected with the current economic situations: unemployment and criminalization of the society. The desire to have a solid base in life has encouraged youths to join the Wahhabis to gain emotional support. In the city of Karachaevsk alone their number is estimated to be between two hundred and four hundred.

A RUSSIAN POLICY FOR THE NORTH CAUCASUS

The situation has been worsened by the fact that Moscow had no strategic policy for the North Caucasus, except the approach to solve all problems by military means. It is urgent for the federal center to thoroughly analyze the situation in the North Caucasus, to clarify its goals, and to delineate how it intends to reach them. The geopolitical situation in the Northern Caucasus is very unstable, and Russian military successes in the second Chechen campaign have not resolved the main issues. The central long-term priorities should be:

In the economic sphere: to stop the economic crisis and to lower the unemployment rate, which reaches 60 to 70 percent in some regions. Most of the disintegrative trends come from the unsatisfactory economic situation. People have stopped believing that Russia is the guarantor of their economic stability and security.

- In the criminal sphere: the restoration of law and order. The level of corruption in the North Caucasus is one of the highest in Russia. It has spread through all levels of political and state structures. No one respects the laws because it is not obligatory for all members of society to obey them. In many cases family rules or traditional clan rules replace the law. In addition, the civil population possesses a great number of weapons.

- In the social sphere: address the migration issue. After the collapse of the Soviet Union, many conflicts resulted. Consequently, many people migrated to the North Caucasus, mainly to Stavropol, Krasnodar, and Rostov territories. Such uncontrolled migration disrupted the traditional interethnic balance of the local population in favor of non-Slavic ethnic groups. This imbalance worsened the criminal situation and created an additional basis for ethnic and confessional conflicts. The second Chechen war created even more acute refugee crisis in Ingushetia.

- In the confessional sphere: support the representatives of traditional Islam and help them consolidate themselves in their struggle against radical extremist groups such as Wahhabism. The state should assist in creating a number of higher Muslim educational institutions to train future Muslim clergy in Russia instead of abroad.

- On the "Russian Question:" address the issue of inter-ethnic balance. The main social pillar of support of Russia in the North Caucasus has always been and will always be the Russian population (the Slavs, the Cossacks in particular, constituted almost 75 percent in the early 90s). Thus, the most disturbing phenomenon that is taking place in the North Caucasus is the ousting of Russians. The balance of ethnic groups in every region of the North Caucasus, including the Stavropol, Krasnodar, and Rostov territories, is shifting against Russians. The diminishing size of the Russian community means the shrinking of Russian geopolitical influence in the North Caucasus. The change is leading toward an outright separation of the North Caucasus from Russia.

• In the nature of Russian federalism: The Russian Federation consists of eighty-nine members, fifty-seven of whom are members without "privileged" (supported by a kind of affirmative actions) ethnic groups, whose formation was based on a territorial principle. The other thirty-two members are either national republics (twenty-one) or national districts (eleven), with one or two privileged ethnic groups that dominate local governments. In the Adygeya, for example, Adigs constitute only 20 percent of the republic's population, but they control the majority of political power because Adygeya is a national republic. This situation creates an official *political* ethnic majority that is not *demographic* majority at all. In general, the national-territorial approach to state formation carries huge destructive potential that creates the grounds for future ethnic conflicts that could lead to the further disintegration of Russia. It serves to create well-organized political ethnic elites who totally control sociopolitical and economic life in their republics. It also inspires further corruption in state structures.

Moscow should develop a proactive policy for the Northern Caucasus. Most titular nationalities of the North Caucasus are in favor of continuing close integration with Russia in the framework of one country. Public opinion surveys published in 1997 show that only in Chechnya (53.6 percent) and Ingushetia (62.3 percent) do respondents no longer believe in the future of a unified Russia. In Adygeya, the number is only 19.2 percent, in Dagestan 14.8 percent, in Kabardino-Balkaria 23.6 percent, in Karachaevo-Chercessia 32.4 percent, and in North Ossetia 18.4 percent.[21] In the near term, the federal government — no matter what its political orientation — must deal with the entrenched ethnopolitical elites who were absent in the Communist period. In most cases these elites are even more radically oriented than their respective populations.

CONCLUSION

Despite the wide diversity of fundamentalist movements, all of them pursue the goal of "political Islam" and are united by the hostile attitude toward the Western model of development, which includes Christian values, such as human rights. They also reject the notion of liberal democracy as a political goal for society. Because Russia directly borders the great area of the Muslim world, it is vital to preserve peace and stability in Russia's southern regions and the security of its southern borders. The situation in the North Caucasus directly concerns Russian national interests. Russia is interested in establishing equal and mutually beneficial relations with the Muslim countries of this region, but at the same time this policy should not exclude a firm resolution to deal with threats to Russian security.

On the whole political Islam has a very limited chance to play a key role in the geopolitics of the North Caucasus, especially in the Caucasus' northwestern sections. There are no well-organized and influential Islamic parties or organizations in these unstable regions; existing organizations do not control economic spheres, financial spheres, or the mass media. There are no charismatic leaders who could compensate for the absence of political parties and consolidate their followers. Additionally, the region already has a well-organized regional-political elite that controls many sources of power. The Islamists will not easily displace these elites.

Aside from the effects of the war, analysis of the religious-political situation in the North Caucasus shows Islamic fundamentalism is not a major force in sociopolitical life. Radical forms of Islamism, such as Wahhabism, are only a small portion of the vast kaleidoscope of Islamist movements. The majority of organizations are moderate Islamic movements that favor preserving the deep historical, political, economic, and social ties with Russia. It seems that the best tack for Russia is not to promote confrontation with moderate Islam, but to find points of interest on the basis of mutual respect. Situated at the junction of West and East, South and North and having a substantial Muslim population, Russia can and should be an integrative force between civilizations. This position seems to be one of the most important points in the Russian national interest.

Part III

Central Asia and
Outside Influences

C h a p t e r   O n e

The Islamic Factor in Relations between Russia and Central Asia

Aleksei Malashenko

INTRODUCTION

It is generally recognized that the "Islamic factor" plays a significant role in relations between Russia and the Central Asian states. However, existing studies are unclear as to what the term Islamic factor actually means. Sometimes Islam alone is used, which might be suitable in the mass media or informal conversation. Nonetheless, a more precise definition of the "Islamic factor" is necessary.

The author understands the term "Islamic factor" to include, first of all, the special role of religious tradition in Central Asia, in social and political life. Second, the term includes the tendency of Muslims to identify themselves with the rest of the Muslim world. Third, the term involves the legitimate existence of Islamic parties and movements in the region, including those whose ultimate aim is to establish an Islamic state, an idea that (although utopian in nature) exerts a tangible mobilizing influence. Failure to take these factors into account makes any analysis of Russian-Central Asian relations unproductive, if not impossible.

It is also important to establish whether the term "Central Asia" is adequate in referring to the entire territory and societies of the former Soviet Central Asian republics. One must understand that today there are two opposing tendencies in Central Asian politics and economics: the centrifugal and the centripetal. The fact that each of the five states in the area is primarily, if not exclusively, guided by its own national interests suggests that the centrifugal tendency is dominant. Regional interests play a role only insofar as they coincide with national interests. While it would be wrong to rule that the centrifugal tendency is the only force in existence there, one cannot deny that the interests and orientation of, say, Tajikistan, Kyrgyzstan, and Turkmenistan are becoming increasingly divergent.

A NEW WORLD VIEW

The 1990s have seen the Central Asian countries drawing closer to the countries of the Middle East and Western Asia, as both sides establish economic contacts and interact politically to form unified information and transportation infrastructures. All this restructuring has made it possible to speak of a new Central Asian macroregion in the making, which will include Turkey, Iran, Pakistan, Afghanistan, the countries of the Persian Gulf, and the Central Asian republics. Although it seems premature to draw such a conclusion, the contours of a new conglomeration of states stretching from the Mediterranean Sea to India, as well as from the Ural Mountains to the Indian Ocean, can already be seen. Among a general geopolitical restructuring, this process appears perfectly logical.

However, within the swirling diversity of economic and political courses in the Central Asian countries, similar domestic sociocultural and sociopolitical conditions can be observed. Some examples are the need for economic reforms; the need for a political system that suits a particular society; and, in general, the need to build a nation-state. All this change is taking place against the background of a growing, though not always discernible, societal confrontation between modernization and traditionalism. A key element of the latter is Islamization — that is, the increasing influence of Islam on society and, broadly speaking, the growing weight of the Islamic factor. This circumstance makes it possible to speak of common sociocultural trends in Central Asia. The newspaper *Neitralnyi Turkmenistan* stated:

> *A religious world view will permit us not only to delve more deeply into the history of the people, and the source of their traditions, customs, behavioral norms, and morals — indeed everything that constitutes the mentality of a nation — but also to develop a set of cultural and ethical values and moral standards that would correspond to the spirit of the times.*[1]

THE ISLAMIC FACTOR: THE VIEW FROM CENTRAL ASIA

What impact then does the Islamic factor have on relations between Russia and Central Asia? It must first be noted that nothing regarding any sort of impact, beneficial or otherwise, has ever been formally mentioned in any official interstate document, nor has a specific civilizing influence in any Central Asian country been recognized.

The Muslim religion is only one factor in the new-found identity of the post-Soviet states. Suddenly outside the grip of the mighty empire that was the second superpower, each of those states found itself facing social and economic problems, and each immediately sensed that it would now be part of a different system of geopolitical coordinates. The era of the double standard — belonging in a sociocultural sense to the Muslim world and at the same time forming a part of the USSR — was definitely over.

When the three "Slavic sisters" (Russia, Belarus, and Ukraine) signed a separate agreement on self-determination based on their ethnic and cultural community, it was natural for the Central Asian republics to react by asserting their national statehood and simultaneously a regional unity based on their religious, cultural, and ethnic commonality.

Identification with Islam is characteristic of Uzbekistan, Turkmenistan, and Tajikistan, with Tajikistan in the uncomfortable position of being the only non-Turkic nation. Though both Kazakstan and Kyrgyzstan are in a relatively advanced process of modernization and *Russification*, an Islamic mentality has begun to awaken there as well.

The question arose of the need to legitimize Central Asia's affinity with the Islamic world, something that was recognized *de facto* by the Soviet authorities, but ignored *de jure* by them as far as sociopolitical life was concerned. For the Central Asian states and societies to recognize the legitimacy of belonging to the Islamic world would be not merely a sociocultural act, it would be primarily a political act. When they declared themselves Muslim countries, they renounced their Sovietness and at the same time distanced themselves from Russia. In the words of Steven Grant, Islam may play the role of a barrier against an extended Russian role in Central Asia.[2] The Islamic factor thus has found its place in the complex new paradigm of Russo-Central Asian relations.

The spontaneous reunification of Central Asia with the Muslim world, from which it had been fenced off in Soviet times, has been encouraged by purely pragmatic motives as well. In the early 1990s, members of the local elite came to the confident conclusion that the basis for their well-being, or at least one of its cornerstones, might be the establishment of economic contacts and political relations with Muslim countries. Candidates for the role of sponsor included Turkey, Iran, and the countries of the Persian Gulf. One of the reasons given for such sponsorship was the religion these countries had in common. A Central Asian analyst in the early 1990s told me that an insight into political life in Central Asia could well be had from a photograph of a head of state flanked by a Turkish technocrat and by an Arab or Iranian in a turban. "Men in turbans" is an ironic term used by Central Asia's westernized intelligentsia in reference to *mullahs* (religious teachers), *ayatollahs* (*Shi'a* religious authorities), *imams* (islamic leaders), and other Muslim clerics.

In 1991 – 1993 policies aimed at reviving Islam, such as constructing new mosques, reestablishing religious education, and promoting adherence to Islamic tradition, became trump cards in the political game that the Central Asian countries were playing with their Muslim partners in the Middle East and Western Asia. Results, however, were not quick in coming. The early returns expected by foreign entrepreneurs and financiers were more often than not disappointing because of the inefficient post-Soviet economic system, the corruption of local officials, and the low professional level of their Central Asian partners. The Central Asian partners, too, expected more from their co-religionists abroad in the way of financial and other support. High hopes for a trans-Asian infrastructure proved illusory, or at least premature. The idea of reviving the Great Silk Route, including its subregional sections, is still on the agenda of many projects and the debates surrounding them. Opened in 1995 in Serakhs, Turkmenistan, the railroad terminal was touted as the cornerstone of a Mideast-Central Asian transport system, but it remains only a symbol in marble of Muslim collaboration, not a functioning enterprise. In a word, there has not been a cardinal change in direction toward Muslim markets. Conversely, the prospect of collaboration with Korea, India, Japan, and the West has begun to look promising. It is evident that, in the sphere of economic and even political collaboration, the Islamic factor is not an absolute, or even required, condition.

Having secured for themselves the status of members of the Muslim community and having joined its various organizations (including the most influential of all, the Islamic Conference), the countries of Central

Asia also consolidated their position as belonging to the Muslim world in *Russian* eyes as well. By the mid-1990s, despite the relatively unsuccessful efforts of Central Asian states to collaborate with the Muslim world, Russian politicians no longer saw them primarily as former Soviet territories. The Islamic factor, in making clear who belonged to what civilization, had helped Central Asia achieve self-determination in its relations with Russia.

Kazakstan stands somewhat apart from the rest of Central Asia. Its drift toward the Muslim world is held in check by the presence of a large proportion of Russian speakers in the population, more than 38 percent in early 1997. Kazakstan is the only country in the region that could be called bidenominational. A still broader, and even somewhat poetic, interpretation of Kazakstan's sociocultural and geopolitical role has been suggested by the Kazak philosopher Nurlan Amrekulov, who defines Kazakstan as "a bridge inside a continent, a link between Slavic North and Turkic South, between the Christian Northwest, Confucian-Buddhist Southeast, Muslim Southwest, and between the Euro-American urban culture of individualism and the Eastern agrarian-communal culture of continental Asia."[3] One argument propounded by some national radical Kazaks is that Kazakstan's unconditional affinity to the Muslim world irks the Russian-speaking population, and mutual antagonism is growing between cultural and religious traditions, thereby destabilizing the country. Attempts to incorporate Kazakstan into the Muslim world are being indirectly opposed by Kazakstan's President Nursultan Nazarbayev and his idea of Eurasianism. This idea could be viewed as endeavoring to preserve and build on stable ties with Russia, in view of Kazakstan and Russia's common history and culture. Consequently, this approach puts Kazakstan in an ambiguous position vis-a-vis the Muslim world.

THE THREE ISLAMIC FACTORS

Because Russia needs to take the Islamic factor into account, it would be beneficial to look into the forms of Islam in the region and their relative significance in the Central Asian paradigm of sociopolitical relations, structures, and ideologies.

In the first place there is state Islam, or state-sponsored Islam. Second is fundamentalist Islam, which is Islam in opposition to the government. Third is popular, or domestic, Islam, which is associated with traditions kept up by the people and which has a formative influence on the population's mass consciousness. All three forms of Islamic ideology are closely intertwined and constantly interacting. Only when they are taken together is it possible to form any true picture of Islam's role in society, political life, and international relations, including relations with Russia.

STATE ISLAM

The function of state, or official, Islam is primarily to interpret secular politics, which in any Muslim country requires a clerical blessing. According to the practice in Muslim countries, almost every purely secular act of a social or political nature is accompanied by an appropriate explanation from the position of Islam. This explanation is readily proffered by clerics cooperating with the authorities and by a member of the Muslim *ulema* (scholars of sacred law and theology). A similar situation, though not so distinct, is taking shape in Central Asia. There the reforms now under way are interpreted by the Muslim authorities as a striving toward universal prosperity and social justice, which from their vantage point was originally characteristic of Islam with principles formed far in the past in the Islamic state of the prophet Muhammad.

Central Asian presidents look to Islam for support significantly less often than their counterparts in other countries. Moreover, those presidents are sometimes prepared to admit that their regimes are "unsatisfactory" from the Islamic point of view. "We do not fit the pattern of an̄ Islamic state," says Islam Karimov, president of Uzbekistan. "We are a secular state. Our constitution has the approval of the most democratc institutions of France, Germany, and Great Britain.... And since we strictly adhere to our constitution in affairs of state, we do not satisfy Islamic norms."[4]

In the early 1990s, Turkmenistan leader Saparmurad Niyazov stated, "We have firmly declared the principle...that Turkmenistan is a secular state.... And we have no grounds to believe that anyone is trying to alter that principle."[5] President Nazarbayev declares proudly that his country "has achieved stability in relations between ethnic and religious groups,"[6] another indication that Kazakstan is not a purely Muslim country.

As for Kyrgyzstan, President Askar Akayev asserts that he is for "harmonious relations between, and inter-penetration and convergence of, civilizations,"[7] a view one would not likely hear from the orthodox head of an Islamic state.

Such words mirror opinions prevalent among today's post-Soviet Central Asian elite, and they reflect the sentiment of the Europeanized or Russified part of the population. At the same time, these views represent the transition to a new, non-Soviet elite, which will likely embrace another set of values. Two possible scenarios exist for the evolution of this elite. The first is a return to traditionalism and the coming to power of men with traditional views — something that is already taking place as provincials, who are less exposed to modernization, make their way into positions of authority.

The second scenario would involve the entrenchment of the present-day Europeanized elite — with the addition of nontraditional standards, particularly standards that could serve as a foundation for some future democratic social system that would take into account local ethnic and cultural features. It seems most likely that the evolution of such a non-Soviet elite would synthesize traditional and modern views and objectives for a new social system. To quote U.S. political scientist Martha Brill Olcott, "The current elites hope to remain in power long enough for their political descendants to take over. Members of the next generation are more worldly; they have traveled and studied in the West and in the Muslim East."[8] For whoever comes to power in tomorrow's Central Asian elite — reformers or traditionalists — the Islamic factor will play a bigger role than before because, in the midst of the religious and cultural revival, political leaders will surely find it important to consider Islam when making policy.

Islam as a state institution may, in the hands of a new elite, turn into a reliable and effective political tool in foreign as well as domestic policy. Although in the mid-1990s the Central Asian leaders ignored appeals for Muslim solidarity by Muslim separatists in Russia's North Caucasus, future leaders may prove more willing to listen. Certain individuals in the United Tajik Opposition who are active in the coalition government have already expressed their sympathy for the Chechen insurgents.

The future political elite will surely be more popular with their co-religionists than their predecessors, who built their careers in their republics' Communist Parties, which formed a part of the Communist Party of the Soviet Union. The new elite can lay much more emphasis on political cooperation with the Muslim world, where members of that elite will be welcomed as closer in spirit and capable of dialogue in the political and ideological categories important to Muslims. This cooperation, in turn, will affect relations with Russia, which will have to take into account the Islamic factor if it hopes to reach certain goals in the region.

FUNDAMENTALIST ISLAM

The second form of Islam, which is associated with religious fundamentalists in the opposition, was at first mostly ignored in Russo-Central Asian relations. In the early 1990s, it was known to exist, but little or no information was available. Russian statesmen initially viewed it as an internal problem of their southern neighbors. Besides, at the time the Islamic opposition did not seem to have much influence, with two possible exceptions: Tajikistan and Uzbekistan. Foreign policy was affected only in Tajikistan, where the Islamic factor did have an impact on relations between that country and Russia.

It was in Tajikistan that Soviet diplomats first encountered Islamic fundamentalists on a territory of the former USSR. The first reaction was to refuse to recognize them because they were seen as an alien force hostile to Soviet interests. What is interesting was that this attitude did not stem from a rejection of Islam or fundamentalism as such. Soviet diplomats and political analysts, at least the most pragmatic of them, did not exclude the possibility of working with fundamentalists, even radical fundamentalists. One may recall the attempts at a rapprochement with Khomeini's Iran in the early 1980s, and the "understanding" attitude to Muslim terrorists in the Middle East. This view was certainly held by Yevgeni Primakov (whose career encompassed both Candidate Member of the Communist Politburo and Prime Minister of the Russian Federation).

By 1991-1992, however, the Russian government ruled out any possibility of dialogue with post-Soviet Islam. This attitude was fostered by its position regarding Tajikistan and other Central Asian republics, who had inherited a Soviet system in which the Islamic opposition was the enemy. It resulted paradoxically from the exaggerated emphasis on European-Christian democratic values made by Russian politicians.

The first wave of the Islamic revival (1990-1993) saw the politicization of Islam. Numerous minor parties proliferated, mass meetings occurred, mosques developed into centers of propaganda, and a new type of religious-political leader heretofore unknown in these republics emerged. This first wave did not result in a powerful Islamic political movement except in Tajikistan.[9] However — and this is particularly important — it was a sign that sooner or later such a movement was *bound* to emerge, if not in all Central Asia, then in its major strategic enclaves, which were vital elements in the alignment of political forces. The lull in religious political activity that followed this first wave of Islamic renaissance gave many experts grounds to downgrade the Islamic factor in the region's politics and foreign policy.

By 1996, as political forces using Islamic slogans became more active, Central Asian Muslims began to demand outlets as evidenced by the determination of Central Asia's ruling class to establish total control over Islam, thereby forcing the clergy into subservience and banishing Islamists from the political scene.

The territory on which Muslim oppositionists were trying to entrench themselves was expanding. Besides the Uzbek part of the Fergana Valley, where the authority of the nonconformist mosques was unassailable, their presence began to be felt in western Kyrgyzstan, primarily in the cities of Osh and Jalalabad, and in southern Kazakstan. Russian embassies informed Moscow of the increasing influence of such groups. Reports began to appear in the media as well. Russian foreign policy could no longer ignore the slow but steady growth of an Islamic opposition in Central Asia. If we consider that such a political force is present in every Muslim society and state, it would have been a mistake to believe this influence could not happen on post-Soviet Muslim territory.

It is difficult to understand the political analysts and journalists who assert that opposition Islam, including that in Uzbekistan, is just the imagination of local authorities working overtime, and that government persecution of dissident clergymen and Muslim political figures is nothing but a way to consolidate an authoritarian regime. Still, there is some truth that regimes in existence today have a right to take such preemptive measures: they are fighting for their survival. Even in Uzbekistan, Islam is the most organized opposition group, with a huge political base and healthy potential chance in the struggle for power, or at least a place in a coalition government.

In Kazakstan and Kyrgyzstan the Islamic opposition will probably continue to exist in isolated enclaves. Its influence extends only to certain areas in southern Kazakstan and western Kyrgyzstan and within certain ethnic groups that tend to drift toward Islamic activism. Political activity under the banner of Islam is more characteristic of the Uzbek population in these republics. Fundamentalism, nonetheless, is looked upon with a degree of favor by some of the more nationalistic Kazaks and Kyrgyzz.

It would be hard to predict how events will play out in Turkmenistan. Even though most experts do not see the social and cultural foundation needed for the emergence of an Islamic movement there, it would be unwise to rule out the possibility of an Islamic resurgence. If the regime of the Turkmenbashi is ever so slightly liberalized, or if President Karimov himself leaves the scene because of illness or death, then potential aspirants to power could likely resort to Islam, so as to rally the politically active traditionalists around themselves. Such a script is all the more plausible because local liberals do not look very commanding, although their courage in defending democratic values inspires respect.

POPULAR ISLAM

The third form of Islam that should be taken into account is traditional, or domestic Islam, which has among its devotees virtually the entire native population of Central Asia. "Central Asian society," writes Russian ethnologist Olga Brusina, "has successfully fought off modernization by adjusting to the new system of relationships, replacing some of its elements with traditional ones. Society still has a hierarchy of social ties and legal relations based on common law and *shari'a* law."[10] Even in Soviet times, popular (or domestic) Islam was extensively studied by linguists and ethnographers, who typically identified it with traditional folk culture and only rarely in the context of political activity. They reduced Islam to just the observance of religious rituals and holidays. In the late 1980s, some atheist officials were in favor of backing this form of Islam so as to counter Islamic fundamentalism, which they claimed was a deviant form of the Muslim religion that was ill suited to Central Asia. Experts among Communist Party functionaries even spoke of the possibility of communists working together with nonfundamentalists in the religious opposition.[11]

Today, popular Islam is not a factor in the power struggle taking place in the countries of the region. As part of the ethnic culture of people's lives, not political life, it remains the object of academic study, not of strategic analysis. However, this type of Islam makes up the sociocultural background for the formation of a nation-state. It is the background against which the ruling elite work out new priorities and alignments, including international alignments.

ISLAM'S INFLUENCE ON RUSSIAN FOREIGN RELATIONS

Each of the three forms of Islam mentioned here — official (or state-sponsored) Islam; opposition (or political) Islam; and popular (or domestic) Islam — has its own functions and works in different contexts. However, all three are part of one whole, with no set boundaries between them. This whole makes up the mindset, the norms of social and individual behavior, and the political culture. All three forms are represented in the region, which makes it possible to speak of a Central Asian Islam. If one allows for the specific religious and cultural features of each of the ethnic groups in Central Asia, then such a Central Asian Islam is incorporated in the pan-Islamic civilization and, consequently, into global Islamic political culture.

"Modern nation building in the Muslim World demonstrates three patterns: secular, Muslim, and Islamic," notes political scientist John L. Esposito. "At one end of the spectrum, Turkey. At the other end of the spectrum, Saudi Arabia. The vast majority of countries in the Muslim World fall in between."[12] It is one of these places "in between" that the Central Asian countries occupy at the end of the 1990s.

How great is Islam's influence on the situation in Central Asia, and what are its limits?

Invoking Islam in the 1990s did not serve to consolidate society, nor could it be used by the regimes in the various states to maintain political stability. The Islamic factor played practically no role in regional consolidation, but it was and continues to be a key regulating factor for relations in society. What is particularly important is that it is exerting an ever-growing influence on political life in Central Asia, especially in the confrontation between the authorities and the opposition.[13] Moscow faces a difficult challenge in taking full advantage of the political potential of the Islamic factor without exaggerating its importance, particularly if the new rulers who come to power in the Central Asian republics believe their future nation-states must be based firmly on Islamic religious and cultural national traditions.

The Russian Empire, and later the Soviet Union, always had a strategic interest in the Muslim world, including Central Asia. Even today, though it has lost influence in Central Asia, Russia has not suffered an irreversible retreat. Moreover, considering Russia's new troubles with the West, where Russia is considered deficient as a European power and will most likely be so regarded in the near future, the Kremlin seems increasingly attracted to the prospect of regaining at least some of its old authority in the East.

This interest in Central Asia coincides with attempts to shore up and build on Russia's influence within the Commonwealth of Independent States (CIS). The policy aimed at reasserting a Russian role in the Middle East was strengthened when Yevgeni Primakov was Foreign Minister.

The Central Asian nations, too, are showing an interest in renewed cooperation with Russia. Following a long and not always successful search for new partners, their governments are beginning to show more enthusiasm for Russia as a possibility. A similar attitude can be seen in the private sector. Interestingly enough, this mutual interest is based at least in part on political considerations, including the fear of radical Islamic fundamentalism both inside and outside these countries. An example is the Taliban movement now entrenched in neighboring Afghanistan.

There is much talk in the Central Asian capitals about the threat of the Taliban expanding northward, although such a turn of events seems improbable if only because the Taliban's army has not been able to claim final victory even over its internal foes, who have the support of Afghanistan's southern neighbors. It would seem that the Taliban's army could not sustain its fighting capacity on foreign soil. Nontheless, if one assumes that the Taliban will be supported by local Uzbek or Tajik Islamic radicals, the threat of Taliban expansion might become real enough.[14] The Taliban's successes must seem to be a graphic demonstration of their might to those in Central Asia who share such values. For that reason, the Taliban threat is seen by rulers of the Central Asian republics as an excellent rationalization for putting down the local Islamic opposition. In this sense, their efforts to secure Russian support against a foreign enemy will likely lead Russia into being a guarantor of their security against any threat from their own domestic fundamentalists.

Russia's decision-makers do not always see eye to eye on the prospect of a stronger Islamic movement in Central Asia, though they all appear to be against such an occurrence. At a meeting of Presidents Yeltsin and Karimov in 1998, the Russian leader spoke in favor of a tripartite agreement between Russia, Uzbekistan, and Tajikistan to "stand firm against the spread of the Islamic threat."[15] The Turkish researcher Gunden Peker expressed a long-established viewpoint when he wrote, "Russian foreign policy must secure both internal and external borders of the CIS as well as good ties with the southern flank. The stability of Central Asia preserves a pivotal role in their security, and conditions the overall security of Russia."[16]

In this connection the security of Russian frontiers is seen as dependent on the ability to keep the Islamic radicals down. This position is widespread in many different political groups in Russia, from democrats to communists and ultranationalists. The danger of radical Islam has repeatedly been noted in numerous memoranda and reports to Russia's National Security Council. The negative attitude toward fundamentalism in the top echelons of the army is also well known. However, this negative attitude to Islamic radicalism is not necessarily applied to how Russia views it in the rest of the world. Russian political leaders and analysts are ambivalent about the movement, which they see could not only harm Russia, but also benefit it.

And so, in 1994 the Russian foreign ministry decided to hold official meetings with the Tajik Islamists. The fateful precedent that those meetings set was to make it possible to negotiate with even this category of Central Asian political leaders. This *de jure* recognition of political Islam was a significant new force in the Central Asian region. Such an attitude expanded the spectrum of Russia's potential partners and made Russia's position more independent and less vulnerable in the future. In addition, dialogue with the Tajik Islamists confirms once again that in the Muslim world at large, Russian policies do not depend on the dominant religious ideology of any country. The most impressive example is continuing relations between Russia and Iran.

THE EFFECT OF THE ISLAMIC FACTOR ON INTERNAL RUSSIAN POLITICS

How does the present-day nationalist and communist opposition inside Russia view Islam and the Islamic factor? This opposition has two approaches that, although contradictory, are intertwined in unlikely ways and converge on several points. The first approach recognizes the Islamic world's hostility — including the hostility of its Central Asian segment — towards Russia. Its proponents insist that Russia must get out of Central Asia for reasons of cultural and religious incompatibility, and claim that no economic collaboration with Central Asia could possibly be beneficial. Relations could be reestablished, they argue, only if the Central Asian countries became Russia's vassals or quasi-client states.

In the other approach, Islam is seen as a sociocultural system, perhaps as the Oriental counterpart of the concept of Russian civilization (the antipode of Western civilization), and is, as such, its natural enemy. This approach is what forms the basis for an alliance between Russia and the Muslim world, particularly the Islamic radicals. Valentin Filatov, an ideologue of the ultranationalist Liberal Democratic Party in Russia, has said that Russian patriotism and Islamic fundamentalism form "a territory on which the foot of Zionism has never trod," and that together they are the last bastion against Western expansion.[17]

Aleksandr Dugin, a proponent of Eurasianism, a movement fairly popular in Russia and parts of Central Asia (Kazakstan, somewhat less so in Kyrgyzstan), maintains that there are two Islams: "Atlantic Islam" (pro-Western) and "Eurasian Islam" (anti-Western). Assessing the importance of the Islamic factor to Russia, he suggests signing a "Russo-Islamic pact and coordinating Moscow's general strategy and those movements within Islam that are pro-Iranian, pro-Sufi, and pro-Fundamentalist in the sense of being fundamental, continental, and anti-Western."[18]

Whatever parties or movements come to power and whatever ideological trends dominate the future political establishment in Russia, the Islamic factor will remain a constant influence, even if not always in the same form, in Russo-Central Asian relations.

This circumstance is determined in the broadest sense by the fact that the Central Asian republics belong to the Muslim world and to Islamic civilization because of the growing role of Islam in their social and political life. The level of this influence, though different in every country, will tend to increase.

Islam's importance may rise or fall depending on the situation in the country itself or in adjacent countries. The immediate reason the Islamic factor is so important is the growing activity of oppositional Islam, which is seeking an ever-higher level of influence in society. This explains why the present regimes in these countries are so tolerant of the Islamic counterelite, even to the point of including the counterelites in their governments, something that has already happened in Tajikistan.

More and more Russian politicians are displaying a rational approach to Islamism in Central Asia, gauging its influence and conceding the need for a productive dialogue with its adherents. Apparently, no longer is it possible to deny that some states of Central Asia are going to legitimize profundamentalist ideas, and these notions may well become part of the official ideology and political practice (again, this is happening in Tajikistan). Conversely, with the unrelenting activity of the Taliban in Afghanistan, some Central Asian states are openly appealing to Russia for help because Russia wants to preserve the status quo in the region.

CONCLUSION

The countries of Central Asia are staking out their claim, with varying success, to a greater degree of participation in the affairs of the Muslim community as a whole; they are looking for a niche in the leading international Muslim organizations. Because the economic weight of such countries, as far as can be predicted, will remain at the same low level as today, they might well emphasize political and ideological consolidation; it would be quite logical on their part to play the Islamic card, especially if a conflict situation arises.

The Russian economist R. M. Avakov once referred to the relations between Russia and Central Asia as "a collection of uncertainties,"[19] and many circumstances confirm his impression. There may be no doubt about the presence of the Islamic factor in Russian–Central Asian relations, but that lack of doubt does not mean this factor is always beneficial or harmful. The Islamic factor remains a sophisticated two-edged weapon that can be used by either side.

Iran, Central Asia and the Opening of the Islamic Iron Curtain

Shireen T. Hunter

INTRODUCTION

Beginning in 1988, the process of reform and political openness that Mikhail Gorbachev initiated in the Soviet Union brought down what can best be characterized as the Islamic Iron Curtain.[1] The establishment of this Islamic Iron Curtain had predated the Soviet Iron Curtain that divided Europe into two antagonistic camps following the end of World War II, and had kept Soviet Muslims separated from the rest of the Islamic world.

The Islamic Iron Curtain was not always or totally impenetrable; Soviet Muslims maintained limited contacts with the rest of the Islamic world throughout the Soviet period as they had during Russian colonial rule. Even Stalin occasionally showed a degree of flexibility in regard to the Muslims when the Soviet Union's interests required it. This was the case during the Second World War between 1942 and 1945, when anti-Islamic propaganda and pressures on Muslims were eased to prevent Central Asian Muslims from falling under German influence. From the mid-1950s onward, the Soviet Union systematically used its Muslim population to advance its foreign policy objectives in the Arab and Islamic worlds. This strategy led both to the relaxing of repression on Islamic practices and to increasing contacts between Soviet and other Muslims. However, those Soviet Muslims who took part in these exchanges were carefully selected.[2] Consequently, until the outbreak of the Afghan War in 1979, most Soviet Muslims remained on the periphery of the Islamic world and were largely out of touch with the major intellectual trends developing there.

The Afghan War exposed Central Asian Muslims to Islamic influences in two ways. First, during the early days of the Afghan War, the Soviets used Central Asian soldiers as part of Russian military forces; this practice soon stopped, partly out of the fear of contamination by Islamic ideas. The second exposure was through Pakistani broadcasts of Islamic propaganda to Central Asia, mostly originating from Peshawar.

Meanwhile, the indigenous — or folk — Islam of Central Asia and other Muslim parts of the Soviet Union proved to be tenacious and resistant to atheist propaganda. This phenomenon was not limited to ordinary people; rather, it extended to the leadership cadre of those regions' Communist Parties.[3]

In 1988, when the Islamic Iron Curtain began to be lifted, Soviet Muslims were reconnected with their Muslim kin, both in the immediate neighborhood and farther afield. As a result Islamic sentiments resurfaced with a new-found vitality. One inevitable question was of intense interest to local elites and outside powers: What role was Islam likely to play in shaping the late-Soviet cultural and political landscape of Central Asian republics and the direction of their external relations?

On the internal level after 1991, the post-communist era leaders (which with great alacrity had turned themselves into democrats and showed every intention of continuing in power) agreed with secular nationalists and pan-Turkist groups on one item. All saw Islam as an ideological rival and potential barrier to their either maintaining or assuming power.

On the international level, the Western countries (notably the United States), their regional allies, and Russia (which despite the end of the Soviet Union considered the post-Soviet space, especially its Asian parts, its exclusive sphere of economic and political influence) adopted a similar outlook. In that view, the potential rise of Islam, particularly its militant and extremist variant, was a serious threat to the stability of Central Asia and to the interests of each of those countries.

IRAN AS A SOURCE OF ISLAMIC RADICALISM

During the period extending from 1988 to mid-1993, the Western powers (especially the United States), Russia, and some regional countries viewed Iran as the primary source of spreading Islamic militancy to the

Muslim republics of the ex-Soviet Union. They also thought Iran would promote the establishment of Islamic states that would be based on its own revolutionary model. However, between 1988 and mid-1993, most entities gradually acknowledged that the political evolution of the Muslim republics of the former Soviet Union would be determined by the interaction of a wide range of indigenous factors and external influences rather than by the mere import of a particular sociopolitical model. Still, many analysts saw the contest for determining Central Asia's sociocultural and political future to be between the Iranian and Turkish models.[4]

The Iranian model was that of the dreaded Islamic fundamentalist state established by the Ayatollah Ruhullah Khomeini, while the Turkish model was that of the progressive, secular, and modernist state created by Mustafa Kemal Ataturk. In other words, during this period the Western view of the coming battle for the hearts and minds of the ex-Soviet Muslims had a dualistic and almost Manichean character. It was a battle between darkness and light represented, respectively, by Iran's Islamic anti-Western fundamentalism and Turkey's pro-Western secularism.

It was assumed that Iran's principal goals in the post-Soviet area would be to spread its revolutionary message and to help set up governments that would be congenial to its own Islamic model. During a 1992 trip to the Central Asian countries, U.S. Secretary of State James Baker III declared that a principal component of American policy toward these newly independent states was to block Iranian inroads into the region.[5] As later became clear, preventing effective Iranian interaction with the ex-Soviet Muslim states was to be part of a broader policy of containing and isolating Iran. This was part of the so-called Dual Containment strategy that was developed and implemented by the Clinton Administration when it assumed power in January 1993.

Between 1992 and 1994, the Russian leadership — with its Euro-Atlanticist vision and expectations of a grand partnership with the West in managing the post-Cold War world — shared the view that the greatest security threat to Russia came from the unstable South and the potential rise of Islamic militancy there. Russia, together with some Central Asian countries (especially Uzbekistan), also viewed Iran as the main source for the spread of Islamic militancy to the region. Hence, Iran was seen as a potential threat to Russian stability. However, for a variety of reasons to be discussed later — most notably, Iran's pragmatic and nonideological approach toward those republics — Russia's attitude toward Iran's role in the region began to change by 1994.

A thorough examination of Iran's policy regarding the Muslim regions of the ex-Soviet Union and the Muslim-inhabited areas of the Russian Federation clearly demonstrates that the desire to spread Islamic militancy to Central Asia or to the Caucasus and to promote the establishment of Islamic states on the Iranian model has played no significant role in its formulation. However, the Iranian media, including the official news agency IRNA, does at times criticize the mistreatment of Muslims and Islamic activists by the authorities of some Central Asian countries, notably Uzbekistan.[6]

Consequently, even countries such as Uzbekistan, which has the least favorable view of Iran, today admit (at least in private conversations) that Iran has not actively pursued the goal of establishing Islamic republics or of fomenting Islamic revolution in Central Asia.[7] Uzbek and Tajik leaders still occasionally accuse Iran of supporting Islamic forces. Iran has provided some support to Tajikistan's Islamic movement, especially the section led by Qadi Akbar Turajonzadeh.[8] Nevertheless, Iran no longer seems to be the main concern of the Uzbeks and Tajiks. Kazakstan, Turkmenistan, and Kyrgyzstan have never seen Iran as a major source of Islamic threat. For example, when asked about the threat of contagion of Islamic fundamentalism from Iran to his Turkmenistan, President Saparmuradt Niyazov said that he could "see neither an exporter, nor anybody who can use such exports...."[9]

The Kazak Ambassador to Tehran also criticized the attitude of some Kazaks, who, he argued, view Iran only through the prism of Islamic fundamentalism. "Unfortunately, to this day we have a perception of this very important strategic partner that is not always objective and is limited to the so-called Islamic fundamentalism. This is a very simplified approach, and it would be a mistake to follow it."[10]

Instead, a decade after Islam burst on the Central Asian social and political scene, the secular leaders of those countries view Wahhabism and Afghanistan's Taliban movement (which espouses the strict and puritanical teachings of Wahhabism) as the most subversive Islamic element. Furthermore, Pakistan is viewed as the country most actively recruiting and training Central Asians according to extremist Islamic ideologies.[11]

As evidence of this perception, Uzbek authorities have complained to the Pakistani government about the activities of a number of groups, including some retired army generals engaged in training exercises.[12] It is beyond dispute that various Pakistani groups support Islamic forces in Central Asia. However, it is not at all certain that the Pakistani government sanctions their actions. On the contrary, Pakistani officials have denied that the government is engaged in such activities. It is also widely believed that Saudi Arabia is the principal source of financing for such activities. What is not clear is whether the Saudi government is behind this financing or the money comes from private sources.

Other Central Asian and Caucasian countries have also focused on Wahhabism as the main subversive Islamic element, rather than Khomeinism or the Iranian form of Islam. During an international conference, "For the Unity of Muslims," held in the Kyrgyz capital Bishkek, the main focus of interest and discussion was the threat that the spread of Wahhabism in the Osh and Djalalabad regions was posing to the unity of Kyrgyz Muslims and the country's security.[13] Because Wahhabis consider the *Shi'as* to be worse than infidels and believe that killing *Shi'as* is no crime, it is inconceivable that Iran would be behind Wahhabi activities.[14] Even Azerbaijan's President, Haidar Aliev, concerned about the potential infiltration of Wahhabis from Chechnya and Dagestan, stated that there was no place for Wahhabis in Azerbaijan.[15]

However, the term "*Wahhabi*" must be used with caution. Although Wahhabi influences have spread in Central Asia through the Afghan connection, some Central Asian governments apply the term *Wahhabi* to any kind of Islamic opposition to discredit it in the public eye. Also, the threat of Wahhabism is sometimes used to forge a coalition among Russia and some Central Asian countries, because other bonds — either through past connections or the Commonwealth of Independent States (CIS) — are fraying.

As a result, nearly all Central Asian countries agree that security and economic concerns, rather than ideological aspirations and the desire to spread Islamic radicalism, have been the principal motivating forces of Iran's foreign policy toward the post-Soviet Muslim area. For its part, Iran has emphasized the nurturing of state-to-state relations, rather than working with Islamic forces. Nothing better illustrates this essentially nonideological Iranian approach toward Central Asia than Iran's position regarding the conflict between Tajikistan's first president, Rakhmon Nabiyev, and the Islamic opposition during the crucial period between May and October 1992. Not only did Iran not provide military assistance to the opposition, but also it failed to give any ideological and rhetorical support. In fact, Iran portrayed the Tajik conflict not as an ideological struggle but rather as an internal conflict caused by regional differences and clan rivalries, which have disturbing regional implications. This Iranian attitude caused tensions in Iran's relations with the Tajik opposition and generated criticism of the foreign ministry by the radical Iranian press.

Iran subsequently played host to President Nabiyev, who visited Tehran in June 1992. Since then, Iran has continued to emphasize state-to-state relations even when the governments of some of those states have not been responsive to its overtures and have even occasionally demonstrated open hostility. This emphasis was the case with the Elchibey government in Azerbaijan during 1992 – 1993, with the Karimov government in Uzbekistan, and, until recently, with the post-Nabiyev Rahmanov government in Tajikistan.

This situation leads to the following questions: Why has Islam played such an insignificant role in shaping Iran's policy toward Central Asia? Why has Iran continued to placate hostile, or at least unfriendly, governments, instead of playing its Islamic card? The answers can be found in the following factors. First, there has been an erosion of the ideological basis of Iran's overall foreign policy and a strengthening of its pragmatic streak since the end of the Iran-Iraq war in 1988. Second, Iran has experienced increased geopolitical and economic vulnerability following the collapse of the Soviet Union. Finally, Central Asia's lack of receptivity to Iranian Islam has been a contributing factor.

REASSESSMENT OF REVOLUTIONARY FOREIGN POLICY

When the process of reform in the Soviet Union removed the Islamic Iron Curtain and brought to the forefront the long-repressed Islamic sentiments of the Central Asian peoples, Iran and its Islamic leadership were in the throes of a political and psychological crisis, caused by Iran's defeat in its war with Iraq. On August 8, 1988, circumstances forced Iran to sign a humiliating cease-fire agreement with Iraq after Iran suffered hundreds of billions of dollars' worth of material damage and sacrificed more than one million dead and wounded. The Iranian defeat not only shook to the core people's confidence in the stewardship of the country's Islamic leadership, but also severely undermined their faith in the country's revolutionary ideology. More importantly, it created serious doubts regarding the justness of their cause.

This last development was particularly traumatic for the Iranians; it initiated the process of disenchantment with the Islamic system, which has continued and intensified ever since. The strength of this emotional reaction was partly because Iran's Islamic leadership had consistently portrayed the war against Iraq not merely as the defense of the Iranian state and its territorial integrity (although in reality these were very important), but actually as a war against falsehood and blasphemy. According to the Islamic leadership — especially the Ayatollah Khomeini — the war with Iraq was a combat between *haq* (righteousness and truth), represented by Iran, and *batil* (falsehood and blasphemy), represented by Iraq and Saddam Hussein. This idea was so inculcated into the hearts and minds of Iranian fighters that they believed that God would be on their side and would secure them victory because they were defending a righteous cause. Thus, until forced to do otherwise, the Iranian leadership maintained that it would not compromise with Hussein and that war must continue until he was removed. Therefore, when Iran failed to win the war, many Iranians concluded that Iran might not be on the side of the righteous after all. Whether or not this conclusion was justified, it did affect the course of social and political developments in Iran during the course of the next decade.

One major consequence of Iran's defeat was questioning the conduct of Iran's foreign policy and its principal determinants. This doubting of the wisdom of Iranian foreign policy and the quality of its diplomacy extended even to the leadership. For example, the Ayatollah Ali-Akbar Rafsanjani, who at the time was Speaker of the Iranian Parliament, admitted that certain aspects of Iran's foreign policy and, in particular, the harsh and revolutionary rhetoric of its diplomacy had unnecessarily alienated its neighbors and other countries and had turned them into enemies. The result was that they had supported Hussein against Iran even though Iraqi aggression had started the war. It was also understood — although not openly stated — that Iran's defeat came about because it had put ideological goals ahead of its security and other national interests. Since the end of the war with Iraq, greater emphasis has been placed on the role that national interest, as opposed to ideological aspirations, should play in determining Iran's foreign policy. Yet, in regard to many areas of its foreign policy, Iran has not been able to apply this principle.

Moreover, there are still those both within and outside the leadership who believe that promoting Islamic causes is in Iran's national interest.[16]

An important occasion to test the new-found pragmatism of Iranian leaders in the field of foreign policy was presented by Iraq's invasion of Kuwait on August 2, 1990. In view of the damage that Hussein had inflicted on Iran, and given the risks involved for Iran's security in a strategy of siding with Iraq, actively supporting Iraq in its conflict with the United States-led international coalition would have been dangerous, even inconceivable, for Iran. Nevertheless, some Iranians perceived the projection of American military power into the Persian Gulf and its consolidation in the region as such a great evil that they argued for Iran's supporting Iraq. A key figure within this group was Ayatollah Sadiq Khalkhali, who during the early years of the revolution was chief justice (because of his summary executions, he was called the "hanging judge"). With a few others, he tried to organize rallies in support of Iraq, but because of the depth of popular animosity toward Hussein and general war-weariness, the effort was unsuccessful. Even Hussein's efforts to wrap himself in the flag of Islam and to portray his struggle with the coalition partners as being between Islam and blasphemy had no impact on Iranian attitudes.

The policy that Iran adopted toward the Persian Gulf War was a compromise between the dictates of national interest and the continued influence of Islamic ideology. To be more precise, the pressures emanating from those people who used ideology to shore up their own hold on power had been greatly diminished because of the fiasco of war with Iraq. Ayatollah Rafsanjani, who was president at the time of the Gulf crisis, clearly appealed to the Iranians' sense of nationalism. He was motivated by national interest when he warned them that an Iraqi victory in the war would truly turn the Persian Gulf into the Arabian Gulf — a long-standing ambition of the Arabs.

Even the more ideologically motivated and less pragmatic Ayatollah Khamenei, who had assumed the mantle of Supreme Religious Leader after Khomeini's death in 1989, clearly stated that the war between Iraq and the coalition was not between Islam and disbelief. Thus it did not qualify as a *jihad* (Muslim holy war). The conclusion drawn from this statement was that Iranians had no Islamic duty to support Iraq.

Iran thus adopted a neutral posture in the war, defended Kuwait's territorial integrity, and abided by UN sanctions. This policy reflected the growing importance of national interest as a determinant of Iran's foreign policy. Nevertheless, ideology continued to have an impact on Iranian policy, thereby preventing Iran from taking advantage of the opportunities that Iraqi aggression presented to enhance Iran's regional and international position. Because of ideological factors, Iran did not seize the opportunity presented by the war to resolve its differences with the United States, join the anti–Saddam coalition, and reap the resulting financial and political benefits.

Throughout the 1990s, tension between the requirements of Iran's national interests and the residue of its Islamic ideology has continued and has affected various aspects of Iran's foreign policy. In some key areas, Islamic ideology and its proponents within the Iranian leadership have exerted the greatest influence on determining the course and content of Iran's foreign policy. Those areas have included relations with the United States, ties with a number of key moderate Arab states, and attitudes regarding Israel and the Arab-Israeli peace process. Even after President Mohammad Khatami came to power in August 1997, accompanied by a greater shift away from ideology and toward pragmatism, such aspects of Iran's foreign policy, with the exception of relations with the Arab states, have proven resistant to change. This resistance stems from the fact that President Khatami's authority is still challenged by hard-line factions.

Iran's inability to determine its policy on the basis of its national interest has been very costly in both economic and political terms. In particular, this inability has prevented Iran from assuming a regional role (including in Central Asia) commensurate with its size, historical connections, and economic potential. Especially damaging has been the continued hostility between the United States and Iran, and the ensuing U.S. determination to contain and isolate Iran. This situation has caused Iran to deal from a weakened strategic position with its neighbors, with Russia, and with other powers such as China. It has also prevented Central Asian countries from fully developing their ties to Iran.

PRIMACY OF NATIONAL INTEREST IN THE SOUTHERN CIS

In the post-Soviet Commonwealth of Independent States (CIS), the policy of Iran has been determined by its perception of what constitutes its national interest, rather than by its Islamic ideology. In addition to the declining role of ideology in Iranian foreign policy, several factors have accounted for the pragmatic nature of Iran's policy toward Central Asia.

First, with regard to the southern Former Soviet Union (FSU), no significant Khomeinist legacy exists as it does, for example, regarding the Palestinian issue or the question of Israel's legitimacy. Therefore, Iranian pragmatists could develop policies toward those regions without being accused by hard-line ideologues of betraying Khomeini's legacy.

Second, Iran has become increasingly vulnerable to security threats emanating from the north while security conditions in the south have remained serious and have worsened in the east. That situation has been the consequence of Iran's geopolitical vulnerability in the post-Soviet era.

Third, Iran wants to find a way out of its isolation and to gain new economic and political partners.

Fourth, Iran's limited economic and financial resources have reduced its ability to sponsor Islamic causes, even if it were so inclined. With respect to peaceful and nonrevolutionary Islamic activities, such as building or repairing mosques and religious schools, Turkey and the Arab countries have done more than Iran. Even in Tajikistan, the country closest to Iran culturally and linguistically, Saudi Arabia has spent more on repairing mosques, sending copies of the Koran, and financing *hajj* pilgrimages to Mecca than has Iran.

POST-SOVIET GEOGRAPHICAL VULNERABILITY AND ITS CONSEQUENCES

The political instability that gripped the Soviet Union in the late 1980s and that finally led to its collapse in December 1991 could not have come at a worse time for Iran. As previously noted, at that time Iran was reeling under the economic and human devastation and the political and psychological crisis caused by its disastrous war with Iraq. Moreover, following the Ayatollah Khomeini's death in June 1989, Iran was engaged in a difficult transition of power.[17] In addition, the Persian Gulf War of January–March 1991, which established a U.S. military presence in the Persian Gulf, caused a dramatic shift in the regional balance of power, thus making Iran potentially more vulnerable on its southern front.

The prospect of instability on its northern frontiers, therefore, was highly disquieting to Iran. This instability was particularly unwelcome because, after two centuries of more or less hostile relations, Iran had finally reached a *modus vivendi* with Russia. This was best exemplified by Soviet Foreign Minister Eduard Shevardnadze's visit to Tehran in February 1989 and his meeting with the Ayatollah Khomeini shortly

before the Ayatollah's death. That historic meeting had significant implications for Soviet-Iranian relations because it meant that Khomeini had
sanctioned close Soviet-Iranian ties, a sanction that extended to Russia
after the Soviet Union's fall.

By 1989, Iran had come to view the Soviet Union as its main economic and military partner and as a major source of much-needed technology and military hardware for the reconstruction of its shattered
economy and military. Iran, therefore, was concerned about all events that
threatened the Soviet Union's stability and the basis of Soviet-Iranian
relations. Because of this concern, when nationalist and Islamic forces
emerged in the Soviet Union's southern republics, Iran reacted with
extreme caution in dealing with them. Even in places such as Azerbaijan,
where the overwhelming majority of people are at least nominally *Shi'a*
and, therefore, likely to be more receptive to the Iranian version of Islam,
the Iranian government reacted cautiously. There were no calls from
Tehran for Muslims to rise up and establish an Islamic republic on the
Iranian model.

This cautious attitude was not supported, however, by all political
factions or by all clerical figures. On the contrary, a number of prominent religious personalities, including some who hailed from the Iranian
province of Azerbaijan, criticized the government's timid approach.
Ayatollah Ardabili, a one-time supreme court judge, stated that Iran's pas-
sivity in responding to the religious yearnings of Soviet Azerbaijanis had
left the field open to other countries, such as Turkey and Egypt, who
might wish to distance them from Iran and their *Shi'a* roots.[18] Iran still
has ties with some Islamic groups in Azerbaijan, including the so-called
Party of Islam (Islam Partisi), which for a time published a newspaper
titled *Islamin Sassi (The Voice of Iran)*. That party has little, if any, influence
in Azerbaijani politics.

Iran did not interfere in the inter-ethnic disputes that erupted in the
Soviet Union's southern republics, instead calling them internal affairs of
the USSR.[19] Iran maintained that attitude even in the face of Soviet
moves such as the introduction of military forces into Baku in January
1990. However, such a cautious attitude did not shield Iran from Soviet
accusations that it was fostering Islamic fundamentalism in Azerbaijan.
That Soviet provocation did not alter Iran's attitude because of the cen-
trality its leadership had conferred on relations with the Soviet Union in
the framework of Iran's overall foreign policy. Iran's attitude also reflected

its growing geopolitical vulnerability, which resulted from the warming of East-West relations and a shift in Soviet foreign policy from a posture of confrontation with the West to one of at least selective cooperation in the context of Gorbachev's "New Thinking."

THE CONSEQUENCES OF SOVIET COLLAPSE FOR IRAN

The collapse of the Soviet Union intensified the systemic changes that the thawing of the Cold War had set in motion in the late 1980s. Those changes further undermined Iran's geopolitical significance and increased its vulnerability to pressures from various international and regional sources. At the international level, eliminating the Soviet counterweight dramatically enhanced the military and economic power of the West, especially that of the United States, along with its ability to project such power without fearing Soviet reaction.

The results of the Persian Gulf War — a conflict that could not have taken place in the manner that it did if the Cold War had not ended by 1990 and if the Soviet Union had not been unraveling economically and politically — further intensified the systemic consequences of the Soviet collapse. The war led to the consolidation of a U.S. military presence in the Persian Gulf and to the establishment of a more open and formal military cooperation between the United States and the Gulf Arab states. This was something those nations had been reluctant to do during the Cold War years, preferring instead to have a U.S. military presence "over the horizon."

In view of the U.S.-Iranian hostility and the declared U.S. policy of containing and weakening Iran, the enhanced U.S. military presence in the Persian Gulf led to a deterioration in Iran's security environment. It should be noted here that the Soviet Union's demise was the main reason the United States was able to pursue a punitive policy toward Iran, when it no longer had to be concerned about potential Soviet gains in Iran.

OTHER REGIONAL ACTORS

The Soviet Union's dissolution also weakened Iran's regional allies while strengthening Iran's rivals. It additionally undermined the cooperative basis of Iran's relations with its neighbors, notably Pakistan and Turkey, and reinforced their competitive and even conflicting dimensions. The reason for this development is quite simple. Eliminating a Soviet threat deprived those countries of their main reason for cooperation: a common fear of Soviet expansion. Moreover, Turkey and Pakistan no longer feared the negative consequences that an Iranian turn toward the Soviet Union could have for their own security. They saw no reason to continue placating Iran, as they had done for most of the postrevolutionary period, despite misgivings about the Islamic Republic's policies and philosophy.

On the contrary, both countries became determined to reduce Iran's regional importance and role — whether in the Persian Gulf or in the southern republics of the former Soviet Union — and to enhance their own position in these areas. This Turkish and Pakistani behavior stemmed in major part from the fact that — at the beginning of the process of East-West rapprochement — both countries had become seriously concerned about their own diminishing importance to their allies. The concerns intensified when, in the late 1980s, some key members of the U.S. Senate said that the United States should reduce its assistance to some countries, including Turkey, because — as East-West tensions eased — they no longer had the same value for the United States. As a result, those countries were trying to find new justification for their continuing value to their allies. One strategy applied by both Pakistan and Turkey was to portray themselves as bulwarks against Iranian influence and the contagious effect of its subversive Islamic ideology, especially in the post-Soviet states.

The negative impact of post-Soviet changes on the character of Iran's regional relations has been most obvious in the case of Pakistan. Through its active support for the viscerally anti-*Shi'a* and anti-Iran Taliban, Pakistan's has pursued a policy of bringing Afghanistan under its own control, and has turned a once close and friendly relationship into one characterized by animosity and mutual suspicion.[20] With Pakistan's development of nuclear weapons and the Taliban's control of areas close to Iran's border, Iran's eastern frontier has become a major security concern.

Until the summer of 1998, Iran's relations with Turkey had not deteriorated to the same extent, although Turkish elements that harbor anti-Iran sentiments have grown stronger. But the coming to power of a coalition government in Turkey, with the participation of the ultra-nationalist MHP, has caused serious deterioration in Turkish-Iranian relations. This was illustrated by the Turkish air attacks on Iranian border areas under the pretext that Iran is harboring PKK terrorists. Turkey has also lent support to political groups in Azerbaijan that have strong anti-Iranian feelings.[21] Iran views the recently concluded Israeli-Turkish alliance, which according to some sources would enable Israel to monitor Iran more effectively, as adversely affecting its security environment.[22]

Two other consequences of the collapse of the Soviet Union have further exacerbated Iran's security problems. The first is the replacement of the Soviet Union, with which Iran had finally achieved reasonably stable relations, with weak and unstable countries, some of which, such as Azerbaijan, have irredentist claims toward Iran.[23] Those countries could cooperate with Iran's other rivals, such as Turkey and the United States, to bring pressure on Iran. To some degree Azerbaijan and Uzbekistan have done so. If the statements of some Azerbaijani officials ever become reality — notably, those made recently by Vafa Gullizade (an adviser to Azerbaijani President Haidar Aliev) that the state would like to host Turkish, NATO, or U.S. military bases on its territory — Iran's encirclement would be complete.[24]

Uzbekistan has portrayed itself as a counterweight to Iranian presence in Central Asia. This strategy has been motivated partly by its desire to ingratiate itself to the West and increase its usefulness. Thus, in 1995 when the United States imposed sanctions on Iran, Uzbekistan was the only regional country that openly supported the U.S. action.[25] Until recently, Uzbekistan justified its animosity toward Iran on the grounds that the latter was spreading Islamic fundamentalism in Central Asia. Although this concern may have played a role in shaping Uzbek views of Iran and its regional role, the more important causes of animosity have been Uzbekistan's regional ambitions and its concerns over the revitalization of Iranian culture in Central Asia, notably in the Tajik cities of Samarkand and Bukhara.[26]

In addition to the direct security threat that Iran could potentially face from some of these new republics, instability in such countries could be a source of security concern, especially in countries that share common borders with Iran, such as Azerbaijan, Armenia, and Turkmenistan. In this context, since the late 1980s, when inter-ethnic conflicts flared up in the South Caucasus, Iran's main preoccupation has been to prevent the large inflow of refugees from the north. Iranian anxiety can be appreciated if we remember that since the early 1980s Iran has been host to more than two million Iraqi and Afghan refugees. Moreover, unlike Pakistan, which received significant amounts of financial assistance to cope with the demands of its Afghan refugees, Iran has received almost no assistance. Only in the past few years has the UN High Commissioner for Refugees (UNHCR) provided some modest help. Therefore, when Armenia captured a significant portion of Azerbaijan's territory in 1993, Iran faced the potential entry of several hundred thousand Azerbaijani refugees and took strict measures to prevent it. Iran did provide assistance to the Azerbaijani refugees and set up tents for them but did so inside the territory of the Azerbaijani Republic.

The upshot of this added sense of vulnerability has been that Iran has viewed any source of conflict and instability in the region, whether of a secular or religious character, as being inimical to its interests. The perception has, in turn, led Iran to adopt an essentially defensive and pro-status-quo strategy. In practical terms, the strategy has led Iran to become active in conflict resolution in the Caucasus and in Central Asia whenever it has been allowed to do so. In Tajikistan the strategy has prompted Iran to promote the theme of regional cooperation in the context of the Economic Cooperation Organization (ECO) and the Organization of the Caspian Sea Littoral States. Given its serious security concerns, Iran could not have afforded to pursue an ideologically inspired policy aimed at fomenting Islamic revolution.

NEW OPPORTUNITIES

The post-Soviet international and regional systems have not been congenial to Iran's interests, as previous paragraphs have illustrated. Nevertheless, the southern belt of the former Soviet Union offered some new opportunities for Iran in both the economic and political fields. Because the Central Asian and Transcaucasian countries are landlocked, Iran offered them the easiest and shortest access route to the outside world. It also portrayed itself as the most convenient gateway to Central Asia and regarded the landlocked countries as potential export markets. Because its relations with the West and its Arab neighbors had been strained, Iran saw these new republics as potential political partners that could help it reduce its isolation.

Perhaps even more important than economic and political considerations was the Iranian belief that because of its long historic and cultural association with the region, Iran has a legitimate role to play in Central

Asia. However, Iran was also aware of the ideological and revolutionary baggage it had accumulated throughout the 1980s and the fact that the West and some regional countries warned the Central Asian states against cooperation with Iran. Before it could establish reasonable ties with the Central Asian countries, Iran had to convince them that it had no subversive or revolutionary intentions. As one observer put it, a major goal of Iranian policy has been to prevent its "demonization" in the eyes of Central Asia. To achieve this goal, Iran has had to pursue a pragmatic policy.[27] Any policy that emphasized the Islamic factor would have been the most serious barrier to achieving Iran's economic, politicocultural, and security objectives in the post-Soviet south.

THE CENTRALITY OF THE RUSSIAN FACTOR

As discussed earlier, the Soviet Union's collapse shifted the balance of international power drastically in favor of the West, especially the United States. Given U.S.-Iranian hostility, this shift has had an adverse impact on Iran's geostrategic conditions. Iran essentially had two choices: one realistic and the other unrealistic. In the realistic option, Iran was to adapt its policies to the new international power equation, to normalize relations with the United States, and to abandon those aspects of its foreign policy that have been principally responsible for its estrangement from the United States. However, Iran's domestic politics, coupled with the ideological residue still prevalent among some members of the Iranian leadership, prevented the adoption of this option despite the increasing pragmatism of Iranian foreign policy during the past decade. The second option, which Iran has chosen, has essentially meant adopting efforts to counteract growing U.S. power and influence by improving ties with other major countries of Europe and Asia.[28]

In the context of Iranian efforts to find counterweights to American power and to sustain a policy of cooperation with the Soviet Union that began in 1989, post-Soviet Russia has continued to occupy an important place in Iran's overall foreign policy, particularly regarding the southern republics of the FSU. Iran has done all it can to maintain good, if not cordial, relations with Russia and to avoid any policy that might antagonize Russia. As noted earlier, Iran pursued this policy even during those times when the Russian leadership was not exactly warm toward Iran.

One certain way for Iran to antagonize Russia would have been to actively support Islamic forces, either in Central Asia or within the

Russian Federation. Iran kept almost completely silent during the Russo-Chechen War, treating the conflict as a Russian internal matter. This silence is perhaps the best example of the priority given to Iranian national interests, as perceived by the leadership, rather than ideological factors or feelings of Islamic solidarity. In addition to factors previously noted, Iran's attitude was determined by its realization that, blocked by the United States and facing stiff competition from other regional powers, it could not play any role in Central Asia without Russia's acquiescence.

It was not until mid-1993, when the Russo-Western honeymoon began to wane and the Euro-Atlanticist theory of Russia's strategic interests began to be challenged by other views, that Russia began to see a certain value in limited cooperation with Iran. The first indication of this reappraisal of Iran's potential role in the post-Soviet south was an article by Dimitri Volsky in the Russian newspaper *New Times*. He argued that in view of Iran's pragmatic and nonideological approach to the post-Soviet Muslim states, Russia should explore the possibility of cooperation with it.[29] Likewise, during a visit to Tehran in 1995, Andranik Mingranyan said "in many areas Iran can be a good and strategic ally of Russia at a global level to check the hegemony of third parties and keep the balance of power." He also reportedly said that "Iran is a big power and Russia can cooperate with Iran and solve many problems in the Transcaucasus region and Central Asia."[30]

Russia has never wanted to treat Iran as a true partner, however, but rather wants to use Iran to the extent that it serves Russian interests. The reasons for this Russian attitude are quite simple. First, Iran could potentially become a rival for Russia in the region. For example, by offering to regional countries some alternative transport links and export outlets for their energy and other products, Iran could reduce those countries' dependence on Russia. Second, Iran's sponsorship of regional cooperation schemes, notably the ECO, could be viewed as undermining Russia's own efforts in the context of the CIS. Third, Russia has been aware all along that — given the U.S. policy of containment and Iran's inability to reestablish ties with the United States — Tehran was dealing with Moscow from a weak strategic position. As a result, Russia has not felt any need to do Iran any special favors to obtain cooperation in areas that Russia has found to be in its interest, such as in bringing peace to Tajikistan.[31]

Russia has made no effort to involve Iran in mediation efforts regarding Nagorno-Karabagh. In Tajikistan, too, Iran was just one of several regional countries, including Pakistan, that were involved in intra-Tajik talks. In 1992, Russia rebuffed Iran's efforts to mediate between the Nabiyev government and the opposition because it wanted to be the principal arbiter in the Tajik dispute and also to use Tajik instability to introduce its troops into the Tajik-Afghan border area.

In the long run, Iran's Russo-centric policy is likely to damage its interests in the region. This would happen if Russia succeeds in tightening its hold on the region, which would mean that it would not need Iranian cooperation, or even if it loses its influence and, therefore, would be of little use or assistance to Iran. If Islamic forces gather strength in some or all of the Central Asian countries, the fact that Iran has not supported them in a tangible way could work against Iran.

LACK OF RECEPTIVITY OF CENTRAL ASIA TO IRANIAN ISLAM

A major reason that Iran has played down the Islamic factor in fashioning its approach toward the Muslim areas of the former Soviet Union has been the lack of receptivity on the part of Central Asian Muslims to Iran's brand of Islam; this derives from four sources.

First is a sectarian divide between Iran and the overwhelming majority of Central Asia's Muslims. Iran is predominantly *Shi'a*, whereas most Central Asians are *Sunni*. Even in places such as Tajikistan, where there is a *Shi'a* minority in the Badakhshan region, these Muslims belong to the *Ismaili* branch of *Shi'ism* rather than to *Twelver Shi'ism*, which is Iran's dominant sect. As a result, since independence and especially in the past five years, the Badakhshanis have increasingly looked to the Agha Khan, the spiritual leader of the Ismailis, for economic and other assistance. The Agha Khan Foundation has been active in developmental and educational activities in the area, such as setting up a university.

Iran's efforts during the past two decades to portray its revolution as a universal phenomenon applicable to all Muslims and to promote *Sunni-Shi'a* reconciliation have not been successful in changing deep-rooted perceptions of Iran's essential character. Therefore, the *Sunni* world — both Arab and non-Arab — has continued to view Iran as essentially *Shi'a*; hence, Iran's model of social and political organization is seen as not being suited to other Muslims. The initial widespread interest in and admiration for the Iranian revolution was produced largely by a feeling that Iran had stood up to the great powers, rather than by accepting its ideology's virtues. The Iranian revolution's failure to deliver on its promises and the ideological backlash that has already begun in Iran against the Islamic system has further eroded Iran's appeal.

Tajikistan's Islamic leaders, including those closest to Iran such as Qadi Akbar Turajonzadeh, have on many occasions stated that deep differences between Iranian and Tajik Islam make establishing an Iranian-style government in Tajikistan unlikely. Turajonzadeh added that Tajikistan will not import the model of another Islamic country, such as Pakistan, and that it must develop its own Tajik model.[32] Another leader of the Tajik Muslims, Said Abdullah Nouri, has said that establishing any kind of an Islamic state in Tajikistan would take at least thirty years. Islam plays a very limited role in the feelings of pro-Iranian Tajiks. Rather, they are motivated by a shared Iranian culture, including a pre-Islamic Iranian civilization and a common language. The most important gathering that brought the Tajiks and the Iranians together was the celebration of the one thousandth anniversary of the famous composer of the pre-Islamic Sassanid court, Barbadh. This cultural bond has led some secular Tajik opposition figures, such as Tajik Democratic Party head, Yousof Shadman, to seek refuge in Iran — at least for a time.

Second, throughout the Cold War, Iran had joined the Western camp, Soviet-Iranian relations were often tense, and contacts between Central Asian Muslims and Iran were limited. For example, in *The Islamic Threat to the Soviet State*, Alexandre Bennigsen and Marie Broxup list a number of visits paid by Soviet Muslims to Islamic countries between 1968 and 1979. The list includes such diverse countries as Morocco, Algeria, Mali, Niger, Saudi Arabia, and even Turkey, but there is no mention of a single visit to Iran. Similarly, while some Central Asians studied in Arab countries (for instance, Turajonzadeh studied in Jordan for a period), no such exchanges took place with Iran. No Soviet Azerbaijanis were studying in Qum.

The situation did not change after the Iranian revolution, as the Soviets increasingly came to see Islam as a political and intellectual rival to communism. Since the Central Asian states' independence, contacts with Iran have increased, but the basic differences in Iranian and Central Asian Islam, combined with Iran's limited financial resources, have meant that, so far, the contacts have not been very extensive.

Third, in the past two decades the principal intellectual influence on the Central Asian Muslims has emanated from Arab sources, Pakistan, and Afghanistan, especially through various Afghan *mujahidin* groups. For a variety of reasons, Iran was not deeply involved in the Afghan War or in training the Afghan *mujahidin*. The most important reason was Iranian preoccupation with Iran's war against Iraq. Equally important is the fact that the United States was the principal power organizing and financing Afghan resistance to Soviet invasion. Given U.S.-Iranian hostility, neither side would have been willing to cooperate closely.

Fourth, most *mujahidin* groups were Sunni and Pushtun and had already been influenced by the Saudi brand of Islam; thus, they were neither well disposed toward Iran nor receptive to its ideology. Even Ahmad Shah Masud, the Persian-speaking Tajik leader of a group of *mujahidin*, was not pro-Iran. The relationship between the two sides improved only after the growth and victory of the Taliban. The only group in Afghanistan that was receptive to Iranian influence and received help from it was the *Shi'a* Hazaras and their group, the Hizb-e-Vahdat.

CONCLUSIONS

Despite the expectation that Iran would use its own model of an Islamic society and polity to fill the ideological and political vacuum created in the southern belt of the former Soviet Union, during the past ten years Islamic ideology and the Islamic factor have played a surprisingly negligible role in determining Iran's policy toward the former Soviet south. In fact, security concerns, followed by economic interests and a desire to be a player in the region's economic and social evolution, have shaped Iran's policy toward Central Asia. Three factors have been primarily responsible for this approach: first, the gradually declining role of ideology in Iranian foreign policy in the post-Iran-Iraq period and the reassertion of the demands of national interest; second, the enhanced geopolitical vulnerability of Iran following the Soviet Union's fall, coupled with the U.S.' policy of containing and isolating Iran; and third, the lack of receptivity of Central Asians to Iranian Islam.

However, Iran's pragmatic and nonideological policy toward Central Asia has not been sufficient to secure Iran an important economic and political role in the region. Iran has been prevented from establishing a significant economic or political presence in the region because of Iran's economic and financial difficulties, the active U.S. discouragement of ties between Iran and the Central Asian states, and the U.S. Dual Containment strategy. The result is Iran's limited ability to be an important economic partner for those countries. Its pragmatic policy, its emphasis on state-to-state relations, and its patience in the face of strong hostility on the part of some countries have, nevertheless, gone a long way to dissipate earlier misgivings of Central Asian countries. Indeed, today Iran is no longer seen as the principal source of Islamic propaganda in Central Asia or as the main provider of assistance to its Islamic groups. This changed view has enabled Iran to counteract some effects of the U.S. policy of isolation and to develop a foothold in the former Soviet south. This achievement should enable Iran to expand its ties further with Central Asia when U.S.-Iran relations improve, and when the United States eases its policy of containment.

However, should Islamic forces gather more strength in Central Asia and perhaps challenge the existing leaderships, Iran's position may suffer. The only exceptions would be Tajikistan (where other ties bind the two countries together and where Iran has developed good ties with the Islamic opposition) and possibly Azerbaijan (where the common *Shi'a* faith could bring the two sides closer together). It is unlikely that fundamentalists would be able to challenge seriously the existing governments; therefore, Iran's cautious policy, which emphasizes state-to-state relations, should prove to be the wisest choice.

193

Chapter Three

Turkish Identity Politics and Central Asia

M. Hakan Yavuz[1]

INTRODUCTION

After the War of Liberation, the modern Turkish Republic, under the leadership of Mustafa Kemal, pursued radical civilizational reorientation to transform the multiethnic and multireligious Ottoman society into a homogenous Turkish nation. In this top-down revolutionary effort, the governing elite used secularism as a constituting and guiding principle, in accordance with the antireligious model of the French Revolution. To create a homogenized, secular nation-state, Turkey used various strategies to eliminate ethnic, religious, and economic differences. Any attempt to challenge this program was perceived as backsliding and referred to as reactionary.[2] The modern history of Turkey, therefore, is the story of a struggle between the state's efforts at social transformation to engineer a new society and its traditional ethnic and religious movements. One of the ironies of the Kemalist project was that as it assaulted ethnic and religious loyalties, it simultaneously stimulated ethnic and religious consciousness.

The foreign policy of Turkey has been subordinated to domestic identity politics. The Republican elite's main goal was to anchor Turkey in the West in order to realize the goal of becoming a civilized (i.e., European) nation-state.[3] The Republican elite quite brutally removed Islam and subregional identities from the public realm and replaced them with a linguistic and territorial-based Turkish nationalism.[4] Since the introduction of the neo-liberal economic policies of Turgut Özal (Prime Minister from 1983 to 1993), and the collapse of the Soviet Union and Yugoslavia, the contradictions and tensions in the national orientation of Turkey have been further highlighted. This domestic and international

conjuncture is crucial for understanding Turkey's ambiguous and competing policies toward Central Asia.

The Europhile Turkish elite (though often only in a superficial sense)
determines official policy, and the Islamo-Turkish masses (who have a
very different conception of the past) seek different headings for the ship
of state. This duality of different cultures and identities is at the center of
the current foreign policy debate in Turkey.[5]

Since the collapse of the Soviet Union and the neo-liberal economic
policies of Özal, Turkey has been struggling to redefine itself with or
without democratic means. This crisis-driven identity debate in Turkey has
greatly shaped its foreign policy toward Central Asia. Turkey's foreign policy is very much conditioned by the domestic fault line between the
Kemalist establishment and the Turkish-Islamic population. To understand
the shifting strategies and orientations of Turkish foreign policy, one needs
to unpack the Turkish identity debate and examine its implications on
foreign policy decisions. Identity politics explain the current disconcerting
sense of betrayal among the ostensibly Westernized elite in Turkey (sadly
though, their understanding of Westernization rarely includes an appreciation for democracy, freedom of thought, and respect for human rights). It
also explains their endeavor to create a community of Turkic states to
overcome Turkey's increasing isolation in the international system.

TURKEY'S FOREIGN POLICY

Turkish state identity is constituted as a result of seismic international
events that have directly affected Turkey's perception of the "self" and the
domestic transformation of elite politics. The historical legacy of the
Ottoman state and its "culture of insecurity" are the two fundamental
constraints in the evolution of a state identity in Turkey. The way in
which the Turkish state perceives itself often depends on the perception
of Turkey by foreign states, particularly by the leading members of the
Western bloc. The European Union's (EU) dismissive treatment of Turkey
affected Turkey's conception of self, and this perception has been reflected in Turkey's conduct of foreign policy. In addition to the self of the
Turkish state there is the self of the Turkish nation, which is more
dynamic and open to change than the official discourse of the state. At
the moment, the Turkish nation is held hostage by its own Kemalist ideology. Its Islamic and Turkic layers of identity have been underscored to
overcome a deep identity crisis.

In the crises in Bosnia and Kosovo, the state stressed its Ottoman and Islamic identity, whereas in Central Asia it stresses the Turkic layer of its identity. These layers of identity are open to internal and external changes. There are three major identity-driven elite factions in Turkey. They are Islamic, Turkic, and European:

- The Kemalist elite has supported Turkey's full integration into the EU, as well as its close ties with the United States. In terms of their ideology, members of this group have professed to view their ties with Europe as being based more on civilization than on national interest. However, they have been quite willing to denounce Europe or the United States whenever pressure has been brought to bear upon the Turkish establishment in terms of respecting democracy and human rights. They tend to treat the "new Turkic world" as a source of increasing Turkey's importance in Europe and in the international system. They present Turkey as a "secular state model" for new independent Muslim states.

- The Muslim/Islamist elite has supported close ties with Muslim countries, thereby subordinating an ethnic identity to a religious one. This group is not inherently anti-Western. Instead, it views Russia and the Orthodox world as its historic rival. Its view toward Central Asia is colored by Islamic solidarity; it also endeavors to present Turkey as a protector of Muslims in the Balkans and the former Soviet Union. Members of this group seek cooperation with the Turkic republics and the Balkan states to form the core of an Islamic bloc. The Islamists see Central Asia as a part of an Islamic community.

- The Turkic elite includes groups who support cultural and political cooperation — and even integration — among Turkic states. This group includes some ultranationalists, who disagree with Turkey's full integration with the EU. This group seeks to form a Turkic world under the leadership of Turkey.

FROM TURKEY *IN* EUROPE TO TURKEY *AND* EUROPE

Since the late nineteenth century, many in the Turkish elite have been reluctant to consider themselves as an integral part of the Middle East or the Islamic world. The demand for acceptance into Europe has been a constant aspect of Turkey's foreign policy. According to a recent survey, Turkish youth prefer that Turkey first become a member of the EU, next a member of a Turkic bloc, and then a member of the Organization of the Islamic Conference and a Balkan regional bloc.[6]

Moreover, the modern Turks measure their achievements through European acceptance. There are two reasons the Turks want to be a part of Europe. First is the Ottoman legacy. The Ottoman social, cultural, and political life was marked and oriented by the Balkan Muslims. The Ottoman Empire was a southeastern European empire more than an Anatolian or Middle Eastern one. The construction of the Ottoman State and Turkish identity took place in the Balkan frontiers rather than in the East; the Ottoman cultural and social networks were the densest between the Danube and the Drina Rivers. Consequently, most of the governing elite and scholars came from the Balkans. There were more Ottoman mosques, cultural institutions, and architectural monuments in the Balkans than in Anatolia or other parts of the Empire.

Second is the identity of the modern Turkish population, which was very much molded and shaped during the disintegration of the Ottoman Empire between 1878 and 1921. The forced mass exodus of Muslims from the Balkans constituted the political elite of the modern Republic.[7]

With modernizing reforms, Kemal sought to Europeanize, at least in its outward forms, the Turkish national identity.[8] The reforms initiated a process of becoming European that was carried out by an ideologically committed elite that consolidated itself by subscribing to a naive Kemalist version of Westernization, such as positivism. The process of becoming European helps to explain why Turkey joined the European Council in 1949, NATO in 1952, and the European Economic Community with the Rome Treaty in 1963. The Cold War and Soviet threats further consolidated the elite's vision of joining all European institutions. The ideological identity of the elite and the Soviet threat helped to create a shared consensus in support of full Europeanization.

In short, although Turkey's Western-oriented foreign policy was an outcome of its struggle to become European, the Soviet threat accentuated the process. During the Cold War years, Turkey's foreign policy became an extension of its relations with NATO. The anticommunist stand of most nationalist and Muslim groups helped to consolidate the legitimacy of the homogenizing Turkish State. However, the Turkish Republic was never considered truly European both because of its undemocratic and illiberal character and because of its Ottoman-Islamic heritage.

After Turkey's integration into NATO, a "European Turkey" became the dominant orientation of Ankara's foreign policy. The Cypriot crisis and other events opened a debate over foreign policy orientation in Turkey, but the fundamental course of foreign policy remained European in direction. The EC's negative response to Turkey's membership application in 1989 constituted a turning point in the evolution of domestic identity, which, in turn, created a confused orientation in foreign policy.[9] Some in the Turkish elite realized the difficulty of integrating into the nascent EU in the late 1980s and decided to find solace in Central Asia and the Balkans.[10] Finally, Ankara would later try to overcome its exclusion from Europe by developing closer ties with the United States through Israel.

The EU's rejection was a major defeat in the Kemalist ideological efforts to create a homogenous (Turkish) and civilized (European) nation.[11] Because there is no possibility of integration with Europe to contain Turkish nationalism, nationalism has been further politicized in reaction to the Kurdish question. The 1997 "soft-military coup," and some shortsighted EU policies, drastically changed the dynamics of Turkish-European relations.

TURKEY *WITH* THE TURKIC REPUBLICS

In the formative years of Turkish nationalism, "outside Turks" played an important role in its formulation and articulation.[12] Tatars developed the first indigenous bourgeoisie and intellectual class in the Turkic world to raise Turko-Islamic consciousness. The leading Tatar intellectuals — Abdunnasir Kursavi (1771 – 1812), Sehabettin Mercani (1818 – 1889), Hüseyin Feyizhani (1828 – 1866) and Kayyum Nasiri (1824 – 1902) — sought to reexamine Islamic teaching to raise religious and national consciousness. This was the first indigenous modernist movement in the Islamic world. Within the discursive tradition of Turkish nationalism, ethnic and religious forms have often been mutually constitutive because of the positive role of *jadid* (Muslim progressive reform movement of the nineteenth century) modernism.[13]

During the disintegration of the Ottoman Empire, there was a great popular desire to free captive Turks from the hegemony of Russia. Some of the most prominent theoreticians of Turkish nationalism — such as Ismail Gaspirali, Yusuf Akçura, Abdürresid Ibrahim, Ali Merdan Topçubasi, Hüseyinzade Ali Bey and Ahmet Ağaoğlu — were émigrés from "outside

Turkish" communities in Russia.[14] This critical group of intellectuals stressed the mutually constitutive role of ethnicity and religion in constructing Turkish nationalism. In short, protonational feelings of collectively belonging to a shared Turkic language and religion were transformed into a national Turkish identity.

The enthusiasm for developing close ties with outside Turks and for freeing them from the Russian yoke came to an end when Kemal decided to focus on domestic politics and to establish close ties with Bolshevik Russia.[15] Between 1923 and 1991, the governments of Turkey pursued a policy that ignored the presence of the Turkic world in Russia, and remained indifferent to the plight of those Turks.[16] However, at the societal level, interactions between the Central Asian diaspora communities outside Turkey and the people still within Turkey continued.

Although pan-Turkism became a motivating force for ultranationalists, and although this idea was institutionalized with the establishment of the Nationalistic Movement Party (MHP), pan-Turkism never shaped Turkish foreign policy and thus remained a marginal movement.[17] With the participation of the MHP in the National Front coalitions during the mid-1970s, the terminology used by outside Turks was partially integrated into the official Turkish discourse. However, neither the diaspora nor the MHP significantly influenced Turkish foreign policy toward the Soviet Union. For a while, any public debate or mention about the existence of outside Turks was disapproved of, as being a sign of ultranationalism. The Turkish governing elite either denied or ignored the existence of the outside Turks. Turkey, therefore, has had very limited formal study of the Turkic world during the Republican period. Any interest or debate over the situation of the outside Turks was treated as backsliding from the Kemalist goal of Europeanization.

The idea of "Turkey *with* the Central Asian republics" is an outcome of the sudden collapse of the Soviet Union, the EU's exclusionary policies against Turkey, and a rising Turkish nationalism. After 1991, Turkey sought to overcome its isolation and the sense of alienation in Europe and the Islamic world by searching for its Eastern roots in Central Asia.[18] Turkey's rediscovery of the Turkic world in the East has opened a new debate over the country's identity and foreign policy. This newly discovered Turkic identity punctuates Ankara's foreign policy and constitutes its self-esteem. This new discovery also affirms the core identity of the Turkish State. When Kurdish and Islamic voices have contested the core identity, foreign policy officials have become embroiled in identity politics. Although the new world system has created windows of opportunities for the Turkish state, its population is experiencing a formative moment, a time when its identity is being contested and reformed. Old identity frames are not useful for understanding new realities within and outside Turkey.

FROM INDIFFERENCE TO BIG BROTHER (1991 – 93)

When the Soviet Union started to collapse and Azerbaijan declared its independence on August 30, 1991, the change took the Turkish government by surprise.[19] The Bush Administration encouraged Ankara to play an active role in Central Asia to counter the fear of Iranian influence in the region. Ankara recognized all the newly independent Turkic states with the blessings of the United States and without defining Turkey's short- and long-term interests in Central Asia.

In 1991, many Western governments supported and even pushed Turkey to play a leading role for the newly independent Muslim states in Central Asia.[20] Turkey was expected to contain Iranian penetration and to supplant the Russian role in the region by offering a Turkish model of secular democracy, market economics, and pro-Western orientation for the new independent Turkic states to pursue.[21] The government in Ankara tried to use this opportunity to stress its strategic importance as an inevitable bridge between Asia and Europe and to consolidate Turkey's position in Europe. By 1999, Turkey's foreign policy toward the Turkic nations had been shaped by the mixed ideological and material interests that are at the center of the evolution of Turkey's Central Asian policy:

- Turkey's search for a new identity in domestic politics and a new role in foreign policy;
- Turkey's attempt to overcome its isolation in the West and in the Islamic world by developing a new Turkic grouping;
- Turkey's attempt to have access to the rich oil and gas reservoirs in Central Asia; and
- Turkey's search for new markets.

Özal was the first Turkish leader with a clear global vision that saw the importance of playing a more activist role in Central Asia and the Balkans. He even argued that the "twenty-first century will be the century of the Turks."[22] He was in favor of creating an economic and cultural union with Central Asian Turkic states. Özal always treated shared cultural norms as the basis for solidarity and cooperation among Turkic people. He argued, "our people are expecting regional cooperation among our countries because we are from the same origin. We are the branches of the same great tree and we are a big family."[23] He developed close ties with Central Asian leaders and did not hesitate to appeal to purported Islamic and Turkish bonds.[24]

Ankara's ultimate goal has been to create a forum for Turkic cooperation, not unity. Turkey took several measures to develop its relations with Turkic states. It first tried to anchor the new republics into the Economic Cooperation Organization (ECO), which Iran, Pakistan, and Turkey founded as a framework of cooperation. Then, in 1992, Turkey established the Turkish International Cooperation Agency, known as TIKA, to "coordinate, navigate, and implement economic, cultural, and social projects" in Turkic republics and other neighboring countries.[25] The goal of this agency is to facilitate a transition to democracy and free markets by helping these countries in the areas of economic and legal reforms; by improving education, transportation, and communication; and by establishing small and medium enterprises. The first act of TIKA was to organize a Turkic summit by inviting the heads of the independent Turkic republics to Ankara on October 20, 1992, to celebrate the seventieth anniversary of the establishment of the Republic of Turkey.[26]

During the first summit, the republic Presidents — Nursultan Nazarbayev, Askar Akaev, Islam Karimov, Safarmurad Niyazov, and Ebulfez Elchibey — signed the Ankara Declaration. In its introduction, the Presidents stressed common history, language, and culture as a basis for developing close cooperation among such states. The Ankara Declaration expressed their intentions to develop closer ties. These rediscovered affinities have not yet been fully translated into solidarity and action. However, on the basis of the Ankara Declaration, Turkey focused on a common alphabet, language, and education to create shared feelings and understanding within the Turkic world. Because of internal differences, it will take a long time to form a security and peace community. The second summit took place in Istanbul on October 18 – 19, 1994, the third one in Bishkek on August 28, 1995, and the fourth summit took place on October 21, 1996, in Tashkent. Although Turkey suggested a formal structure of Turkish cooperation, Kazakstan and the other Turkic republics did not support it. These informal summits have continued as discussion forums, but without many formal results.

The most crucial step that Ankara took in the early 1990s was establishing air links with most of the Turkic Republics and Tatarstan. Ankara helped these states establish their own independent digital phone system, and some of the states still use Turkish communication satellites.

Ankara also used its limited resources to create a shared cultural language and to consolidate the Turkish aspect of their shared history.[27] It introduced a transnational television channel, TRT Avrasya, to beam Turkish cultural and language programming to the region. Although TRT Avrasya sought to raise the consciousness of the people of Central Asia to realize their common heritage with the Turks of Turkey, it highlighted sociocultural differences. Moreover, Ankara offered 10,000 university scholarships to the students of Turkic republics, and thousands of these students traveled to Turkey to study. (See Appendix Two.)

In addition, the Ministry of Education has opened eighteen high schools in the Central Asian Republics and Azerbaijan. The community of Fethullah Gülen, a leader of a Nurcu movement, opened 110 high schools and several universities in the Turkic Republics and other autonomous regions in the Russian Federation.[28]

These schools have become very popular in the republics because of their bilingual programs in English and local languages and because of the high quality of teaching in the physical sciences.[29]

Although Turkey made some long-term investments in the field of education, a number of factors helped to dissipate Turkish romanticism toward Central Asia. The year 1993 was critical because Ankara was forced to reexamine its ties with the region. Because of their geographical connections, and their linguistic and cultural affinity, Turkey developed close ties with Azerbaijan, and those relations were treated as a model for other Turkic republics.[30] However, Russia used all means to intervene in Azerbaijani domestic politics in order to test Turkish resolve and to demonstrate Ankara's weaknesses. The major setback to Turkey's rising influence was the Armenia-Azerbaijan conflict, which highlighted the failure of Turkey to help Baku against an Armenian invasion in 1993. The removal of the pro-Turkish Ebulfeyz Elchibey from power further demonstrated the limits of Ankara's abilities. Thus, the Azerbaijan-Armenia conflict and its political consequences derailed the Turkish dream of becoming a big brother in the region.

After Turgut Özal, Süleyman Demirel — who was the most timid, subservient, and least visionary Turkish politician — dominated relations with the Central Asian states. Demirel personalized the relations with the Turkic states. During the Demirel era, some of Turkey's approaches to the region were similar to Russia's colonial attitude. It did not take long for people to realize that not Turks but rather Kazaks, Kyrgyz, and Uzbeks lived in this region and had their own perceptions of history and culture.[31] At the same time, many Turks became aware of the gap between the imagined Turkish world and the reality of six different sovereign nation-states with their own particular interests. Moreover, as Turkey insisted that the Central Asians be renamed as *Türk*, they insisted that a *Türk* meant a citizen of Turkey more than the generic name of the Turkic peoples of Central Asia.

FROM BIG BROTHERLY ASPIRATIONS TO NORMALIZATION (1993 – PRESENT)

After realizing both its limits and the differences within and between different Turkic states and regions, Ankara pursued a more cautious policy. Its main goal is to create a Turkish space by using economic and cultural factors in what is still an unfolding and very dynamic region. However, Ankara was confronted with a set of obstacles in consolidating its relations with Central Asia. The main internal obstacles are the domestic divisions and the weak coalition governments, limited economic resources, and lack of proper information about the region. Externally, Turkey's conduct in Central Asia has been conditioned by the human rights question and by Russian policies to restrict Turkey's influence.

Turkey's ties with Central Asian states are not totally determined by the foreign ministry; sizeable and influential civic pressure groups have an effect. These diverse economic and social groups ask Ankara to meet their needs in the region. Moreover, there is a growing tension within different sectors of these pressure groups. The ideological and social fault lines of Turkey have been carried out to the region by the official and unofficial Turkish presence there. It is easy to find many competing and conflicting circles of Turkish interest groups, which range from pan-Turkish nationalists to pan-Islamists, and from short-sited carpetbaggers to long-term investors. The diversity and complexity of Turkey have been reflected in the 1,616 Turkish firms and 134 Turkish associations in

Central Asia. The Turkish reality with all of its complexity now exists in Central Asia.

By 1998, the Turkish Eximbank offered $1.2 billion credits to develop trade between the Central Asian states and Turkey. Trade between the Central Asia republics and Turkey is currently above $1 billion. Turkish construction firms have more than $1.7 billion worth of projects within the Turkic republics.[32] In addition to the limited economic resources of Turkey, geographic distance and transportation problems have constrained the development of trade between Turkey and Turkic republics.

One of the major external constraints, in addition to human rights problems, is the Russian factor. For several reasons, Russia wants to develop closer ties with Turkey. Turkey is Russia's main trading partner in the Middle East. Trade between the two countries ranges between $11 billion and $12 billion a year. Turkish construction firms have been involved in major projects, and they even reconstructed the Duma, which was damaged during the abortive anti-Yeltsin coup in 1993. Many Russian tourists are visiting Turkey, and they have rejuvenated the small goods trade in Istanbul. Turkey is the major purchaser of gas from Russia, which encourages the powerful Gasprom conglomerate to promote Turko-Russian ties and to promote better understanding between the two countries. Moreover, Russia is a new and unconditional source of military hardware because some European countries refuse to sell arms to Turkey because of the Kurdish conflict.

Sets of factors, however, do create a constant tension between the two countries, such as the intense competition over gas and oil pipelines in the Caucasus and Central Asia. Turkey is lobbying for a Kazak and Azerbaijani oil pipeline to go through Georgia to the Turkish port of Ceyhan rather than to the Russian port of Novorossisk through Chechnya. To prevent environmental damage and to protect Istanbul, the government of Turkey is already regulating traffic along the Bosporus and Dardanelles. Russia has offered a new route through Bulgaria to Greece, thereby bypassing Turkey. Finally, the major source of tension is Russia's wariness of Turkey's support for the Chechen fighters and other ethnic Muslim groups in the North Caucasus. Because of the lack of centralized authority in Moscow, Russia has been pursuing conflicting policies toward Turkey.

As Turkey's economic ties with Russia rapidly expand, Ankara becomes more sensitive to Russian needs and influence in Central Asia.

In other words, Turkey's identity and interest-based politics are in conflict as far as its policies toward Central Asia and Russia are concerned.

SOURCES OF IDENTITY POLITICS IN TURKISH FOREIGN POLICY: TURKISH-ISLAM[33]

Islam and Turkic identity inhibits Turkey's behavior toward Russia and facilitates close ties with the Central Asian states. Turkey's policy toward the region evolves more slowly than one might otherwise expect because the role and meanings of Turkish identity are still very much contested at home. With its multiple identities, Turkey is acting differently in the international system. The Turkified-Islamic identity, or Turkish-Islam, has been the most powerful cognitive identity map to define national interest and it is used as a tool to promote the interests of Turkey. Turkish-Islam has three major differentiating characteristics among the five major zones of Islam: Arabic, African, Malay, Persian, and Turkic. These characteristics are Sufi-oriented, state-centric, and more mixed with vernacular cultures.

Although it was Arab invaders who took Islam to the region in the eighth century, the conversion patterns and sociocultural structure created a vernacular Turkic-Islam. Saman and Kam, as legendary religious and charismatic leaders, converted to Islam and became Sufi dervishes, known as *baba* and *ata*.[34] They personified the old religion and became the agents of Islamization in Central Asia. The new faith was internalized through vernacular narratives and the syncretization of older traditions. Islam, as a new faith, was regarded as a part of native culture because of its ability to enhance and build upon important facets of the old shamanism.[35] This symbiosis between different cultures and religions in the region helped to produce three major Sufi orders: Yeseviyye, Kübreviyye, and Naksibendiyye.

Ahmet Yesevi (d. 1166), the founder of Yeseviyye order, became very influential among tribes of Kazaks and Kyrgyz by reinterpreting Islam to accommodate nomadic lifestyles.[36] He did not seek to negate old customs and traditions, but rather he used them to disseminate Islamic teaching. His followers collected his teachings in a book, known as the Divan-I Hikmet. This work heavily influenced the Anatolian Sufi poet Yunus Emre, which was one of the first literary Turkish works on Islam. Although he knew Arabic and Persian, Yesevi wrote his teachings in the vernacular Turkic dialect to communicate with the people of the region. Many Central Asian Turks regard the teachings of Ahmet Yesevi as a part of their shared Turkic tradition. Yeseviyye became the intellectual origin of Naksibendiyye and Bektasiyye, an Anatolian syncretic Sufi order, in Turkey. Thus, Yesevi and his vernacularized understanding of Islam has been the dominant form of Islam in the Turkic world.

Because the first converts were the local *khans* (tribe leaders) and because the population followed the top-down conversion, Islam has always been an ideology of power and social control. Some nomadic societies treated Islam as the conquering ideology of a sedentary population. Islam mixed with local customs (*Adat*) and set the parameters of social interactions in the Turkic world. One main characteristic of Islamization was localizing the religion within the region, thus creating a powerful connection between local culture and Islam.

When the dynastic states weakened between the sixteenth and nineteenth centuries, Islam became the glue of civil society and social capital. This connection was reproduced with the age of nationalism in the nineteenth century. Sufi orders became the major institutions for reconciling the local culture with universal Islamic norms. The same orders were at the center of an ethnoreligious revival, known as *jadidism* in Russia and the Turkic world. This would greatly influence Turkish nationalism.

Against the colonial penetration of the elite, the *jadid* movement sought to construct a Turkistani identity by reimagining a modernist Islam. The *jadid* movement played a key role in articulating of national identities. In short, the Turkistani identity and the local identities were reimagined within this spiritual domain of Islam. Turkic and Islamic identity were used interchangeably which, in turn, played a constitutive role in forming national identities of the new Central Asian states. Therefore, religious networks played an important role in Turkish relations with Central Asia.

Islam in Central Asia and Russia does not easily denote a religious category *per se*; instead it is an ethnocultural category. Thus, the boundary between religion and ethnicity is blurred and in flux, similar to that of Turkey. The overwhelming population of the region is *Sunni* and belongs to the Hanafi (one the four branches of *Sunni* Islam) school of law. Ethnic or cultural revival usually takes Islamic forms without necessarily being religious. The Islam of Central Asia in the late nineteenth century (*jadidism*) was the engine of modernism and helped to highlight the difference between the Turkic groups and the dominant Russians.[37] Under communist rule, the peoples of the region created a sacred territory through imagined and invented holy places and cemeteries to maintain and perpetuate their conception of Islam. They also maintained their distinctions from the ruling Russian colonialism through circumcision, wedding ceremonies, and burial rites. Therefore, Russian academics and politicians frequently labeled all cultural revival and identity claims as reactionary and fundamentalist.

Because of this symbiotic relationship between ethnicity and religion in Central Asia, the Soviet Union engineered a number of national identities to curb the potential unification of the region along Islamic or Turkistani lines. In the 1920s Moscow divided the region into five independent republics by highlighting ethnic and cultural nuances, and by creating territorial national identities. Disparate dialects were made standardized national languages, and national histories were even constructed in Moscow to be consumed by the elites of the region. Moreover, the construction of separate economies and administrative units helped to consolidate separate national identities. In the 1980s a weak and fragmented national awakening punctuated major sociopolitical events.[38] This national revival took Islamic coloring, and Islam became the language of opposition against the heavy-handed Soviet policies and the local communist elites who sought to take over.

During the 1970s and 1980s many Western scholars looked to Islam as the force that would undermine communist rule. Throughout the Soviet period, the scholarship of the Central Asian peoples was dominated by Cold War convictions, and Alexander Benningsen (1913-88) dominated the field of study. He constantly presented Muslims as being the weakest integrated part of the Soviet system because of the role of Islam. Scholars also presented ambiguous Islamic loyalties as being a form of Muslim nationalism.[39] In 1982, Benningsen argued that:

> Soviet Muslims . . . are likely to be influenced by the ideas (perhaps even by the political terrorism and guerilla methods) adopted from the newly radicalized Middle East. These ideas, ranging from the most conservative religious fundamentalism to the wildest revolutionary, share one common characteristic: the potential for destabilizing Soviet Islam, thereby undermining the stability of the USSR itself.[40]

This orientalizing thesis dominated studies in the area, and American scholar Michael Rywkin of the City University of New York even popularized this view. A closer examination indicates that Islam did not play a significant role in the demise of the Soviet Union. Its collapse resulted from groups in the European part of the Soviet Union rather than its Muslim borderlands. Most of the Central Asian Republics, which were dominated by cliques of notoriously corrupt *nomenclatura*, were in favor of preserving the Union.

The conflicts between Uzbeks and Meskhetian Turks in 1989, and between Kyrgyz and Uzbeks in 1990, indicated that not Islamic loyalty but rather more narrow loyalties were more dominant.[41] The modern revival of Islam in the Central Asian context means the rebirth and consolidation of ethnocultural identity, not the appropriation of Islamic fundamentalism from the Middle East.[42]

In Turkic-Islam, the boundary between ethnic and religious identity is codeterminant and fluid. As the nations of Central Asia seek to construct their collective memories to consolidate their selfhood, Islam is used as a leading source for that purpose. The Islam of Central Asia is a historical partner to nation building. However, with the collapse of the Soviet Empire, the people of the region are searching for another partner to consolidate their national identity. Those peoples have been trying to nationalize and parcel out the shared legacy of the region. For instance, the Kyrgyz stress their mythical hero, Manas, who illustrates the pre-Islamic origins of the Kyrgyz. The Kazaks bring Abai, their writer and poet, as a synthesizer of Islamic and Kazak roots. Turkmen are seeking to embody their roots in terms of pet Machtumquli. The Uzbeks have been busily differentiating themselves from other Central Asiatic nations by highlighting Amir Temur as a state-builder and as the founder of the Uzbek nation.

TURKEY'S ISLAMIZATION PROJECT

Turkey has been trying to use this commonly shared ethnoreligious culture to create a number of institutions that will develop cooperation. Institutionalization in the religious domain is well advanced and still developing. Turkey has developed ties with the first two of three layers of Central Asian Islam. These layers are official, folk (Sufi brotherhoods), and the *efsanevi* (legendary) Islam.[43]

Official Islam

Establishment Islam was articulated in the form of the four Spiritual Boards of Directorate set up in Tashkent, Baku, Makhachkala, and Ufa in 1943 by Stalin. They aimed for the secularization and ultimate dissolution of Islam. These boards had administrative authority to regulate religious affairs of the state. They stressed that Islam is not opposed to Communism but rather could coexist in harmony. With new-found independence, the states formed their own national religious administration, and the government of Turkey has been more active in the distribution of religious material and training of religious functionaries. In other words, the Directorate of Religious Affairs of Turkey has tried to carry out a re-Islamization of Central Asia.

The Foundation of Turkish Religious Affairs, known as Türk Diyanet Vakfi (TDV), is an official state-run foundation. It has been at the forefront for exporting a "soft and nationalized Turkish Islam" to Central Asia. The head of the Directorate, Mehmet N. Yilmaz, defines Turkish national identity in terms of Islam. Yilmaz argues, "if we take those acquired Islamic characteristics out of Turkish national identity, there will be a little left behind. Islam molds Turkish national identity. Islam is both reason and guarantor of our national existence."[44]

Turkey has been very active in Central Asia. Before the soft coup in Turkey on February 28, 1997, the Directorate was the most powerful institution in the region. It organized the first Eurasian Islamic Congress on October 23 – 25, 1995, by inviting the heads of twenty-one countries and autonomous regions. The Second Eurasia Congress, which included thirty-two countries and autonomous regions, took place during October 21 – 24, 1996, and institutionalized itself by establishing a permanent secretariat in Ankara.[45] The Third Eurasia Islamic Congress took place between May 25 – 29, 1998, in Ankara. The Republic of Turkey has managed to become the main center for Islamic activism and a source of support for Turkish and Muslim communities.[46] Turkey has constructed thirty mosques in the newly independent Turkic regions.[47] Between 1992 and 1998, the TDV spent three trillion Turkish lira for different mosque building projects in Central Asia. No organization has been as active as the TDV.[48]

Folk Islam

Sufi groups in Turkey have established close ties with old Sufi networks to revise Sufism throughout the region. This unofficial Islam is a hybrid ideology made up by combining Sufism and local traditions. During Soviet rule, longhaired Sufis, known as *Ishans*, appeared in the1960s. They constituted the largest Sufi group in the area and resisted atheistic propaganda.[49] People visited holy places, and mystical tombs became centers for religious performances. Turkey-based religious groups continued to be very active in the region. For instance, the Istanbul-based Iskenderpasa Naksibendi order has a number of centers in Central Asia and has managed to integrate some prominent personalities into the order.

The Nurcu community of Fethullah Gülen (b. 1938) has carried out the most effective re-Islamization process.[50] In spite of all the efforts of Saudi-backed Wahhabi Islam and of Iranian ambitions in Central Asia, Nurcus have been the most influential in that region for several reasons. Many people perceive the Nurcu interpretation of Islam as a "national Turkic understanding of Islam." One reason is the close connection between folk Islam and the narrative-based texts of Said Nursi (1873-1960).[51] Nursi, who authored several volumes of *Koranic* exegesis known as the *Risale-I Nur Kulliyati (The Epistles of Light)*, transmitted Islamic information and knowledge through narrative stories about the family of the Prophet or about major events. Similar patterns of transmission exist between legendary or oral Islam and the print-based narrative Islam of Gülen. First, Islamic knowledge and lessons are rooted in narrative stories. Second, because of the heavy-handed atheism of the Soviet period in Central Asia, Islam could survive only by reconciling reason and science.[52]

The writings of Nursi reflect the attempt at the reconciliation between Islam and modernity and between reason and revelation. The *Risale-I Nur Kulliyati* is referred to as Zamangah in Uzbekistan. Zamangah is understood as a place where contemporaneousness is located to meet modern challenges and to understand faith within modern means. This Sufi-oriented and softer Turkish-Islam has been more appealing to the younger people of Central Asia as they reconstruct their faith rather than the Saudi-based Wahhabism or the Iranian version of a rigid Islam. Knowledge in the *Risale-I Nur* is not transmitted in terms of rigid rules but rather through narratives. The schools of Gülen have managed to distribute the writings of Nursi and to mark the geography of Central Asia with Sufi Islam. The activities of the Directorate of Turkish Religious Affairs and Nurcu networks have been reconstituting the meaning and role of Islam in Central Asia and have been undermining oral and mythical Islamic practices in the region.

Efsanevi Islam

Efsanevi, or legendary Islam, was the major carrier of Islamic tradition in Central Asia. This mythical Islam is common among villagers and some city dwellers. It derives its core beliefs from the Koran and incorporates much-older religious rites and rituals that predate Islam. Mythical oral-based Islam incorporates pre-Islamic tradition and seeks to create a sacred canopy through stories, mythologies, tales and legends. These stories indirectly dealt with authority, community, and everyday life experiences. The oral tradition of Central Asia is very much infused with Islamic history, ethics, and theology. In preserving and perpetuating this oral tradition, the itinerant minstrels of Turkic culture, known as the *ashik, dzyrshy, aqyn,* and *baqsy,* played an important role.[53] Minstrels traveled from one region to another and helped to create a Turkic cognitive and shared code of conduct and tastes. They embodied their understanding of religion linked to geography by creating narratives around key mountains and rivers. Most of the Kyrgyz and Kazak communities are still under the influence of this oral-mythical Islam because they never achieved an Orthodox Islamic establishment. There are, for example, several purported graves of Ali, the Prophet's cousin and fourth Caliph, in the Fergana Valley. The most critical means for promoting communal ethical life are narratives, which are used and mobilized for several purposes.[54] Finally, Turkish groups and the government institutions have been reconstructing the tombs of some prominent religious leaders. For instance, the tombs of Shah-i Zindeh in Samarkand, Bahattin Naksibend in Bukhara, and Ahmad Yesevi in Cimkent are reconstructed with this aid from Turkey.

CONCLUSION

Ankara developed a new framework of thinking in its ties to Central Asia following an initial period of confident euphoria and then subsequent failure and disappointment. Ankara's policies today have created a framework of cooperation between Turkey and the Turkic Republics and other Turkic communities within the Russian Federation.

In the evolution of relations between Turkey and the Turkic Republics, ethnicity and religion are the two cultural resources that Ankara uses. Because of the effects of Stalinist secularization in Turkic communities, ethnicity or ethnoreligious affinity, rather than purely religious solidarity, have become significant. The strategies and policies of Turkey have been more guided by societal groups (such as Turkish businessman, cultural institutions, and ethnoreligious Islamic networks) than the state itself.

The identity of the Turkish State is partly defined by the identity of others in Central Asia and by that of the EU. Turkey's three layers of identity have been in flux because of the changing international system. Different identities such as Islamic, Turkish, and European (or Balkan) have different meanings. In Central Asia and Turkey, Islam and ethnic identity are co-determinant. One becomes a Turk if he or she becomes Muslim. Different identities are likely to produce different — or even competing — foreign policies. Identity is not only a tool to promote interest but also a set of views from which issues are examined and made meaningful. Turkish-Islamic identity operates at a very deep level by allowing individuals to give meanings to actions and aspirations.

In the formation of Turkey's Central Asian policy, Islam plays a subordinate role. The most important identity that shapes these relations is Turkism, not Islam. However, Islam is an essential part of the Turkish identity. Islamic connections are more spread out and deeper, but not quite decisive. The ties with Turkic groups are articulated within the discursive tradition of Turkish nationalism. Therefore, Islamic and Turkish layers should not be seen as utterly opposing forces but as mutually constitutive tendencies within Turkish nationalism. The two layers of identity imperceptibly merge and shape Turkey's orientation. In other words, Turkish, Uzbek, Kazak, and Tatar nations are not elsewhere, but rather are rooted in Islamic symbolism and are shaped by political conditions.

Because of the recent rise of nationalism in Turkey, new governments in Ankara have had a strong Central Asian orientation. The major foreign policy goal of the newly ascendant Nationalist Movement Party (MHP) has been to consolidate ties with Central Asia at the expense of Turkish-EU relations. Again, the party program aims to turn Turkey into a leader of the Turkic states.[55] The election program of the party used "the Turkish World" rather than "Turkic World" to illustrate the special role that Turkey has to play in consolidating ties among the Turkic communities and states. Through the theme of the Turkish World they stress not only the ties at the state level but also — and perhaps more significant for the future on the communal level — the ties among the various Turkic communities around the world. The party treats cooperation within the Turkic world as compulsory and vital, and it calls for the establishment of a "ministry of the outside Turks."

Chapter Four

Islam in Central Asia: Afghanistan and Pakistan
Ahmed Rashid

INTRODUCTION

After spending nearly seventy years cut off from mainstream Islamic
trends and ideas, Central Asian Muslims received their first reintroduction
to the wider *ummah* (the community of Muslims based on a common
faith) through the Afghan *Jihad* against the Soviet Union in the 1980s.
The Afghan *mujahidin* (rebels), backed by Pakistan and the United States,
were to play a major role in clandestinely reopening the borders between
Central Asia and Afghanistan and South Asia that Stalin had closed in the
late 1920s. Hundreds of Uzbek, Tajik, and Caucasian Muslims came clandestinely to fight alongside the *mujahidin* and to study in Pakistani
madrasas (Muslim secondary schools).

The one-way trickle became an extensive two-way flood after the
breakup of the Soviet Union, when Pakistani, Saudi, and Afghan missionaries traveled in Central Asia preaching radical Islamic theology and funding the construction of mosques and *madrasas*. Compared with other outside states, Pakistan and Afghanistan have had the most significant impact,
both with regard to helping revive Islam in Central Asia and to radicalizing Central Asian Muslims with new ideas of Islamic revolution.

ORIGINS OF RADICALISM

In 1986 Central Intelligence Agency chief William Casey made three significant secret decisions. These decisions not only escalated the *mujahidin's*
war effort against the Soviet Union, but also had profound implications
for Central Asia in the decade ahead.

First, Casey persuaded the U.S. Congress to provide the *mujahidin*
with American-made Stinger antiaircraft missiles to shoot down Soviet

planes, and to provide U.S. advisers who would train the guerrillas. Before this time no U.S.-made weapons had been directly delivered through the CIA arms pipeline to the *mujahidin*. Pakistan's Interservices Intelligence (ISI) distributed these arms, which provided the bulk of the weaponry to the most radical Afghan Islamic groups, such as Gulbuddin Hikmetyar's Hizbe Islami, with its Pan-Islamist agenda.

Second, the CIA, Britain's MI-6, and the ISI agreed on a provocative plan to launch guerrilla attacks into the Soviet Republics of Tajikistan and Uzbekistan, the soft Muslim under-belly of the Soviet state, and into locations from which Soviet troops in Afghanistan received their supplies. This task was given to Hikmetyar. In March 1987, small Hizbe units crossed the Amu Darya from bases in northern Afghanistan and launched their first rocket attacks against villages in Tajikistan.

Third, Casey committed CIA support to a long-standing ISI initiative to recruit radical Muslims from around the world to fight with the Afghan *mujahidin*. The ISI began this program in 1982. By 1986, Western states had their own reasons for encouraging the initiative. Pakistan's military ruler, President Zia ul Haq, aimed to cement Islamic unity, to turn Pakistan into the leader of the Muslim world, and to foster an Islamic opposition in Central Asia. The Saudis saw an opportunity to promote both Wahhabism and dispose of its disgruntled radicals. Washington and London wanted to demonstrate that the entire Muslim world was fighting the Soviet Union alongside the Afghans and their Western benefactors, and the United States and the United Kingdom thus promoted the idea of a global *jihad* against the Soviet state and communist system.

Pakistan had issued standing instructions to all its embassies abroad to give visas, with no questions asked, to anyone wanting to come and fight with the *mujahidin*. In the Middle East, the Ikhwan ul Muslimeen (Muslim Brotherhood), the Saudi-based World Muslim League, and the Palestinian Islamic radicals organized recruits and put them in contact with the ISI. The ISI and Pakistan's Jamaat-e-Islami Party set up reception committees to welcome, house, and train the foreign militants. Then the two encouraged militants to join the *mujahidin* groups, usually the Hizbe Islami. Much of the funding for this enterprise came directly from Saudi Intelligence, which was partly channeled through the Saudi radical Osama Bin Laden, who was then based in Peshawar. At the time, French scholar Oliver Roy described the enterprise as "a joint venture between the Saudis, the Muslim Brotherhood, and the Jamaat-e-Islami, put together by the ISI."[1]

Between 1982 and 1992, approximately 35,000 Muslim radicals from fifty-three Islamic countries in the Middle East, north and east Africa, Central Asia, and the Far East passed their baptism under fire with the Afghan *mujahidin*. Tens of thousands more foreign Muslim radicals, including hundreds of illegal students from Central Asia, came to study in the thousands of new *madrasas* that the Zia government began to fund both in Pakistan and along the Afghan border. Eventually, more than 100,000 Muslim radicals from around the world were to have direct contact with Pakistan and Afghanistan and to be influenced by the Afghan *Jihad*.

While in Pakistan and Afghanistan, the radicals networked, studied, trained, and fought together. It was the first opportunity for most of them to learn about Islamic movements in other countries and to forge tactical and ideological links that would serve them well in the future. The camps became universities for Islamic radicalism. Western intelligence agencies failed to consider the future repercussions of bringing together thousands of Islamic radicals from all over the world. "What was more important in the world view of history? The Taliban or the fall of the Soviet Empire? A few stirred-up Muslims or the liberation of Central Europe and the end of the Cold War?" said Zbigniew Brzezinski, a former U.S. National Security Adviser.[2]

Other American commentators were less sanguine. Samuel Huntington wrote:

> *The war left behind an uneasy coalition of Islamist organizations intent on promoting Islam against all non-Muslim forces. It also left a legacy of expert and experienced fighters, training camps and logistical facilities, elaborate trans-Islam networks of personal and organization relationships, a substantial amount of military equipment including 300 to 500 unaccounted for Stinger missiles, and, most important, a heady sense of power and self-confidence over what had been achieved, and a driving desire to move on to other victories.[3]*

Uzbek and Tajik radicals, whom this writer met along the Pakistan-Afghanistan border in 1989 and who later established branches of the Islamic Renaissance Party (IRP) in both former Soviet Republics, were convinced that an Afghan victory would lead to the renewal of Islam in Central Asia and of anti-Soviet state movements.

THE HISTORY OF CENTRAL ASIA

The linkages between Central Asia and Afghanistan were seen as a renewal of a common history because for centuries northern Afghanistan was considered an integral part of Central Asia. The territory comprising modern-day Tajikistan, southern Uzbekistan, and northern Afghanistan was one contiguous territory that had been ruled intermittently by Persian, Turkic, Mongol, and Mogul conquerors and later by the Amirs (kings) in Bukhara, Khokand, and Kabul. The Amir of Bukhara depended on Afghan mercenaries for his army, while persecuted tribal chiefs, bandits, and mullahs (religious teachers) sought sanctuary in each other's territory, often crossing a nonexistent border.

In the nineteenth century the Great Game between the expanding empires of Russia in Central Asia and of Great Britain in India made Afghanistan the center of competition for both powers. The British feared a Russian thrust on Herat from the Turkmen region that could threaten British Baluchistan, while the Russians were concerned with potential British support for revolts by Muslim tribes that would undermine the Russian position. In other areas the British had concerns that Russian gold could turn Kabul's rulers against the British. Conversely, the Russians feared the British might even lend support to the rulers of Bukhara and Kokand against Russia.

Today, one can see that the competition between the two empires was over communication links; both indulged in massive railway projects. The Russians built railway lines across Central Asia to their borders with Afghanistan, Persia, and China, while the British built railway lines across India to the Afghan border. Afghanistan's contiguity with Central Asia came to an end after the 1917 Bolshevik Revolution, when the Soviet Union sealed its borders with its southern Muslim neighbors. The reopening of these borders in 1991 heralded the start of the new Great Game.

THE GREAT GAME

Modern-day Afghanistan today borders Turkmenistan, Tajikistan, and Uzbekistan. Along the Pamir Mountains the Amu Darya marks the rugged 640-mile Tajik-Afghan border, which divides Tajikistan's five million Persian-speaking people from Afghanistan. A quarter of Afghanistan's estimated twenty million citizens are Tajiks. In ancient times, Tajikistan and northern Afghanistan were the military and economic center of the region, becoming a peaceful gateway for the Silk Route and a less-peaceful gateway for Turkic nomadic invaders who rode west into Iran, Russia, and Europe and south into Afghanistan and India. Russia annexed the northern part of present-day Tajikistan in 1868, merging it with the Russian-controlled province of "Turkestan." As the Great Game intensified, the British and Russians demarcated the border between Afghanistan and Central Asia in 1884; Russia then annexed southern Tajikistan as well.

After Stalin created the five Central Asian Socialist Republics in 1924 – 1925 by arbitrarily drawing lines on a map, he handed over Bukhara and Samarkand, the two major centers of Tajik culture and history, to Uzbekistan. Thus, modern-day Tajikistan possesses none of the major population or economic centers of ancient Tajik glories. Stalin also created the Gorno-Badakhshan Autonomous Region in the Pamir Mountains, a region that contains 44 percent of the land area of Tajikistan but only 3 percent of the population. While the Tajiks are *Sunni* Muslims, Gorno-Badakhshan contains various Pamiri ethnic groups, the majority of whom are *Shi'a* Muslims. They include the Ismaelis (followers of the Agha Khan) who also inhabit the contiguous Badakhshan region of Afghanistan. A few months after the 1917 Revolution, Muslim guerrilla groups, or *Basmachis* (bandits), sprang up across Central Asia to resist the Bolsheviks. The movement stood for Islam, nationalism and anti-communism. Sixty years later the same inspiration motivated the *mujahidin* in Afghanistan. Determined to undermine Soviet power, the British helped the *Basmachis* in 1919 by paying Kabul's rulers to send camel caravans of arms and ammunition to the *Basmachis*. (This strategy of supporting Central Asian Islamic rebels was to be repeated in 1986.) The *Basmachi* struggle continued until 1929. As the Bolsheviks slowly defeated them, thousands of Tajik and Uzbek *Basmachis* took refuge in northern Afghanistan.

TAJIKISTAN

The civil war in Tajikistan (1992 – 1997) between the neo-communist government and an array of Islamist and nationalist forces devastated the newly independent country. Once again, thousands of Tajik rebels and refugees found a haven in northern Afghanistan where both the radical Pushtun leader Hikmetyar and the Tajik *mujahidin* commander Ahmad Shah Masud, whose forces then controlled Kabul, initially helped them.

The two men were at war with each other but wielded considerable influence in radicalizing the rebel Tajik leaders, at least until the Taliban soundly defeated Hikmetyar in 1996. After that defeat, Masud's influence in Tajikistan became predominant. Ultimately, the two sides in the Tajikistan civil war agreed to a UN-brokered peace settlement, but neither side had been able to promote a national identity for the fragmented Tajik clans.

The internal clan cleavages, the opposition from Tajikistan's Uzbeks who account for some 25 percent of the population, and the lack of an indigenous intelligentsia to formulate a Tajik nationalism to heal the wounds of the civil war — all left Tajikistan vulnerable to influences from Afghanistan. Both sides in the civil war cooperated with Masud, who to many Tajiks became a symbol of Tajik nationalism and a political and military hero as he battled the obscurantist and predominantly Pushtun Taliban. The Taliban only strengthened Masud's image by accusing him of trying to divide Afghanistan and to create a Greater Tajikistan by joining Afghanistan's Badakhshan province with Tajikistan. Masud has always denied such claims.

For Tajikistan the Taliban represented not only an alien ethnic group (the Pushtuns were at odds with Tajik aspirations), but also an extremist Islamic fundamentalism that was at odds with the mainstream moderate *Sufi* spiritualism (mysticism) of Central Asia. Masud's Islamist model inspired Tajikistan's Islamic opposition because it was closely interlinked with energizing Tajik nationalism. Toward the end of the civil war in Tajikistan, Masud played the role of mediator between the government of President Ali Rakhmanov and the opposition movement. After the UN had mediated an end to the civil war, President Rakhmanov rewarded Masud by allowing him to build a rear base for his forces in Tajikistan. After the Taliban evicted Masud's forces from Kabul in September 1996, the Tajik government gave Masud an air base in Kuliab in southern Tajikistan, where he received military supplies from Iran and Russia, who were rearming the anti-Taliban alliance. Thus, Tajikistan became locked into the Afghan conflict, supporting the anti-Taliban alliance.

UZBEKISTAN

In Uzbekistan, Islamic militancy — partly fueled by Afghanistan — is the most serious challenge to President Islam Karimov. The Uzbeks — the most numerous and influential ethnic group in the region — occupy

Central Asia's Islamic heartland and political nerve center. Uzbekistan has borders with all of the Central Asian states of the former Soviet Union and Afghanistan. Its principal cities of Samarkand and Bukhara have played host to countless civilizations during the past 2,500 years and have become the largest centers for Islamic learning after Arabia. Medieval Bukhara contained 360 mosques and 113 *madrasas*, and even in 1900, 10,000 students were studying at 100 active *madrasas*. For centuries many of these students came from Afghanistan. The 250-mile-long Fergana Valley, with its long associations with Islamic learning and militancy (such as the *Basmachis*), is both the richest agricultural region in Central Asia and the center of Islamic opposition to Karimov.

With a population of twenty-two million, Uzbekistan is the largest Central Asian Republic. Some six million Uzbeks live in the other Central Asian countries, and form substantial minorities in Tajikistan, Turkmenistan, and Kazakstan. Consequently, Karimov has many ethnic allies to pursue his agenda of dominating the region. Additionally, some two million Uzbeks live in northern Afghanistan, the result of migrations before and during the *Basmachi* rebellion. Another 25,000 Uzbeks live in China's Xinjiang province.

Well before Soviet troops withdrew from Afghanistan in 1989, Moscow and Tashkent were cultivating Afghan Uzbeks to create a secular Uzbek-controlled "cordon sanitaire" in northern Afghanistan that would resist any *mujahidin* takeover. That policy was successful for nearly a decade. Afghan Uzbek General Rashid Dostum controlled six northern provinces and, with military aid from Moscow and Tashkent, proved successful at holding off the *mujahidin* and later the Taliban. Meanwhile, Karimov led the attempt to forge an anti-Taliban alliance among the Central Asian Republics and Russia after 1994. However, with the fall of Dostum's capital, Mazar-e-Sharif, to the Taliban in 1998, Karimov's policy collapsed and the Taliban became Uzbekistan's immediate neighbors. Since that time Uzbekistan's influence in Afghanistan has waned considerably; Karimov is unwilling to back Masud, a Tajik.

The most significant political opposition to Karimov has come from underground radical Islamic groups (such as the Islamic Renaissance Party), who are entrenched in the Fergana Valley. Many of these Uzbek militants and mullahs, who set up alternative mosques and *madrasas* to the state-controlled Islamic network of mosques, have studied in Pakistan and Saudi Arabia and have been influenced by Saudi Wahabbism. As early as

1992, the Wahhabis had set up mosque-*madrasa* centers in nearly all the major towns in Fergana, of which the authorities seem to be unaware.[4] These Uzbek Wahhabis developed links with the Taliban, the Arab Afghans based in Afghanistan and led by Bin Laden, and Pakistan's Jamiat-e-Ullema Islam (JUI). This party followed the Deobandi creed of *Sunni* Islam and was deeply sympathetic to Wahhabism. It became the main inspiration for the Taliban. The JUI increasingly encouraged Uzbek militants to study at its *madrasas* in northern Pakistan.

Since 1995, Karimov has passed the most stringent laws of all the countries of Central Asia against Islamic fundamentalism, with provisions ranging from restricting *madrasa* education to determining the length of beards. He has subsequently blamed all political unrest against his regime on the "Wahhabis," a blanket term that Uzbek authorities now use inaccurately to describe all Islamic activism. However, Fergana is imbued with other Islamic radical trends, which are opposed to Wahhabism, while in urban centers there is a growing underground democratic and nationalist opposition to Karimov.

TURKMENISTAN

Afghanistan's 500,000 Turkmen population also arrived as a result of the civil war in the Soviet Union in the 1920s. The first migration into Afghanistan was by the Esari tribe in the early nineteenth century, followed by the Tekke tribe after their revolt against the Bolsheviks failed. Before the nineteenth century, borders were meaningless for the Turkmen nomads, who migrated freely across the region. As a result of their wanderings some 300,000 Turkmen still live in Iran, 170,000 live in Iraq, 80,000 live in Syria, and several thousand live in Turkey.

The Tekke, the largest Turkmen tribe, began to resist Russian advances into their territory in 1870 and wiped out a Russian army at the oasis fort of Geok Tepe in 1881. A year later, a Russian retaliatory force killed 6,000 Turkmen horsemen. In 1916, under the charismatic leadership of Muhammad Qurban Junaid Khan, the Turkmens began another long and bloody resistance, first against Czarist Russia and then against the Bolsheviks. The resistance continued until Khan's defeat in 1927 when he took refuge in northern Afghanistan. Turkmenistan was the poorest and least-developed Soviet Republic until the 1960s, when Moscow began to exploit Turkmenistan's rich natural gas resources. After independence, a weak and impoverished Turkmenistan, which had no military force to defend its long borders with Iran, Afghanistan, and rival Uzbekistan, opted for a foreign policy of neutrality. This neutrality gave the Turkmens the justification to keep their distance from Russia and to avoid being sucked into the economic and military pacts that arose out of the breakup of the Soviet Union.

Neutrality even allowed Ashkhabad to avoid taking sides in the Afghan conflict. This neutrality angered Moscow and Tashkent when Turkmenistan refused to join the anti-Taliban alliance. Unlike the other Central Asian Republics, Turkmenistan maintained working relations with all the Afghan factions. Ashkhabad provided the communist regime in Afghanistan with diesel fuel until Kabul fell in 1992. It proceeded to do the same for the warlord Ismael Khan, who controlled Herat until 1995 when Herat fell to the Taliban. Turkmen President Saparmurad Niyazov then cultivated the Taliban and helped them with supplies of fuel, foodstuffs, and consumer goods.

While the Turkmen Consulate in Herat maintained good relations with the Taliban, its Consulate in Mazar-e-Sharif did the same with the anti-Taliban alliance. Turkmenistan was the only country in Central Asia that wooed the Taliban rather than confront them. Despite having close relations with all the Afghan factions, the authoritarian control exercised by Niyazov prevented radical Islamic ideas from influencing the population of Turkmenistan. While Niyazov did deal with the Taliban, he kept them at a distance. The Turkmens were the least likely to be influenced by either Pushtun or Tajik-generated Islamic radicalism, while the Turkmen population in Afghanistan was too small, too secular, and too vulnerable to Taliban pressure to play a role in exporting radical Islamic ideas to Turkmenistan.

Turkmenistan's policy was driven not just by its neutrality but also by its desperate need to export gas. As Niyazov saw his economy crumble in part because the former Soviet Republics were unable to pay for Turkmen gas, he sought alternative export routes. By 1994, Turkmenistan had drawn up plans for a 5,000-mile-long oil and gas pipeline that would run eastward to China. The cost was estimated to be more than U. S. $20 billion. A U. S. $2.5-billion gas pipeline would also run through Iran to Turkey, and an oil and gas pipeline that would run south through Iran to the Persian Gulf. None of these projects ever came to fruition because the United States forbade Turkmenistan and Western oil companies from dealing with Iran, and the oil companies were reluctant to

invest in Turkmenistan where there were few laws or guarantees to protect foreign investments. However, Bridas, a small Argentine oil company,
did take the risk. It took up oil and gas concessions in Turkmenistan and
invested some US$400 million in developing them. After discovering a
huge new gas field at Yashlar in 1994, Bridas proposed building a gas
pipeline that would cross southern Afghanistan (which was controlled by
the Taliban) and would deliver gas to Pakistan and India. With support
from Washington and later from Pakistan, the U.S. company Unocal proposed a similar pipeline in 1995. The battle between the two companies
to build this pipeline sucked in the Taliban and the other Afghan warlords. Thus, Afghanistan became the fulcrum of the first test in the
pipeline war in the new Great Game.

AFGHANISTAN

For centuries Islam has been a major unifying factor in Afghanistan,
which is a complex multiethnic, multitribal society and is one of the
poorest nations in the world. The Pushtuns, who compose some 40 percent of the population and inhabit southern and eastern Afghanistan,
have ruled the country since the seventeenth century. However, they
have done so only by yielding considerable autonomy to the minority
ethnic groups, who are largely of Central Asian origin.

The Soviet invasion of Afghanistan in 1979 — the devastating war in
which one million Afghans died — and the infusion of billions of dollars
of weapons and multiple external paymasters, who all wanted to cultivate
their own Afghan proxies, helped undermine both the traditional tribal
society and the legitimacy of tribal and clan hierarchies. The civil war
became even more brutal after the *mujahidin* captured Kabul in 1992 and
could not reach consensus on ruling the country. The worsening civil
war steadily destroyed the tolerance and consensus among Muslim sects
and ethnic groups. Masud's massacre of the *Shi'a* Hazaras in Kabul in
1995, the Hazaras massacre of the Pushtun Taliban in Mazar in 1997, and
the Taliban massacres of Hazaras and Uzbeks in 1998 have no precedent
in Afghan history and irreparably damaged the country's national and
religious identity. For the first time in Afghanistan's history the unifying
factor of Islam was instead a lethal weapon in the hands of extremists —
a force for division, fragmentation, and enormous bloodshed.

Ninety percent of Afghans belong to the *Sunni* Hanafi sect, the most
liberal of the four *Sunni* schools of thought.[5] The minority sects are few

and scattered along the fringes of the country. *Shi'a* Islam is predominant among the Hazaras in the Hazarajat, a handful of Pushtun tribes, a few Tajik clans, and some Heratis. The *Sunni* Hanafi creed is essentially non-hierarchical and decentralized, which has made it difficult for twentieth century rulers to incorporate their religious leaders into strong central-ized state systems. However, for centuries this way of life admirably suited the loose Afghan confederation.

Traditional followers of Islam in Afghanistan believed in minimum government, where state interference is as little and as far away as possi-ble. The tribe and the community carried out everyday decisions. Among the Pushtuns, village mullahs, although largely uneducated, ensured that the mosque was the center of village life. *Talibs* (students) studied at the small *madrasas* scattered through the tribal areas. In medieval times, Herat was the center of Afghanistan's *madrasa* system, but from the eighteenth century Afghan students traveled to Central Asia, Egypt, and British India to study at more renowned *madrasas* to join the ranks of the ulema (scholars of sacred law and theology).[6]

Islamic *shari'a* law governed the legal process until 1925, when King Amanullah first began to introduce a civil legal code and when the state took on the role of training *ulema* to become *qazis* (Muslim judges). In 1946 a *shari'a* faculty opened in Kabul University, which became the main center for integrating the new civil code with the shari'a. Thus, after the 1979 Soviet invasion, the Pushtun mullahs joined — not the radical Islamic *mujahidin* parties which had been fostered by Pakistan since 1975 but the more traditional tribal-based parties such as Harakat Inquilabi Islami, headed by Mawalana Muhammad Nabi Muhammadi, and Hizbe Islami, led by Maulvi Younis Khalis. Both men were *maulvis* (Islamic scholars) who had studied at the Haqqania *madrasa* in Akhora Khattak in northern Pakistan and later established their own *madrasas* inside Afghanistan. Their parties were loose organizations that were decentralized, unideological and nonhierarchical, but they rapidly lost out as the CIA-ISI arms pipeline supported the more radical Islamic parties.

A tolerant and moderate Islam in Afghanistan was a result of the enormous popularity of Sufism, the trend of mystical Islam that had originated in Central Asia and Persia. The two main Sufi orders in Afghanistan are Naqshbandiyah, which originated in Uzbekistan, and Qaderiyah, which played a major role in uniting the anti-Soviet resis-tance as the orders provided a network of associations and alliances. The leaders of these orders set up their own parties: the Mujaddedi family led the Naqshbandiyah order and the Gailani family headed the Qaderiyah order. Sibghatullah Mujaddedi and Pir Syed Ahmad Gailani remained the most moderate of all the Mujahidin leaders, but were also sidelined by the CIA-ISI arms pipeline, as well as by Hikmetyar, Masud, and, later, the Taliban.

THE BEGINNINGS OF WAHHABISM IN AFGHANISTAN AND CENTRAL ASIA

Before the advent of the Taliban, Islamic extremism had never flourished in Afghanistan. Among the Pushtuns were small pockets of Wahhabis, followers of the strict and austere Wahhabi creed of Saudi Arabia. Begun by Abdul Wahhab (1703-1792) as a movement to cleanse the Arab Bedouin from the influence of Sufism, the spread of Wahhabism became a major plank in Saudi foreign policy after the oil boom in the 1970s. The Wahhabis first came to Central Asia in 1912 when a native of Medina, Sayed Shari Muhammad, set up Wahhabi cells in Tashkent and the Fergana Valley. From Fergana the creed traveled to Afghanistan, where it had miniscule support before the Afghan *Jihad*.

However, as Saudi arms and money flowed to Saudi-trained Wahhabi leaders among the Pushtuns, a larger following emerged. In the early stages of the war, the Saudis sent Abdul Rasul Sayyaf, an Afghan long settled in Saudi Arabia, to set up a Wahhabi party, the Ittehad-e-Islami (Islamic Unity) in Afghanistan. The Afghan Wahhabis became active opponents of both the Sufi and the traditional tribal-based parties, but were intensely disliked by ordinary Afghans. Arab *mujahidin*, including Osama Bin Laden, who were practicing Wahhabis and who joined the Afghan *Jihad*, won a small Pushtun following, largely because of the lavish funds and weapons at their disposal.

Because of the CIA-ISI arms pipeline, the engines of the *Jihad* were the radical Islamic parties. Hikmetyar and Masud had both participated in an unsuccessful Islamic uprising against President Muhammad Daud in 1975. They then fled to Pakistan, where Islamabad patronized them as a means to pressure future Afghan governments. President Zia ul Haq insisted that the bulk of CIA military aid be transferred to these parties, at least until Masud became independent and fiercely critical of Pakistani control. These radical Islamic leaders were drawn from a new class of educated university students (Hikmetyar studied engineering at Kabul

University; Masud studied at Kabul's French Lycée) who took their inspiration from the most radical and politicized Islamic party in Pakistan, the Jamaat-e-Islami. The Pakistani Jamaat, in turn, was inspired by the Ikhwan ul Muslimeen (the Muslim Brotherhood), which was formed in Egypt in 1928 with the aim of bringing about an Islamic revolution and creating an Islamic state. The founder of the Ikhwan, Hasan al-Banna (1906 – 1949), was a major influence on Abul-Ala Maududdi (1903 – 1978), who founded the Pakistani Jamaat in 1941.

The Ikhwan movements in Muslim states visualized an Islamic revolution rather than a nationalist or communist movement to overthrow colonialism. Opposed to the traditional mullahs, these Islamists also refused to compromise with the indigenous neo-colonial elite and wanted radical political change, with the goal of creating a "true" Islamic society. They rejected nationalism, ethnicity, and feudal class structures in favor of a new Muslim internationalism that would reunite the *ummah*, the community of Muslims based on common faith.[7] To achieve this goal, parties such as the Pakistani Jamaat and Hikmetyar's Hizbe Islami set up highly centralized parties organized along communist lines that established a cell system and conducted political indoctrination and military training in extreme secrecy. The Jamaat was to play a major role in educating the first recruits from Soviet Tajikistan and Uzbekistan and in introducing them to the outer world of Islam and revolutionary ideology.

These radical Islamists, as compared to the later Taliban, were relatively modern and forward-looking. They favored women's education and participation in social life. They developed theories for an Islamic economy, banking system, foreign relations, and the development of a more equitable and just social system. However, the radical Islamist discourse suffered from the same weaknesses and limitations as the Afghan Marxist discourse, in that as an all-inclusive ideology they rejected rather than desired integration with the different social, religious, and ethnic identities that constituted Afghan society. Both the Afghan communists and Islamists wanted to impose radical change on a traditional social structure through a revolution from the top. They wished to do away with tribalism and ethnicity by fiat — an impossible task. After 1992, the Afghan Islamists failed to work out their differences and reconstitute Afghan society, ensuring the continuation of the civil war.

The devastating impact of the civil war utterly destroyed Afghan society and created warlordism on a large scale, leaving an enormous political vacuum in the Pushtun belt. In 1994-1995, the Taliban, a movement of young Afghan students who studied at *madrasas* in Afghan refugee camps in Pakistan, swept through the Pushtun belt, and promised to reconstitute Afghan society in a truly Islamic manner. They were supported by Pakistan, who wanted to create a more pliable and unified Pushtun movement to combat the Tajik grip on Kabul, to secure peace in southern Afghanistan, and to open up trade routes and gas pipelines from Turkmenistan.

However, the Taliban's interpretation of Islam, *jihad*, and social transformation was an anomaly in Afghanistan because the movement reflected none of the leading Islamist trends that had emerged through the anti-Soviet war. The Taliban were neither radical Islamist inspired by the Muslim Brotherhood, nor mystical Sufis, nor traditionalists. They simply did not fit anywhere in the Islamic spectrum of ideas and movements that emerged in Afghanistan between 1979 and 1994. Their initial victories were a result of the war weariness of the Pushtun population and their uncompromising honesty, rather than a popular commitment to the Taliban creed.

DEOBANDI ISLAM AND THE TALIBAN

The Taliban's Islamic ideology sprang from an extreme form of Deobandism, which was being preached by Pakistani Islamic parties in Afghan refugee camps in Pakistan. The Deobandis, a branch of *Sunni* Hanafi Islam, had a minor history in Afghanistan but none in Central Asia. The Deobandis arose in British India in the nineteenth century as a movement that would reform and unite Muslim society as it struggled to live within the confines of a colonial state ruled by non-Muslims. Its main ideologues were Muhammad Qasim Nanautawi (1833-1877) and Rashid Ahmed Gangohi (1829-1905), who founded the first *madrasa* in Deoband in central India. The Indian Mutiny of 1857 was a watershed for Indian Muslims, who had led the anti-British revolt and whom the British had defeated severely. In the aftermath of the mutiny several philosophical and religious trends emerged among Indian Muslims in a bid to revive their standing. These philosophies ranged from the Deobandis to pro-Western reformers.

All the reformers saw education as the key to creating a new, modern Muslim. The Deobandis aimed to train a new generation of educated Muslims who would revive Islamic values based on intellectual learning, spiritual experience, and *shari'a* law. By teaching their students how to interpret *shari'a*, they aimed to harmonize the classical *shari'a* texts with current realities. The Deobandis took a restrictive view of the role of women, opposed all forms of hierarchy in the Muslim community, and rejected *Shi'as* — but the Taliban were to take these beliefs to an extreme the original Deobandis would never have recognized. The Deobandis set up *madrasas* all over India, and Afghan students — themselves searching for a better understanding of how Islam could cope with colonialism — arrived to study.[8] The Afghan state established a few Deobandi *madrasas*, but they were not popular even in the Pushtun belt.

Deobandi *madrasas* developed much faster in Pakistan after their creation in 1947. The Deobandis set up the Jamiat-e-Ullema Islam (JUI). In 1962 the Deobandi leader in the North West Frontier Province, Maulana Ghulam Ghaus Hazarvi, turned the JUI into a political party; it quickly split into several factions. The dynamic Maulana *Mufti* Mehmood quickly took over the Pushtun faction of the JUI in the province and reshaped the organization in a populist mold. The JUI, which now began to take part in electoral politics, were bitter opponents of the Jamaat-e-Islami; the rift between the two largest Islamic parties persists to this day.

The Deobandi creed became the primary religious and ideological influence on the Taliban. During the 1980s, Pakistan's Afghan policy was conducted with the help of the Jamaat-e-Islami and Hikmetyar's Hizbe Islami, who were both rivals of the JUI. Pakistan's Interservices Intelligence (ISI) gave no political role to the JUI, and largely ignored the small pro-Deobandi Afghan *mujahidin* groups.

However, the JUI used this period to set up hundreds of *madrasas* along the Pushtun belt in the North West Frontier Province and Baluchistan, where it offered young Pakistanis and Afghan refugees the chance of a free education, food, shelter, and military training. These *madrasas* were to train a new generation of Afghans for the post-Soviet period. As Pakistan's state-run educational system steadily collapsed, these *madrasas* became the only avenue for boys from poor families to receive any semblance of an education. The interpretation of *shari'a* in these *madrasas* was heavily influenced by Pushtunwali, the tribal code of the Pushtuns, while funds from Saudi Arabia to madrasas and parties that were sympathetic to the Wahhabi creed, as were the Deobandis, helped these *madrasas* expand.

In Pakistan's 1993 elections the JUI allied itself with the winning Pakistan Peoples Party (PPP) led by Benazir Bhutto, thus becoming a part of the ruling government coalition. The JUI's access to the corridors of power for the first time allowed it to establish close links with the army, the ISI, and the government. JUI leader Maulana Fazlur Rehman was made Chairman of the National Assembly's Standing Committee for Foreign Affairs. He used his position to visit Washington and European capitals to lobby for the Taliban, and to visit Saudi Arabia and the Gulf States to enlist their financial support.

Maulana Samiul Haq, a religious and political leader whose *madrasa* became a major training ground for the Taliban leadership and Central Asian radicals, now leads one breakaway faction of the JUI. In 1999, at least eight Taliban cabinet ministers in Kabul were graduates of Haq's Dar-ul-Uloom Haqqania, and dozens more graduates served as Taliban governors in the provinces, military commanders, judges, and bureaucrats. Earlier, Younis Khalis and Muhammad Nabi Muhammadi, leaders of the traditional *mujahidin* parties, had also studied at Haqqania.

Haqqania in the North West Frontier Province's Akhora Khatak was set up in 1947. It has a boarding school for 1,500 students, a high school for 1,000 day students, and twelve affiliated smaller *madrasas*. Haqqania offers an eight-year Master of Arts course in Islamic studies and a Ph.D. after an additional two years of study. Funded by public donations, it does not charge its students. It has become the most popular *madrasa* in the North West Frontier Province, with some 1,500 applicants for 400 new places every year. Since 1991 some 400 places are reserved for Afghan students, and another sixty places are reserved for students from Central Asia. These latter students tend to belong to the Islamic opposition in these countries, and they enter Pakistan without passports or visas. Haq was the godfather of the Taliban movement, urging his Afghan students as early as 1992 to start a student movement that would sweep through the country, eliminate the warlords, and reconstitute Afghan society in the Deobandi mold. Haq does not believe that the recognized Muslim *ulema*, or scholars of sacred law and theology, can bring about a pure Islamic revolution. He believes only poor students who have no vested interest in the status quo can do that. He now teaches his Central Asian students the same message.

Haq and Haqqania have become the principal organizers for recruiting Pakistani and Central Asian students to fight for the Taliban. Tens of thousands of Pakistani students and several hundred Central Asians sent by Haqqania have fought alongside the Taliban since 1994. At any given moment some 30 percent of the Taliban's standing army of some 25,000 men is made up of Pakistani recruits. Meanwhile, another JUI faction runs the Jamiat-ul Uloomi Islamiyyah in Binori town, a suburb of Karachi. It was established by the late Maulvi Muhammad Yousuf Binori and has 8,000 students, including hundreds of Afghans and dozens of Central Asians.

The JUI was to benefit immensely from its Taliban proteges. For the first time the JUI developed international prestige and influence as a major patron of Islamic radicalism. Pakistani governments and the ISI could no longer ignore the party, nor could Saudi Arabia and the Arab Gulf states. Camps inside Afghanistan were used for military training and refuge for the non-Afghans, particularly Arab recruits. At first, Hikmetyar ran the camps, but after his defeat the Taliban took over and in turn handed the camps over to JUI groups. In 1996 the Taliban gave Camp Badr, near Khost on the Pakistan-Afghanistan border, to the Harkat-ul-Ansar, another small splinter group from the JUI, which had sent members to fight in Afghanistan, Tajikistan, Kashmir, Chechnya, and Bosnia.[9] Camp Badr was the site of the U.S. cruise missile attack in August 1998, following the U.S. embassy bombings in Africa; it is where the United States suspected that Bin Laden was hiding.

The Taliban have clearly debased the Deobandi tradition of learning and reform with their rigidity, but in doing so they have advanced a new, radical, and — to the governments of the region — extremely threatening model for any forthcoming Islamic revolution. The Taliban are poorly tutored in Islamic and Afghan history, knowledge of the *shari'a* and the Koran, and the political and theoretical developments in the Muslim world during the twentieth century. While Islamic radicalism in the twentieth century has a long history of scholarly writing and debate, the Taliban have no such historical perspective or tradition. There is no Taliban Islamic manifesto or scholarly analysis of Islamic or Afghan history. Their exposure to the radical Islamic debate around the world is minimal; their sense of their own history is even less. This lack of knowledge has created an obscurantism, which allows no room for debate even with fellow Muslims.

The Taliban's new model for a purist Islamic revolution has created an immense backlash in Pakistan and to some extent in the Central Asian

Republics. Pakistan is already a fragile state and is currently beset by an identity crisis, an economic meltdown, ethnic and sectarian divisions, and an inept ruling elite that has been unable to provide good governance. Pakistan now faces the spectre of a new Islamic wave, which is led not by the older, more mature, and accommodating Islamic parties, but by neo-Taliban groups. Pakistan's support for the Taliban is thus coming back to haunt the country itself, even as Pakistani leaders and the army appear to be oblivious of the challenge and as they continue to support the Taliban. The Taliban and their supporters present the Muslim world and the West with a new style of Islamic extremism, which rejects all accommodation with Muslim moderation and the West. They have given Islamic fundamentalism a new face and a new identity for the next millennium — one that refuses to accept any compromise or political system except their own.

The Deobandi-Taliban influence over a new, younger generation of Islamic militants in Uzbekistan and Tajikistan has reestablished links between these militants and the Pushtun radicalism that Hikmetyar had fostered in the 1980s, but which had weakened steadily as ethnicity became more significant (particularly in Tajikistan). The Pushtun Taliban have no ethnic allies in Central Asia, and they are closely linked to Pakistani Pushtun radicals and to funding from Saudi Arabia. This linkage makes their influence in Central Asia all the more remarkable and threatening and, thus, a major cause for concern among the Central Asian regimes.

Throughout the 1980s Moscow tutored the communist parties in Central Asia to strongly resist the Pushtun-generated and Pakistan-Saudi-supported brand of Islamic fundamentalism. Moscow viewed such beliefs as wholly alien and foreign inspired, while the Central Asians were averse to this form of fundamentalism because the Pushtuns had no ethnic or cultural ties with Central Asia. This view persists even more strongly in the Uzbek and Tajik regimes today. President Karimov's blanket condemnation of all Islamic radicalism as Wahhabi-inspired is, therefore, more complicated than meets the eye. What the Uzbek authorities are clamping down on is not so much the pure Wahhabi influences emanating from Saudi-educated Uzbek mullahs, but the Pushtun and Pakistan-Saudi-backed form of Deobandi Islam that is becoming more influential.

The Central Asian states are thus even more committed to back the anti-Taliban alliance led by Masud, because it is now wholly made up of non-Pushtuns from Afghan ethnic groups that have close links to Central Asian ethnic groups. Thus, even as Karimov clamps down on Islamic radicalism at home, he deals with it in Afghanistan in the shape of the anti-Taliban alliance. Ethnicity and Islam have become intertwined — better the Islamic radical who speaks a language you understand and is historically related to Central Asia than an Islamic radicalism that is ethnically and culturally alien and is supported by outside powers.

Deobandism is not the only influence radicalizing Central Asian Muslims. Although Pakistan's Jamaat-e-Islami lost influence in Afghanistan because of the enhanced role of the JUI and because of Deobandi influence over the Taliban, the Jamaat has maintained its close links with Central Asia, which it had developed throughout the Afghan *Jihad*. The Jamaat's network of *madrasas*, particularly its principal *madrasa* and Islamic University at Mansoora in Lahore, educates dozens of Uzbeks, Tajiks, Caucasian Muslims, and Uighurs from China's Xinjiang province every year. The majority of these students are illegal, arriving without documents but receiving them in Pakistan through the Jamaat's extensive contacts within the Pakistan government.

The Pakistani state is no longer supporting Central Asian Muslim radicals and instead has tried to develop extensive formal diplomatic, trade, and cultural links with the Central Asian states. However, leaders such as Presidents Karimov and Rakhmanov continue to believe that the ISI is supporting the Islamic underground opposition in their countries for several reasons. First, the fact that President Zia encouraged Afghan *mujahidin* attacks in Central Asia in the 1980s is not easily forgotten, and Central Asian leaders believe the relationship between the ISI and radical groups continues. Second, Pakistan's support for the Taliban and rejection of the non-Pushtun minorities in Afghanistan is seen as a Pakistani-inspired threat to stability in Afghanistan and Central Asia. Third, successive Pakistani governments have repeatedly promised the Central Asian Republics to curb the links and movements between Pakistani Islamic parties and militants in Central Asia and to forbid militants from studying illegally in Pakistani *madrasas*, but Islamabad has repeatedly failed to implement such measures.

OSAMA BIN LADEN

A major new factor in Central Asian leaders' perspective of Islamic fundamentalism originating from Afghanistan and Pakistan is the growth of terrorism associated with the Arab Afghans and Osama Bin Laden. Among the thousands of foreign recruits who came to fight in the Afghan *Jihad* was a young Saudi student, Osama Bin Laden, the son of Yemeni construction magnate Muhammad Bin Laden. The senior Bin Laden was a close friend of the late King Faisal; his company became fabulously wealthy on contracts to renovate and expand the Holy Mosques of Mecca and Medina.

Osoma Bin Laden, although not a royal, was close enough to the Saudi Royal Family and certainly wealthy enough to lead the Saudi contingent in Afghanistan. Bin Laden developed close contacts with the CIA, the ISI, and Saudi Intelligence, providing the Afghan war effort with money, Arab recruits, and extensive help in constructing bases, underground storehouses, and roads for the CIA-ISI arms pipeline. Bin Laden later said:

> To counter these atheist Russians, the Saudis chose me as their representative in Afghanistan. I settled in Pakistan in the Afghan border region. There I received volunteers who came from the Saudi Kingdom and from all over the Arab and Muslim countries. I set up my first camp where these volunteers were trained by Pakistani and American officers. The Americans supplied the weapons; the Saudis, the money. I discovered that it was not enough to fight in Afghanistan, but that we had to fight on all fronts, communist or Western oppression.[10]

Abdullah Azam, a Jordanian Palestinian, ran the center for the Arab Afghans that also functioned as the offices of the World Muslim League and the Muslim Brotherhood in Peshawar. During the 1980s, Azam forged close links with Hikmetyar and Abdul Rasul Sayyaf, the Afghan Islamic scholar; the Saudis then sent Azam to Peshawar to promote Wahhabism. Saudi funds flowed to Azam and the Makhtab al Khidmat (Services Center), which he created with Bin Laden in 1984, to service the new recruits and to receive donations from Islamic charities and Saudi intelligence. A decade later the Makhtab would emerge at the center of a web of radical organizations that helped carry out the World Trade Center bombing in New York and the U.S. embassy bombings in Africa in 1998.

After spending nearly a decade with the *mujahidin*, Bin Laden left Afghanistan in 1990 for Sudan. He returned to Afghanistan in May 1996 and lived under the protection of the Jalalabad Shura, which controlled three provinces in eastern Afghanistan until the conquest of Kabul and

Jalalabad by the Taliban in September 1996. In August 1996, Bin Laden issued his first Declaration of Jihad against the Americans, whom he said were occupying Saudi Arabia. Striking up a friendship with Mullah Omar, the reclusive leader of the Taliban, Bin Laden moved to Kandahar in 1997 and came under the protection of the Taliban. He reestablished his links with Central Asian radicals who had fought with the *mujahidin* and the Arab Afghans in the past. The Taliban handed over several training camps around Khost in eastern Afghanistan to Bin Laden and Pakistani Islamic groups, where Islamic radicals from many countries, including Uzbekistan and Tajikistan, received training.

By now the Arab Afghans were playing a major role in the Muslim world fomenting Islamic movements in Algeria, Sudan, and Egypt. Bin Laden maintained contact with them as well as with senior figures in the National Islamic Front in the Sudan, the Hezbollah in Lebanon, the radical Islamic Palestinian movement Hamas in Gaza and the West Bank, and the IRP leaders in Uzbekistan and Tajikistan. In Kandahar he had Chechens, Uzbeks, Bangladeshis, Filipinos, Algerians, Kenyans, Pakistanis, and African American Muslims for followers and bodyguards. Several hundred non-Afghan militants under his command lived in camps in Kabul and Khost. It was only after the bombings in Africa that the United States began to unravel this network by launching a global operation. The result was the arrest of more than eighty Islamic militants in a dozen different countries, ranging from Tanzania, Kenya, Sudan, and Yemen to Pakistan, Bangladesh, Malaysia, and the Philippines.

Bin Laden developed considerable influence with the Taliban, especially in encouraging a Pan-Islamic ideology among Taliban leaders. The Taliban became increasingly vociferous against the United States, the UN, Saudi Arabia, Iran, and the Central Asian Republics that backed the anti-Taliban alliance. Taliban statements increasingly reflected the language of Islamic defiance that Bin Laden used and that was not originally a Taliban trait. Bin Laden endeared himself further to the Taliban by sending several hundred Arab Afghans to participate in the 1997 and 1998 Taliban offensives in the north against the anti-Taliban alliance, and by building houses for Mullah Omar and other Taliban leaders. Bin Laden's extensive network grants global connections to Central Asian Islamic radicals who are associated with him. The Bin Laden network links these radicals more firmly in the politics of radical Islam within the Muslim world, gives them a financial and military support base as well as sanctuary in Afghanistan, and allows them to clandestinely travel in and out of their respective Central Asian states.

AFGHANISTAN'S DRUG TRADE

Another major destabilizing factor for Central Asia is the drug trade emanating from Afghanistan, now used by all the Afghan factions to fund their war effort. Afghanistan is now the largest exporter of heroin to Western markets. Drug export routes, which used to run solely through Pakistan in the 1980s, now extend through Iran, the Central Asian Republics, and China. Western intelligence agencies and the Chinese government believe that the drugs routes through Central Asia are run both by secular mafia closely linked to senior government officials, as well as by local Islamic radical movements. The drug trade is extremely beneficial to the latter because it provides a relatively risk-free and clandestine financial base for political activism. The drug trade generates money for arms, training, and other equipment, as well as travel through the region. The same network that smuggles in drugs can also smuggle in weapons and explosives. Drug smugglers, who are regularly hauled up on the Afghanistan-Tajikistan-Uzbekistan borders by border guards, are often linked to Islamic radical groups.

The Taliban gave heroin trafficking virtual Islamic immunity in 1995. Ironically, the Taliban banned hashish because Muslims consumed hashish, but allowed opium production because they said non-Muslims consumed heroin. The Taliban imposed a tax on all opium traffic through their territory, thereby legitimizing it as an official source of revenue for the Taliban government. Nevertheless, heroin addiction has grown enormously in the region. Pakistan has some five million heroin addicts, Iran has three million, and addiction is growing in Central Asia and China as these export routes develop.

The combination of drug and weapon smuggling has become the most potent trade in the region that is helping fund and fuel Islamic radicalism. In a region where state controls are evaporating, where economic crises worsen, and where the smuggling of consumer goods in an ever-expanding black economy destroys local industry and deprives states of revenues, the drug trade has become an ideal and ever easier means to fund anti-state political movements.

CONCLUSION

The growing economic crises in Pakistan, Afghanistan, and the southern Central Asian region are helping fuel Islamic radicalism as a new generation of younger, educated, inspired, but unemployed youth become attracted to models of Islamic revolution. Unless the Central Asian states are able to generate economic development by building the oil and gas pipelines and the road and railway links for their exports to the outside world, they will face continuing economic crises that will, in turn, encourage Islamic radicalism. At the same time the longer Central Asian leaders delay in allowing opposition politics and parties to coexist within more democratic and tolerant state structures, the more they will force opposition politics — particularly Islamic radicalism — underground. This, in turn, will legitimize terrorism and radical revolution as the only alternative.

However, the continuing civil war in Afghanistan remains the most destabilizing external factor affecting the countries of Central Asia. The Afghan war has exacerbated ethnic and sectarian tensions in the region, fueled Islamic radicalism, created a vast network of drug and weapons smuggling, and transformed Afghanistan into the world's largest sanctuary for international terrorism. With the civil war showing no signs of coming to an end, all these factors will increase instability in the already fragile Central Asian states. Since 1992 the international community has paid little attention to trying to end the conflict, either by pressuring the neighboring states to halt weapons supplies to their Afghan proxies or by sufficiently empowering the UN to negotiate among the warring factions.

In particular, the United States walked away from Afghanistan after the Soviet withdrawal, and its involvement in trying to end the civil war since that time has been intermittent, inconsistent, and inconsequential. Moreover, with the Clinton Administration's foreign policy, which is driven largely by domestic concerns, topical issues relevant to U.S. domestic politics rather than an overall strategic policy for the region have dominated the U.S. focus on Afghanistan. Thus, between 1994 and 1997, the United States quietly encouraged its allies of Pakistan and Saudi Arabia to back the Taliban to provide access to U.S. oil companies and to build a gas pipeline from Turkmenistan to Pakistan that would avoid Iran.

Since that time the Clinton Administration has been forced to distance itself from the Taliban because of the highly effective campaign by the U.S. Feminist Majority that condemns the Taliban's discrimination against Afghan women. The latest single-issue focus of Washington has been Osama Bin Laden and the factor of international terrorism emanating from Afghanistan. These issues have still not galvanized Washington to have a more forceful strategic vision of the region, a view that should hinge on pushing for peace in Afghanistan.

The continuing civil war has polarized the region, with Iran, Russia, and the Central Asian states supporting the anti-Taliban alliance, and with Pakistan and Saudi Arabia backing the Taliban. This acute polarization has made it much more difficult for multinational energy projects to be achieved in the region. The civil war has given Russia the excuse to increase its military presence in Central Asia and to retain influence on the foreign policies of the Central Asian Republics. The civil war is helping destabilize Iran by exacerbating Iran's drug problem, increasing Sunni-Shi'a tensions while 1.6 million Afghan refugees remain in Iran, thereby creating a major burden on the exchequer at a time of economic recession. Iran's confrontation with the Taliban has also worsened its previous close ties with Pakistan.

There are even greater risks to those who support the Taliban. The increasing Talibanization of Pakistan is adding to the country's instability, and Pakistan could well face a Taliban-style Islamic revolution led by a multitude of Islamic groups that could lead to anarchy and divide the Pakistan army. The sanctuary given to Bin Laden provides those Saudi extremists opposed to the Saudi royal family a convenient and secure base for the first time in the Kingdom's history. Radical Wahhabism has come back to haunt the Wahhabi state. Unless there is a greater international and, in particular, U.S. commitment to try to end the Afghan civil war, the Central Asian region will become more polarized and radicalized.

Part IV

About the Contributors

About the Contributors

Ms. Susan Eisenhower has been the chairman of the Center for Political and Strategic Studies since its founding in 1991. During this time she has focused on US-Russian relations and European Security. She has also helped administer the Center's project on Central Asia. During this time she has edited three collected volumes and has written two books and co-authored another. She is a regular contributor to op-ed pages at such papers as the *Washington Post* and the *L.A. Times* and she has appeared on all the network news programs. She has also testified to Congress on numerous occasions. In 1998, she was elected to the National Academy of Sciences' standing Committee on International Security and Arms Control (CISAC), and during that fall she spent the semester at Harvard as a visiting fellow at the Kennedy School of Government's Institute of Politics. In 1998, she was also appointed to the National Advisory Council of the National Aeronautics and Space Administration (NASA) and recently was appointed by the Secretary of Energy to sit on his task force to assess U.S. funded non-proliferation programs in Russia.

Dr. Shireen T. Hunter is the Director of Islamic Studies at the Center for Strategic and International Studies in Washington, DC, with which she has been associated since 1983. From 1993-97, Dr. Hunter was Visiting Senior Fellow at the Center for European Policy Studies (CEPS) in Brussels. Prior to joining CSIS, Dr. Hunter was a political and economic consultant for the Board of International Broadcasting and a wide array of other corporations; Guest Scholar at the Brookings Institution; and Research Fellow at the Harvard University Center for International

Affairs. From 1966-1978, she was a member of the Iranian Foreign Service, serving in London, New York (UN), and Geneva. She has submitted Congressional testimony as well as written a number of books, book chapters, and articles on arms control, international economics, technology transfer, refugees, human rights, the Middle East (especially the Persian Gulf region), Central Asia, and the Transcaucasus. Dr. Hunter holds a BA in international law from Teheran University, an MSc in international relations from the London School of Economics, and a Ph.D. in international relations from the Institut Universitaire de Hautes Etudes Internationales in Geneva.

Dr. Aleksei Malashenko is currently the Head of the Sector of the Islamic Studies in the Institute of the Oriental Studies at the Russian Academy of Sciences, and the Scholar-in-Residence in the Ethnicity and Nation-Building program at Carnegie Moscow Center. From 1982 to 1986, Dr. Malashenko was an editor of the *World Marxist Review* (Prague), and in 1990 he was a visiting professor at Colgate University. Dr. Malashenko retains his affiliation of Professor at the Institute of the International Relations (Foreign Ministry of Russian Federation), and is a member of the editorial board of *Acta Eiirasica* (Moscow) and *CeHtra Haja Asia I Kav,kaz* (Stockgoliii). He is the author of eight books and over 200 media and academic articles and chapters. Dr. Malashenko earned his Ph.D. from the Institute of Asian and African countries at Moscow University.

Mr. Murat F. Murtazin has been the rector of the Moscow High Islamic College (where the future imams of Russian mosques receive their education) since 1994. Mr. Murtazin is also rector of the Moscow Islamic University and *imam-hatyb* of Moscow Memorial mosque. After his graduation from Leningrad State University in 1981, he taught Arabic at several colleges in Moscow while concurrently studying the history of Ancient Arabia and the morthology of Semitic languages. In 1989 he became the head of the *madrasa* at Moscow Cathedral Mosque (an elementary Islamic school), the first one in Russia. Mr. Murtazin's books include *V molitve spasenie (Prayer Is Our Salvation)*, a translation from Old Tatar of *Mufti* Gabdurahman Rasuli's *Islam*. He is also the editor of a collection of articles *Islam and Muslims in Russia*. Mr. Murtazin is a specialist in the field of Arabic philology and Islamic sciences and author of a number of books on religion.

Ms.Saodat Olimova is co-founder and co-director of the Center "Sharq," a nongovernmental think tank in Dushambe, Tajikistan.

Dr. Victor N. Panin is the director of the Scientific Research Center for Social, Economic and Political Studies of the North Caucasus at Pyatigorsk State Linguistic University (PSLU). His academic career began in 1985 as a lecturer at PSLU. From 1987 until 1990 he worked as the director of the Department for International Relations for the Pyatigorsk City Administration. In 1993, he was an Assistant Professor and Deputy Director of the Department for International Relations at PSLU. Dr. Panin has written extensively on international relations, strategic policy, conflict management, U.S.-Russian relations, the Middle East conflict, and the North Caucasus. He has received two fellowships from the USIA: in 1994 for participation in a summer institute on the American political system, and in 1998 as a participant of the Regional Scholar Exchange Program administered by IREX. He received an M.A. in Linguistics from PSLU in 1982 with a specialization in English and French, and in 1995 he earned his Ph.D. in Philosophy of Politics from Rostov State University.

Dr. Abdumannob Polat has been a political analyst since 1998, in addition to his roles as human rights and democratic activist. He is a founding member and current Chairman of the Human Rights Society of Uzbekistan (HRSU) and has been the Director of the Union of Councils' Central Asian Human Rights Information Network (CAHRIN) since 1992. In 1988 he was also a founding member of Birlik (Unity), the primary democratic movement in Uzbekistan. Dr. Polat is the author of over sixty articles, reports, and essays on democracy, human rights, and political developments in Uzbekistan and Central Asia. These articles have been published in many countries, including the United States, Russia, and Uzbekistan, in the English, Russian and Uzbek languages. Dr. Polat holds the Heinz R. Pagels Human Rights of Scientists Award of the New York Academy of Sciences and Hellman-Hammet Award of the Human Rights Watch. Dr. Polat was forced to leave Uzbekistan in June of 1992. In December 1992 Dr. Polat co-sponsored an international conference on human rights in Central Asia in Bishkek, Kyrghyzstan. Immediately after the conference, he was abducted by an Uzbek security detail and jailed in Uzbekistan on charges of "insulting the President of Uzbekistan." Only after strong international protests and two months' imprisonment did he receive amnesty.

Mr. Ahmed Rashid is a Pakistani journalist based in Lahore. He is the Pakistan, Afghanistan, and Central Asia correspondent for the *Far Eastern Economic Review* and the *Daily Telegraph* (London). He also writes for Pakistani newspapers and broadcasts regularly on international radio and TV stations. Mr. Rashid is the author of *The Resurgence of Central Asia: Islam or Nationalism?* Mr. Rashid contributed or co-authored a number of books including *Fundamentalism Reborn: Afghanistan and the Taliban, Contemporary Issues in Pakistan Studies*, and *Afghanistan: Essential Field Guides to humanitarian and conflict zones*. His most recent work is *Taliban: Islam, Oil and the new Great Game in Central Asia* published in 2000 by Yale University Press.

Dr. Roustem Yurevich Safronov is the special correspondent to the United States of *Novaya Gazeta* (Moscow), and a frequent contributor to the BBC's Russian and Central Asian Services. During his employment with the State Archives in Ashgabat during the Soviet period, he published many articles and hosted television and radio programs about the history of Turkmenistan. Later, while with the Central Committee of Komsomol of Turkmenistan, he traveled extensively throughout the Republic as a lecturer. In 1992 Dr. Safronov was a correspondent and commentator for Open Radio in Moscow. From 1993 – 1996 he was special correspondent to the Duma and political commentator for Russian State Television's "Vesti" program. Dr. Safronov received the Medal for Personal Bravery for his coverage of the battle for control of the Russian White House; he was wounded during these events. He has written, hosted and directed two television programs about Turkmenistan, which were broadcast nationally on RTR. Dr. Safronov has published widely in all of the major Russian press, as well as authoring a number of books on Russian issues. He received his M.A. from Moscow State Historical Archive Institute, and graduated from Moscow's Super Komsomol School's Department of Journalism.

Dr. Roald Sagdeev has been elected a member of many national scientific academies and societies around the world, including the National Academy of Sciences (USA), the Royal Astronomical Society (UK), and The Max Planck Society (Germany). Dr. Sagdeev is also the recipient of the Lenin Prize, the Tate Medal (from the American Institute of Physics), and most recently the Leo Scillard Award (from the American Physical Society). In addition to his work to promote international cooperation in science, Dr. Sagdeev also played an outspoken political role during the first five years of *perestroika*. Elected to the Supreme Soviet in 1987, he served as a summit advisor to Mikhail Gorbachev at three summits: Geneva (1985), Washington (1987) and Moscow (1988). From 1987 – 1991 he served as a deputy in the USSR's parliament. Roald Sagdeev serves as a Senior Associate of the Center for Political and Strategic Studies (CPSS). He uniquely holds a joint appointment as Distinguished Professor of Physics at the University of Maryland and Director Emeritus of the Space Research Institute, the Moscow-based center of the Soviet — and now the Russian — space exploration program. He has been the Principal Investigator on CPSS' project on Central Asia for the last five years.

Dr. Anara Tabyshalieva is the co-founder and director of the Institute for Regional Studies, a NGO in Kyrghyzstan. She is also currently a lecturer at Kyrghyz-Slavonic University, where she conducts research on regional cooperation in Central Asia. Dr. Tabyshalieva was a senior fellow at the United States Institute of Peace in 1996 – 97. She has authored several works including *Faith in Turkestan* (1993), *Reflection in Time* (1995), and more recently *The Challenge of Regional Cooperation in Central Asia: Preventing Ethnic Conflict in the Fergana Valley* (1999). Dr. Tabyshalieva holds a Ph.D. equivalent in history from Kyrghyz National State University.

The Archbishop Vladimir is Head of the Russian Orthodox Church in Central Asia. (Kazakstan is not included.)

Dr. M. Hakan Yavuz is an assistant professor of political science at the University of Utah. Dr. Yavuz is a columnist in weekly Turkish *Aksiyon* and an editorial member of *Critique, Silk Road, Journal of Muslim Minority*

Affairs, and *Cemoti*. His current projects focus on transnational Islamic networks in Central Asia and Turkey; the role of Islam in state building and nationalism; and ethnoreligious conflict management. Dr. Yavuz has also carried out extensive field-work in the Fergana Valley of Uzbekistan to examine the relationship between Islam and nationalism and the preservation and dissemination of Islamic knowledge under socialism. He is widely published as an author with more than 20 articles on Islam, nationalism, the Kurdish question, and modern Turkish politics. He has lectured in Tashkent, Ankara, Istanbul, and Sarajevo. Dr. Yavuz earned his B.A. from Siyasal Bilgiler Fakultesi, in Ankara; his M.A. from the University of Wisconsin-Milwaukee; and his Ph.D. in political science from University of Wisconsin-Madison, 1998.

Endnotes

PART I

Chapter One

[1] "The Legacy of Marjani and Contemporaneity," *Proceedings of the Conference*, Institute of History, Tatarstan Academy of Sciences, Kazan, 1998.
[2] A.Bennigsen, "Les Musulmans oublies: L'Islam en Union Sovietique," Paris, 1981.
[3] Qadi Akbar Turajonzoda, "Religion: The Pillar of Society," Central Asia. *Conflict, Resolution and Change*. CPSS, 1995.
[4] Turkestan Newsletter, March 29, 2000.
[5] Turkestan Newsletter , March 31, 2000.

Chapter Two

[1] According to other stories, the name "Osh" is connected with the cult of a river deity Bakhsha-Oakhsha, Okhsho. It is also known that in the tenth century AD in Osh there existed the Gates of the shrine of fire-worshipers. Maklaev, K. "The Ancient History of Osh, Renesans ili regres," Tsentr issledovanii mira, Bishkek, 1996, p. 193.
[2] *Kyrgyz Rukhu*, 7 October 1998.

Chapter Three

[1] One of the four interpretations of Islam generally recognized to be legitimate among *Sunni* Muslims (the main sect in Islam). Founded by *Abu Hanifa an-Nu'mon ibn Sobit, Imam A'zam* in the eighth century, *Hanafi* is considered to be the most liberal, modest, and convenient as far as rituals are concerned, among other interpretations of Islam. Also, this form of Islam is the most tolerant of local traditions and customs, and even occasionally incorporates them.
[2] An Islamic-political movement founded in Saudi Arabia by *Abdul Wahhab* in the eighteenth century, which adheres closely to the Koran, and advocates a "true" Islam that existed during the life of the Prophet Muhammad. In 1953, *Wahhabism* became the official ideology of Saudi Arabia. It has followers in many countries.
[3] Bobokhonov, who earned his Ph.D. in Arabic language and philology, was educated both in secular and Islamic disciplines, and is a member of a family of respected Islamic leaders in Tashkent. In the mid-1990s, he became the first Ambassador of Uzbekistan in Egypt.

[4] *Lashkari Islom* (Troops of Islam) was the main movement that fought against the Russians and Bolsheviks in Central Asia in 1918-1932. However, unlike the national-religious resistance of decades ago, the movements that emerged in the early 1990s were nonviolent. In early and mid-1990s, there has not been a single credible report on military activities associated with this organization.

[5] For instance, see *FBIS*, Document ID: FTS19990412001808.

[6] A *qori* is an individual who is able to recite the entire Koran from memory.

[7] Recently President Karimov promised that the *som* would be freely exchangeable with foreign currencies beginning in the year 2000.

Chapter Four

[1] A.V.Vishnevsky. *Serp i rubl'. Konservativnaya modernizatsiya v SSSR [The Sickle and the Ruble. Conservative Modernization in the USSR]*, Moscow, 1998, p. 281.

[2] *Tajikistan. Otchet po chelovecheskomu razvitiyu. [Tajikistan. Report on Human Development.]* 1997, Dushanbe. UN Mission in Tajikistan, 1997, p. 10.

[3] The national poll conducted by IFES and the SHARK Center covered 1,500 people in 134 communities located in 30 districts of Tajikistan. It followed internationally approved procedures with a 2.5% margin of error. The results were published by IFES in: S. Wagner, *Public Opinion in Tajikistan*, 1996, Washington, D.C., 1997.

[4] A.Malashenko, *Rossiya i islamskiy faktor [Russia and the Islamic Factor]*, Moscow, Russia, 1997, p. 22.

[5] R. Hassanov, "An Underground Regional Communist Party Committee... under the Banner of Islam," *Pravda*, May 16, 1991.

[6] A. Lukin, "Allah Akbar: Notes from the first convention of the Islamic Revival Party of Tajikistan," *Soglasie*, November 1, 1991.

[7] *Soglasie*, November 1, 1991.

[8] Evgeny Primakov. *The Years in Big Politics.* (in Russian). Publishing House "Strictly confidential", Moscow, 1999

[9] K. Hassanov, "The Way It Was: The Truth About the Registration of the Islamic Revival Party's Rules," *Narodnaya Gazeta*, Apr. 27, 1993.

[10] Courtesy of the Ministry of the Economy and Foreign Relations of Tajikistan.

Chapter Five

[1] S. M. Demidov, *Istoriya religioznykh verovanii narodov Turkmenistana (History of Religious Beliefs of the Peoples of Turkmenistan)* (Ashgabat: Ylum, 1990) 140 [in Russian].

[2] See *Turkmeny: Nauchno-publitsisticheskii al'manakh. (The Turkmens: An Almanac of Scholarly and Sociopolitical Essays)* (Moscow: Turkmen Azat, 1995) 12 [in Russian].

[3] Ibid, 12.

[4] *Basmachi* (from the Turkish word *besmach*, which means to attack) was an anti-Soviet rebellion movement in the 1920s and 1930s in Central Asia.

[5] Giorgy Mirsky, "*Islam i natsiya: Brizhnii Vostok i Tsentral'naya Aziya*" ("Islam and the Nation: The Middle East and Central Asia"), Polis no. 5 (1998): 82 [in Russian].

[6] Ibid, 82.

[7] Wahhabism is the teaching of Abd al-Wahhab, who lived in Arabia in the eighteenth century and founded a puritanical fundamentalist movement within Islam. In the twen-

tieth century, his followers came to power in Saudi Arabia. At a certain point, a Wahhabi-type Islamic republic was about to emerge in the Fergana Valley (in Uzbekistan), but the Karimov regime succeeded in crushing the Wahhabis. Today, the movement is gaining momentum in Chechnya and Dagestan. Wahhabis in Chechnya oppose both the traditional *Sunni* Muslims and adherents of the two popular *Sunni* orders — the Nakshbandiya and the Qadiriya. These *tariqats* (orders) are successfully vying for influence with the *Sunni* clergy, but G. Mirsky believes that today the greatest threat to Sufism in Central Asia comes from Wahhabis affiliated with the Arab Islamites.

[8] Shokhrat Kadyrov, *Otkroi Turkmenistan! (Discover Turkmenistan)* (Bergen: Azar Press, 1997) 3 [in Russian].

[9] In Turkmenian Sufi tradition, certain tribes (such as the Khodja, Shikh and Ata) are considered to be direct descendants of the prophet Muhammad. In traditional Turkmenian society these tribes have sacred status and in pre-[Soviet] revolutionary times were granted special privileges such as land ownership and access to water. Their mission was to spread Islam. (For details see S. M. Demidov, *Turkmenskie Ovliady* (Ashgabat, Ylym, 1976) 196 [in Russian].

[10] See *Transcripts of the Soros-Kyrghyzstan Seminar, Tsentral'naya Aziya (Central Asia)*, no. 6, (1997): 18 [in Russian]

[11] See *Aziya (Asia)*, 113 no. 23 (1997): 7 [in Russian].

PART II

Chapter One

[1] The Russian scholar, Sablukov, rendered this verse as follows: "The Muslim has no better friend than a Nazarene (Christian)."

Chapter Two

[1] M. Khudiakov, *Ocherki po istorii Kazanskogo khanstva (Essays on the History of the Kazan Khanate)* (Moscow: 1991), 163 [in Russian].
[2] Ismail bei Gasprinsky, "Russkoe musul'manstvo" ("The Muslim Community in Russia"), in collected volume *Rossiya i Vostok (Russia and the Orient)* (Kazan: 1993), 39 – 40 [in Russian].

Chapter Three

[1] "Does pan-Islamism and Islamic Fundamentalism Threaten Russia?" *Asia i Africa segodnia*, 2 (1996).
[2] V. Shpak, "Theory and Practice of Political Process in the North Caucasus," Proceedings of the conference "The ways of socio-political development of Russia," Stavropol (1994).
[3] *Pravda*. 11 August 1993
[4] *Nezavisimaya Gazeta*. 31 January 1992.
[5] Time magazine, August 14, 1992
[6] Press conference of Turkey's Secret Service agent I.Kasap in Makhachkala, Dagestan. *"North Caucasus"*, March 10, 1999.

[7] De Pau F. Policy of Turkey in Transcaucasus: Disputed borders in the Caucasus. Institute of Oriental Studies, Moscow, (1996)

[8] According to the Iranian ambassador to Russia, Saffari Mehdi, "Turkish regional diplomacy in the Caucasus directly reflects American interests in the region." *North Caucasus*,10 March, 1999.

[9]. *North Caucasus* 11 March, 1999.

[10] V. Akaev, S. Magomadov, "Sufi Brotherhoods in Chechnya,..", *Scientific Life of the Caucasus*, March, 1999

[11] "Factors of Destabilization of the religious-political situation in Dagestan." *Assalam Aleikum* 2 (1998).

[12] The first Islamic institution of this type in the North Caucasus opened in 1993 in Nazran (Ingushetia). Soon after this they appeared in all national republics of the region.

[13] I. Dabaev. "Radical Ideology on Political Process." Rostov-on-Don (1999).

[14] I. Dobaev. "The Islamic Factor in the Ethno-Political Processes in the North Caucasus. News of Higher Institutions." *North Caucasuan Region*, 2 (1998).

[15] "The Geopolitical Situation in the Transcaucasus and Ways of Providing Regional Stability," International Conference on Regional Security of Caucasus and Perspectives for the Twenty-first Century",Tbilisi, March 13 – 14, 1999.

[16] *Al Kaff.* April 1999.

[17] *North Caucasus*, 39 (1998).

[18] Tagaev M., Our Struggle of Insurrectional Army of Imam. Kiev: Nauka Press, (1997).

[19] A. Koichueva. "Some Problems of the North Caucasian Region." Materials of the II International Congress "Peace in the North Caucasus through Languages, Education, Culture." Pyatigorsk, 1998, P. 34.

[20] From the speech of V. Mirko, associate ataman of the Pyatigorsk division of the Tersk Cossack Forces at the Congress of Small Towns of Russia. Pyatigorsk, (1998).

[21] L. Choperskaya. "Modern Ethnopolitical Processes in the North Caucasus." Rostov-on-Don (1997).

PART III

Chapter One

[1] Bairamgul Shaniyazova, E. Stepanova, in *Neitralnyi Turkmenistan* (Ashgabad, 12 August 1997).

[2] Steven Grant. "Faith in Central Asia: Kazakstan, Uzbekistan, and Islam," *USIA Opinion Analysis*, 14 February 1995.

[3] *Aziya-EZh* (Almaty), no. 22 (December 1995): 17.

[4] *Narodnoe Slovo* (Tashkent), 12 November 1997.

[5] *Nezavisimaia Gazeta* (Moscow), 20 January 1992.

[6] N. A. Nazarbayev, "Message of the President of the Republic of Kazakstan to the People of Kazakstan. On the State of the Nation and the Priorities of Domestic and Foreign Policy: Democratization of Society and Economic and Political Reform in the New Century," 30 September 1998: 6.

[7] "The Difficult Road to an Open Society: Kyrghyzstan's Way." Speech by President Askar Akayev at the Carnegie Foundation, in *Nasha Gazeta* (Bishkek), 18 July 1997, 4.

[8] Martha Brill Olcott, "Central Asia's Political Crisis," in ed. Dale F. Eickelman *Russia's Muslim Frontiers: New Directions in Cross-Cultural Analysis* (Bloomington: Indiana University Press, 1993), 60.

[9] See, for example, *The Post-Soviet Muslim Territory: Religion, Politics, Ideology*; (Moscow: Nauka, 1994); A.V. Malashenko, *The Muslim World of the CIS*, (Moscow: Ariel Corporation, 1996); Dmitri Trofimov, *Central Asia: Problems of Ethno-Religious Development*, Studies of the International Research Center, Moscow State Institute of International Relations (MGIMO), Russian Foreign Ministry, no. 3 (March 1994); D. B. Malysheva, *Islam in the CIS* (Moscow: Nauka, 1998); Liudmila Polonskaia and Aleksei Malashenko, *Islam in Central Asia* (Reading, Great Britain: Ithaca Press, 1994); *Russia's Muslim Frontiers: New Directions in Cross-Cultural Analysis*, ed. Dale F. Eickelman, (Bloomington: Indiana University Press, 1993).

[10] Olga Brusina, "Social Traditions in the Newly Independent States of Central Asia as a Factor in the Exodus of the Russian-Speaking Population," in *Current Ethno-Political Processes and Migration in Central Asia* (Moscow: Moscow Carnegie Center, 1998), 47.

[11] I. Makatov, "Speeding Up Reform in Communist Education," *Kommunist Uzbekistana* no. 11 (1990): 64.

[12] John L. Esposito, Islam. *The Straight Path* (Oxford: Oxford University Press, 1988), 166.

[13] Aleksei Malashenko, "The Muslim States from the Caspian Sea to Lake Issyk-Kul," *Commonwealth of Independent States* no. 6 (1998), 3.

[14] Curiously enough, in spite of the official anti-Taliban propaganda throughout Central Asia, favorable opinions of the Taliban are voiced from time to time, such as this one: "They are seeking to achieve peace and reconciliation in their country," quoted in *Nasha Gazeta* (Bishkek), 4 July 1997.

[15] *Delovaia Nedelia* (Moscow), 15 May 1998.

[16] Gunden Peker, "Islam: Myth or Reality in Central Asia," *Eurasian Studies* no. 3 (fall 1996): 82.

[17] Valentin Filatov, *Den*, May 30 – June 6, 1993.

[18] Aleksandr Dugin, "Islam vs. Islam," *Zavtra* no. 31 (August 1998): 4 – 5.

[19] R. M. Avakov, "Russia and Central Asia: Independence or Economic Interdependence?" *Central Asia and Reform*, reports delivered at an international academic seminar, Paris, 1996, 40.

Chapter Two

[1] Alexandre Bennigsen and Marie Broxup first referred to this notion in their book, *The Islamic Threat to the Soviet State*, (London: Croom Helm, 1983).

[2] See Karen Dawisha and Helene Carrere d'Encausse, "Islam in the Foreign Policy of the Soviet Union: A Double-Edged Sword," in *Islam in Foreign Policy*, ed. Adeed Dawisha (Cambridge: Cambridge University Press, 1983).

[3] Some of these communist officials became very devout after retiring from government service. In 1981, Dinmuhammed Kunaev, secretary of the Central Committee of Kazakstan's Communist Party and member of the Soviet Politburo, lamented that the observance of religious rituals was not declining in Kazakstan, and that even Communist Party leaders participated in those rituals. According to reports at the time, Kunaev himself had been guilty of the same sin by holding a lavish feast to mark the circumcision of his son. See Alexei V. Malashenko in *Russia's Muslim Frontiers*, ed. Dale F. Eickelman,

(Bloomington, Ind.: Indiana University Press, 1993); Bess Brown, "The Phenomenon of Self-Appointed Mullahs" *Radio Liberty Research* 220181, 29 May 1981.

[4] There were, however, exceptions. See, for example, Shireen T. Hunter, "The Muslim Republics of the Former Soviet Union: Policy Challenges for the United States," *Washington Quarterly* 15 no. 3 (Summer 1992): 55 – 71.

[5] See Thomas L. Friedman, "United States to Counter Iran in Central Asia," *New York Times,* 6 February 1992.

[6] See "Mashhad Radio: Uzbekistan Persecuting Islamist's Family," *FBIS/SOV-98-301,* 28 October 1998.

[7] This view is based on my conversations with Uzbek officials and academics.

[8] Turajonzadeh lived in Iran for several years.

[9] Quoted in Kirill Nourzhanov, "Turkmenistan: Halfway through to the Golden Age," *Central Asia Monitor,* no. 1 (1995): 12.

[10] "Zholdasbekov on Future Relations with Iran" *FBIS/SOV-25-120,* 22 June 1995.

[11] In February 1998, the Uzbek foreign minister stated that recruits from Fergana Valley were indoctrinated and trained by groups based in Peshawar. "Uzbeks say Pakistan Islamist groups train fighters," *Reuters,* 16 February 1998.

[12] According to some sources, General Hamid Gul (ret.), former chief of Pakistan's intelligence services, in 1993 visited the headquarters of the Islamic Renaissance Party (IRP), the main opposition in Tajikistan (which has an Uzbek branch located in Afghanistan). Those contacts have continued. See Barnett R. Rubin, "The Fragmentation of Tajikistan," gopher://gopher.soros.org:70/00/Af...I NY/Tajikistan Project/rubin3.txt, February 2, 1998. Tajikistan has complained that Pakistani nationals have been involved in promoting puritanical Islam and the philosophy of the Taliban. In August 1998, the Tajik government expelled four Pakistani nationals because the four had been inviting the Tajiks to follow a more puritanical Islam and had been supporting advances made by the Taliban in their fight against opponents. "Tajiks to expel four Pakistanis for praising Taliban," *Reuters.* 24 August 1998.

[13] See T. Turdubayev, "For Islamic Unity, but without Wahhabis," *The Central Asian Post* no. 9 (3 September 1998)

[14] For Saudi clerics' anti-Shi'a comments and Iran's reaction, see Seyyed Mohammad Safizadeh, "Diplomacy with a Smile," in Tehran daily *Abrar* reproduced in *FBIS/NES 98-071,* 13 March 1998. The author argues that — given the fact that the Wahhabi Sheikh called the *Shi'as* worse than infidels in front of Ayatollah Ali-Akbar Rafsanjani — the latter should have cut his visit short. Also see "Iranian Clerics Sanei, Lankarani Respond to Saudi Shaykh," *FBIS/NES-98-071,* 13 March 1998.

[15] Referring to efforts to spread Wahhabism to Azerbaijan, Haidar Aliev said, "The Wahhabi religion belongs to another country....The Azerbaijani nation has never been devoted to the theory of Wahhabism....There is no place for Wahhabism in Azerbaijan." See "President Aliev: Azerbaijan No Place for Wahhabism," *FBIS/SOV-98-196,* 15 July 1998.

[16] On the tension between Islamic ideology and national interest as determinants of Iran's foreign policy, see Seyed Ali Ghazvini, "On the Foreign Policy of Islam: A Search into the Juridical Dimension of Iranian Foreign Policy," *The Iranian Journal of International Affairs* VII, no. 4 (1996): 780 – 796.

[17] On the transition of power and the constitutional changes, see Shireen T. Hunter, *Iran After Khomeini.* (Washington, DC: CSIS/Praeger, 1992).

[18] See "Musavi Aradabili Delivers Friday Prayer Sermon," *FBIS/NES*, 22 April 1991.

[19] In a letter to the Soviet foreign minister, Iran's foreign minister, Ali Akbar Velayati, emphasized Iran's "adherence to the principle of non-interference in other nations' affairs." See "Velayati on Helping Resolve Azerbaijan Crisis," *FBIS-NES*, 8 February 1990.

[20] Following the killing of the Iranian diplomats by the Taliban, Iranian newspapers and media were full of comments on Pakistan's treachery toward Iran, while the Pakistani media talked about Iran's arrogance. See, for example, "Pakistani Daily Condemns Iran for Arrogance," *FBIS/NES-98-262*, 5 October 1998.

[21] For example, Turkey was one of the major backers of the ultranationalist government of Abul Fazl Elchibey, who was very anti-Iran.

[22] On Israeli-Turkish alliance and its regional implications, see Daniel Pipes, "A New Axis: The Emerging Turkish-Israeli Entente," *National Interest*, no. 50 (Winter 1997 – 1998): 31-36.

[23] On Azerbaijan's views of Iran, and the Iranian province of Azerbaijan, see Shireen T. Hunter, "Greater Azerbaijan: Myth or Reality," in *Le Caucase Post-Sovietique: La Transition Dans Le Conflict*, ed. M. R. Djalili (Bruxelles: Bruylant, 1995): 115 – 142.

[24] See "Azerbaijan Views U.S., NATO or Turkish Base," *FBIS/SOV-1999-0214*, 29 January 1999.

[25] On President Karimov's statement supporting United States sanctions against Iran, see "An Iran Embargo" *OMRI* no. 88 (5 May 1995). However, after a few days the Uzbek foreign minister denied that his country had backed United States sanctions; see "Denies Backing United States Embargo," *FBIS/NES-95-141*, 24 July 1995.

[26] Uzbekistan has been actively suppressing the Tajik language and culture in Tajik-speaking areas and does not allow the entry of Persian language books from Iran. Recently, Uzbekistan even prevented the transit of Persian language books through its territory to Tajikistan.

[27] See Seyed Kazem Sajjadpour "Iran, the Caucasus and Central Asia," in Ali Banuzizi and M. Weiner *The New Geopolitics of Central Asia*, (London: Tauris, 1994): 198.

[28] On views regarding search for counterweights to United States power, see "Iran: Nabavi on U.S.-Iran Relations," *FBIS/NES-98-065*, 6 March 1998.

[29] Dimitri Volsky, "A New Look at Cooperation with Iran," *New Times*, no. 15 (June 1993): 27.

[30] "Iran Said Crucial Partner in Region," *FBIS/NES-95-045*, 8 March 1995.

[31] See Shireen T. Hunter, "Closer Ties for Russia and Iran," Transition 1, no. 24 (29 December 1995): 42 – 45; see also Mohiaddin Mesbahi, "Iran's Emerging Partnership With Russia," *Middle East Insight* 9, no. 5 (July-August 1995): 84 – 87.

[32] In an interview, Turajonzadeh said, "The Iranian model does not exactly suit us. Iranians are *Shi'ites*, and we Tajik are *Sunnis*.... But I would not take other Islamic states as a model either. We have to create our own Tajik model." *The Jamestown Foundation-Fortnight in Review*, (24 January 1997): http://www.jamestown.org, 2/2/98.

Chapter Three

[1] The author wishes to thank Süleyman Hayri Bolay, Edibe Sözen, Mujeeb R. Khan, and Ömer Turan for their assistance as I wrote this article.

[2] Nilüfer Göle, "Islami Dokunulmazlar, Laikler ve Radikal Demokratlar," *Türkiye Günlüğü*, no. 27 (March-April 1994): 13 – 18.

[3] M. Hakan Yavuz, "The Abrading of the Turkish Republican Myth," *JIME Review* 12, no. 41 (1998): 18 – 34.

[4] According to article 66 of the 1982 Constitution, "[E]very person who is bound with the citizenship to Turkish Republic is a Turk." Yet in everyday life, being Turk is very much defined in terms of being Muslim and belonging to the Turkish ethnicity.

[5] M. Hakan Yavuz and Mujeeb R. Khan, "A Bridge Between East and West: Duality and the Development of Turkish Foreign Policy Toward the Arab-Israeli Conflict" *Arab Studies Quarterly*, 14, no. 4 (Fall 1992): 69 – 95.

[6] The Konrad Adenauer Foundation conducted this survey, *Turkish Youth 98: The Silent Majority Highlighted* (Ankara: Tasarim, 1999).

[7] Mujeeb R. Khan, "The 'Other' in the Balkans: Historical Construction of Serb and 'Turks,'" *Journal of Muslim Minority Affairs* 16, no. 1 (1996): 49 – 64.

[8] For more on the identity debate in Turkey, see Edibe Sözen, "Modernite ve Kültürel Kimlik," Sosyoloji Konferansları, no. 25 (Istanbul: Cantay Kitabevi, 1998): 153 – 60.

[9] Birol Yesilada, "The Worsening EU-Turkey Relations," *SAIS Review* 19, no. 1 (1999): 144 – 62.

[10] Cengiz Candar, "Değişmekte olan Dünyada Türkiye'nin Bağımsızlığını Kazanan Yeni Türk Cumhuriyetleriyle İlişkileri," In *Yeni Dünya Düzeni ve Türkiye* (Istanbul: Baglam, 1992): 133 – 42.

[11] Haluk Özdalga, "Avrasya Seçeneği var mi?" *Milliyet*, 6 March 1999.

[12] For more on those "outside Turks" who played a critical role in Turkish culture and politics, see Ertuğrul Yaman et al., *Türkiye'deki Türk Dünyası* (Ankara: D.I.B. Yayınları, 1998).

[13] For more on ethnicity-based Turkish nationalism, see the special issue on Turkish nationalism in the twenty-first century in *Türk Yurdu* 19, no. 139 – 141 (March – May 1999). This issue has one hundred essays on different aspects of Turkish nationalism.

[14] M. Hakan Yavuz, "Nationalism and Islam: Yusuf Akçura, Üç Tarz-i Siyaset," *Oxford Journal of Islamic Studies* 4, no. 2 (1993): 175-207.

[15] A. Suat Bilge, "Analysis of Turkish-Russian Relations," *Perceptions: Journal of International Affairs* 2, no. 2 (June – August 1997): 66 – 92.

[16] Ahat Andican, *Değişim Sürecinde Türk Dünyası* (Istanbul: Emre Yayınları, 1996).

[17] Jacob Landau, *Pan-Turkism: From Irredentism to Cooperation* (Bloomington, Ind.: Indiana University Press, 1995); Hakki Öznur, *Ülkücü Hareket I-VI* (Ankara: Alternatif Yayınları, 1999).

[18] Ahmet Kuru, "Türkiye'nin Orta Asya'ya Yöneli?i," *Geçis Sürecinde Orta Asya Türk Cumhuriyetleri*, ed. Mim Kemal Oke (Istanbul: Alfa, 1999): 128 – 151.

[19] Ali Faik Demir, "SSCB'nin Dağılmasından Sonra Türkiye-Azerbaycan İlişkileri," *Değişim Dünya ve Türkiye*, ed. Faruk Sönmezoğlu (Istanbul: Baglam, 1995): 221 – 48.

[20] John Palmer, "Rule of Ottoman Empire," *The Guardian*, 3 April 1992. More editorial, see "The Sick Man Recovers," *The Times*, printed in *Newspot Turkish Digest*, 13 February 1992.

[21] Paul Kubicek, *Nation, State, and Economy in Central Asia: Does Atatürk Provide a Model?* Occasional paper, no. 14 (The Henry M. Jackson School of International Studies, The University of Washington, Seattle, 1995).

[22] Turgut Özal set the guidelines of Turkey's Central Asian policy in his opening speech at the Turkish Grand National Assembly, See *TBMM Tutanak Dergisi*, Dönem: 19 – 1, Cilt

1, no. 3, p.25. In this speech, Özal asked the Parliament to capitalize this new opportunity of establishing close ties with Turkic states and autonomous regions in Russia.

[23] For more on Özal's statement, see *Dünya*, 6 November 1992.

[24] Graham E. Fuller, "Turkey's New Eastern Orientation," in *Turkey's New Geopolitics: From the Balkans to Western China*, eds. Graham E. Fuller and Ian O. Lesser (Boulder, Colo.: Westview Press, 1993): 37-98.

[25] Necati Utkan, "Türk İşbirliği ve Kalkınma Ajansı (TIKA) Hakkında Bir Değerlendirme," *Yeni Türkiye*, 15 (May-June 1997): 946-951.

[26] *Milliyet*, 31 October 1992.

[27] Mustafa Öner, "Ortak Türk Alfabesi," *Yeni Türkiye*, no. 15 (1997): 207 – 11.

[28] M. Fethullah Gülen, "Orta Asya Eğitim Hizmetleri," *Yeni Türkiye*, no. 15 (1997): 685 – 95. Gülen examines the reasons of his educational activism in Central Asia and other regions of the world.

[29] M. Hakan Yavuz, "Osta Asya'daki Kimlik Olusumu: Yeni Kolonizatör Dervisler-Nurcular," *Türkiye Günlüğü*, no. 33 (1995): 160 – 4. During my field work in the Fergana Valley, I examined the impact of the Nurcu community of Fethullah Gülen.

[30] Turkey shares a twelve-kilometer border with the Azeri enclave of Nakcivan.

[31] Cenk Başlamış, "10 Yil Sonra Orta Asya," *Milliyet*, 15 – 22 July 1998.

[32] Ali Coşkun, "Türk Dünyasi ve Komsularımız," *Yeni Türkiye*, no. 15 (1997): 764; Sükrü Elekdağ, "Avrasya'nin Balkanları," *Milliyet*, 5 April 1998.

[33] For several studies about the role of Islam in Central Asia, see Mehrdad Haghayeghi, *Islam and Politics in Central Asia* (New York: St. Martin's Press, 1995); Alexander Bennigsen and Marie B. Bennigsen, *Islamic Threat to the Soviet State* (New York: St. Martin's Press, 1983); Dale Eickelman ed., *Russia's Muslim Frontiers* (Indianapolis: Indiana University Press, 1993). For a typical orientalist treatment of Islam, see Sergei Poliakov, *Everyday Islam* (London: M.E. Sharpe, 1992).

[34] Osman Türer, "Türk Dünyasında Islam'ın Yayılması ve Muhafazasında Tasavvuf ve Tarikatler," Yeni Türkiye, 15 (May-June 1997): 174 – 181; Fuat Köprülü, *Türk Edebiyatında ilk Mutasavvıflar* (Ankara: D.I.B Yayinevi, 1984): 14 – 20.

[35] M. M. Blazer, ed., *Shamanism: Soviet Studies of Traditional Religion in Siberia and Central Asia* (Armonk, N.Y.: M. E. Sharpe, 1990).

[36] In recent years, the Kazak government has sought to nationalize his work as "Kazak."

[37] Adeeb Khalid, *The Politics of Muslim Cultural Reform: Jadidism in Central Asia* (Berkeley, Calif.: University of California Press, 1998).

[38] Yaacov Ro'i, "The Impact of the Islamic Fundamentalist Revival of the Late 1970s on the Soviet View of Islam," *The USSR and the Muslim World*, ed. Yaacov Ro'i (London: George Allen and Unwin, 1984): 149 – 77.

[39] Bennigsen and Bennigsen, *The Islamic Threat*, 114; Rywkin, *Moscow's Muslim Challenge* (London: M. E. Sharpe, 1990): 85.

[40] Bennigsen and Bennigsen, *The Islamic Threat*, p. 117.

[41] In 1989, the leadership of the Central Asian Spiritual Administration changed, and Muhammad Sadik Muhammad Yusuf took over from conformist Samsuddin-Quari Babakhanov. Sadik was educated in Libya and was from the Fergana Valley. The most religiously active cities are Andijan and Namangan. Two groups — *Adalat* and *Tawba* — were formed in 1991 and had very radical views. They captured several buildings and

were later crushed by Karimov. Events turned against Sadik in mid-1992. In February 1993 the All-Muslim Kurultai elected Muktar Abdullayev to replace Muhammad Sadik. Sadik was forced into exile. He first lived in Saudi Arabia and is currently in Turkey. Karimov seeks to exert his power and de-politicization through institutionalizing the mahalla (neighborhood) as a unit of administration.

[42] For one of the best works on Islam in Central Asia, see Yaacov Ro'i, ed., *Muslim Eurasia: Conflicting Legacies* (London: Frank Cass, 1995).

[43] M. Hakan Yavuz, "Efsanevi Islam: Atatalar Dini ve Modern Baglantilar," *Türk Dünyasinin Dini Meseleleri* (Ankara: D.I.B. Yayinlari, 1998): 11 – 24. This book includes the proceedings of the conference on Islamic institutions in the Turkic world. For more on Islam, see Yaacov Ro'i, "The Islamic Influence on Nationalism in Soviet Central Asia," *Problems of Communism* (July – August 1990): 49 – 64.

[44] For more on Yilmaz's speech, see *Birinci Avrasya Islam Surası* (Ankara: Diyanet Isleri Başkanlığı, 1996), 30. During the congress, the Turkish representatives, in particular, Bülent Ecevit, constantly stressed the virtues of *Turkish* Islam as Sufi Islam. Ecevit identifies two major characteristics of Turkish Islam as Sufi and love-based versus fear-based Arab Islam and more popular and democratic Islam.

[45] For more see *Birinci Avrasya Islam Surasi.*

[46] *Ikinci Avrasya Islam Surasi* (Ankara: Diyanet Isleri Baskanligi, 1998). This book includes basic information about Islamic institutions and activities in thirty-two countries and regions. It is heavily focused on Muslims in the former Soviet Union and in Yugoslavia.

[47] Kemal Güran, "Vakıf Hizmetleri," In *Birinci Avrasya*, 1996, 156.

[48] I would like to thank Ömer Turan, who provided the information from the TDV. The figures are from the Annual Report of the TDV.

[49] Alen Hetmanek, "Islamic Revival in the USSR," *Religion in Communist Dominated Areas* (Keston, UK) (Summer 1968): 83-86.

[50] M. Hakan Yavuz, "Towards an Islamic Liberalism?: The Nurcu Movement and Fethullah Gülen," *The Middle East Journal* 53, no. 4 (1999): 584-605.

[51] M. Hakan Yavuz, "Efsanevi Islam: Atalar Dini ve Modern Bağlantılar," In *Türk Dünyasının Dini Meseleleri* (Ankara: Turkiye Diyanet Vakfı Yayınları, 1998), 11 – 24; M. Hakan Yavuz, "Turkistan'da Halkının Manevi Dünyasi: Efsanevi Islam," *Dergah* 62 (April 1995).

[52] More on the Soviet atheistic policies and their impact, see Nazif Shahrani, "Islam and the Political Culture of 'Scientific Atheism' Post-Soviet Central Asia: Future Predicament," *Islamic Studies* (Pakistan) 33, no. 2 – 3 (1994): 139-60.

[53] For more on oral literature in Central Asia, see Thomas Gustav Winner, *The Oral Art and Literature of the Kazaks of Russian Central Asia* (Durham, N.C., Duke University Press, 1958).

[54] Maria Eva Subtelny, "The Cult of Holy Places: Religious Practices among Soviet Muslims," *The Middle East Journal* (Autumn 1989): 593 – 604.

[55] Sibel Utku, "MHP Foreign Policy: 'Turkish World' and Cyprus." *The Turkish Daily News*, 21 April 1999.

Chapter Four

[1] Olivier Roy, *Afghanistan, from Holy War to Civil War* (Princeton: Princeton University Press, 1995).

[2] Ibid.

[3] Samuel Huntington, *The Clash of Civilizations and the Remaking of World Order* (New York: Simon and Schuster, 1996).

[4] Ahmed Rashid, *The Resurgence of Central Asia: Islam or Nationalism?* (London and New York: Zed Press, 1994). In Chapter 4 on Uzbekistan, I extensively discuss the early role of Wahhabism in Fergana when no one in the Uzbek government appeared to know either who these Wahhabis were or where they came from. During trips to Fergana in 1992 and 1993, I met dozens of Uzbek Islamic militants who were mostly Wahhabis and were preparing to launch an opposition movement against Karimov. They admitted that most of their funding came from Saudi Arabia.

[5] The four schools of Islamic law that evolved in the ninth century were Hanafi, Maliki, Shafi, and Hanbali. Hanafi was based on customary practices and is the easiest to follow.

[6] The syllabi of these *madrasas* include, and still include, memorizing and interpreting the Koran; studying Islamic jurisprudence and Islamic law, the life and sayings of the Prophet Muhammad, Islamic philosophy, the Arabic language, and mathematics; and spreading the word of God.

[7] Roy.

[8] Ibid.

[9] Included are mullahs Khairkhwa Minister of Interior, Abbas Health, Mutaqqqui Information, Ahmed Jan Industries, Haqqani Frontier Affairs, Qalamuddin Religious Police, Mansur Agriculture, and Arif Deputy Finance Minister.

[10] After the Clinton Administration classified them as a group supporting international terrorism in 1998, they changed their name to Harkat-ul-Mujheddin. In, "Laden planned a global Islamic revolution in 1995," *AFP 27* August 1998.